A Logical Introduction
to Philosophy

A Logical Introduction to Philosophy

RICHARD L. PURTILL

Western Washington University

PRENTICE HALL, *Englewood Cliffs, New Jersey 07632*

Library of Congress Cataloging-in-Publication Data

Purtill, Richard L.
  A logical introduction to philosophy/Richard L. Purtill.
    p. cm.
  Includes index.
  ISBN 0-13-539917-3
  1. Philosophy—Introductions. 2. Logic. I. Title.
BD21.P86   1989   88-16641
100—dc19   CIP

Editorial/production supervision and
  interior design: **Susan E. Rowan**
Cover design: **Ben Santora**
Manufacturing buyer: **Peter Havens**

To my students
who have learned from me
and from whom I have learned

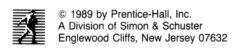 © 1989 by Prentice-Hall, Inc.
A Division of Simon & Schuster
Englewood Cliffs, New Jersey 07632

Printed in the United States of America
10 9 8 7 6 5 4 3 2 1

ISBN 0-13-539917-3

PRENTICE-HALL INTERNATIONAL (UK) LIMITED, *London*
PRENTICE-HALL OF AUSTRALIA PTY. LIMITED, *Sydney*
PRENTICE-HALL CANADA INC., *Toronto*
PRENTICE-HALL HISPANOAMERICANA, S.A., *Mexico*
PRENTICE-HALL OF INDIA PRIVATE LIMITED, *New Delhi*
PRENTICE-HALL OF JAPAN, INC., *Tokyo*
SIMON & SCHUSTER ASIA PTE. LTD., *Singapore*
EDITORA PRENTICE-HALL DO BRASIL, LTDA., *Rio de Janeiro*

Contents

——————————— **7** ———————————

——————————— **8** ———————————

——————————— **9** ———————————

——————————— **10** ———————————

APPENDICES

——————————— **I** ———————————

II

III

IV

Preface

Logic was originally developed by philosophers to serve as a tool in dealing with philosophical problems. Logical arguments are still important in philosophy, but on the introductory level, logic and philosophy are usually taught separately and in isolation from each other. This is bad for both subjects. In introductory logic classes, logical principles are applied to trivial examples, and it is hard for students to see the usefulness of logic. In introductory philosophy classes, fairly complex arguments have to be analyzed without the use of logical techniques. Some teachers and a few textbooks try to give a "mini-course" in logic as a preliminary to the introductory philosophy course, and some teachers and textbooks use philosophical examples in teaching logic. Such approaches are helpful, but they do not entirely solve the problem.

In this book I develop and discuss logical principles *along with* an introduction to philosophy so that the two subjects are learned together and cast mutual light on each other. Thus, this book could serve as a text for an introduction to philosophy course *or* for an introduction to logic course, depending on which subject is given more emphasis. The student will be able to see that logic can be applied to some important problems and be useful in solving them, and the student will also have a better insight into the logical structure of philosophical arguments.

Another separation that I find an obstruction rather than a help in teaching logic is the separation between formal and informal (or "practical") logic. The analysis of the formal structure of arguments is confined to formal logic and separated from such "informal" topics as definition or fallacies. But if we look at actual instances of philosophical argument, we often find "formal" and "informal" techniques mixed. For instance, in Plato's dialogue *Euthyphro*, Socrates urges Euthyphro to formulate a definition of righteousness then criticize the definition by arguments that can easily be expressed by the machinery of formal logic. However, in the way logic courses are often structured today, definition is discussed in the informal logic or "critical thinking" course and logical argument patterns in the "formal" or "symbolic" logic course.

I begin this book by discussing definition, because definition is a valuable help to clarity, and unless we are clear as to what we are arguing about, we will often be arguing at cross-purposes. I then proceed in Chapter 2 to introduce some simple patterns of argument that can be analyzed by means of propositional logic. My philosophical texts in these two chapters are all drawn from the early dialogues of Plato, where Socrates is often trying to get a definition of a key term such as "piety" or "knowledge" and using simple arguments to reject proposed candidates.

The logical system introduced in Chapter 2 gives proof techniques, but a simple and effective way of mechanically checking arguments for validity is also needed. I have used a cancellation system based on the work of Professor Fred Sommers of Brandeis University, which is far less cumbersome and time-consuming than such techniques as truth tables or "trees." An extension of this system is used for syllogistic logic, which would not be possible for other methods. The advantages of the cancellation system, you will find, more than compensate for the fact that it is less familiar than more standard techniques.

In Chapter 3 I apply the same methods of analysis to various arguments from Thomas Aquinas and other medieval philosophers. But because syllogistic logic was the distinctive logical system used in the Middle Ages, in Chapter 4 I introduce syllogistic logic, using examples from Aquinas and other medieval philosophers. Chapter 5 shows how a mixed system of statement logic and syllogistic logic can be used to deal with arguments from Descartes and Leibniz.

In Chapters 6 and 7 I discuss the elements of probability theory and the logic of causation. My examples here are taken from David Hume, the great philosophical skeptic and critic of religion.

Chapter 8 is in some ways the most advanced chapter, both philosophically and technically. It covers part of the philosophy of Immanuel Kant and the basic parts of modal logic—the logic of possibility and necessity. However, every effort has been made to make both of these topics clear and understandable, and they are both of great philosophical and logical interest. Kant's philosophy was clearly influenced by the logic he used, which makes it an especially valuable topic for a book of this kind.

The final two chapters of this text attempt to draw together all of the techniques learned in earlier chapters and apply them to the analysis of extended arguments. Students are shown how to take a philosophical argument, define key terms, identify assumptions, look for fallacies, and analyze formal and informal arguments. They are expected to show validity or invalidity for deductive arguments and assess the strength of inductive arguments. The philosophical texts are taken from a number of contemporary philosophers.

In any given chapter, only short excerpts from individual philosophers are presented. This book could be used in an Introduction to Philosophy class in connection with complete editions of the philosophical texts (available inexpensively in paperback). At the ends of chapters there are a number of exercises on logic drawn from a variety of philosophers. Thus, this book could be used on its own as a text for an introductory logic class or for a formal or symbolic logic class, or it could be supplemented with further exercises such as those found in *Arguments: Deductive Logic Exercises* by Howard Posposel and David Marans (Prentice Hall, 1978).

Logic and philosophy were born together and have pursued parallel careers ever since. But lately they have become separated and even estranged. If this book does something to bring them together again and shows the advantages of using them together, then it will have justified my efforts in writing it and your efforts in reading it and working with it.

My thanks to the Bureau of Faculty Research at Western Washington University for assistance in the preparation of this book, and especially to Gail Fox and to Dabney Bankert who did the typing. Thanks also to Joe Heider, Linda Albelli, and Susan Rowan at Prentice Hall and to my students, my own teachers, and my colleagues who have all, in different ways, helped make this book better.

Richard L. Purtill

Introduction for Students

In this book you will be introduced to both philosophy and logic. The philosophical statements and arguments will serve as subject matter for the application of logical techniques, and the logical techniques will help to clarify and organize the philosophical statements and arguments. Thus, you will understand the philosophical material better and learn techniques that can be applied in other areas to make your thinking clearer, more critical, and more organized.

Philosophy is the study of some of the deepest and most fascinating questions that human beings have asked, questions such as "What can we know?" "Is there a God?" "How should we judge right and wrong?" Philosophers investigate these questions by three basic techniques: First, they *analyze* questions and statements to get the clearest possible understanding of each question and statement; second, they *criticize* every statement and assumption, trying to take nothing for granted until it has passed the test of critical questioning; third, they *argue* and examine arguments on both sides of any question, trying to determine on which side the arguments are strongest, or where they must suspend judgment or look for further arguments.

The logical study of definition is especially useful at the stage of clarification, but the techniques that enable us to symbolize arguments and lay them out in an organized way also help in the analysis of philosophical positions. These techniques are also invaluable at the critical stage, for we can see exactly what is needed to reach a certain conclusion and ask whether each step is justified. By the study of various arguments and how each can be tested, we acquire valuable tools for seeing on which side of a question the arguments are strongest, or where the arguments are inconclusive.

By working through this book with a good teacher you will get a sound knowledge of some important parts of the history of philosophy and of some of the basic techniques of logic. You may be motivated to take other classes to extend your knowledge of philosophy and your mastery of logical techniques. Even if you do not continue your study of logic, the skills you acquire here should help you think in a clearer, more critical, more rational way about problems you face in other areas: your other studies, your work, and your personal life.

Logical thinking is only part of life; sensation, emotion, and aesthetic, moral, and religious experiences all have a part to play in our lives. In certain areas, such as choosing a person to love, there may well be "reasons of the heart" not subject to logical examination. But in many areas of our life clarity, a critical attitude and a search for rational evidence can save us both headaches and heartaches. It is my hope that your study of logic and philosophy with the aid of this book will be interesting in itself and will also enhance your ability to make judgments and decisions that are reasonable and wise. For philosophy is the love of wisdom, and logic is at least one road to wisdom.

1

Socrates and the Search for Definitions

Philosophy in the modern, Western sense really began when a Greek stone-cutter refused to accept the idea that nobody was wiser than he was. This man, Socrates, was in the habit of discussing ideas with his friends, and one of them was so impressed by Socrates' wisdom that he went to the Oracle at Delphi and asked whether Socrates was the wisest man in the world. The Oracle replied, "No one is wiser than Socrates."

But when his friend returned with the message, Socrates was honestly puzzled. Like most Greeks of his time he believed that the god Apollo spoke through the Delphic Oracle and that although the Oracle was often ambiguous it never lied. But Socrates felt quite sure that *he* was not wise: There were too many things he didn't know, didn't understand. So he began to talk with anyone he could find who had a reputation for wisdom, trying to test the Oracle's statement. He found that statesmen could not explain the political concepts they made speeches about, that poets and artists could not interpret their own works adequately, and that people who did have expertise in some area assumed that this gave them the right to make pronouncements in areas they knew nothing about.

Eventually Socrates came to the conclusion that what the Oracle had meant was that all human wisdom was flawed: that no one was wiser than Socrates, even though Socrates was not wise, because no one was really

1

wise. The only advantage that Socrates had over others was that he realized his own lack of wisdom and had the humility to admit it.

Socrates could have drawn a skeptical conclusion from all this and simply given up all hope of wisdom. Instead he took the attitude that in recognizing our own lack of wisdom we should try to become wiser. He came to the conclusion that the first step in becoming wiser was to understand the ideas we used and that the best way of doing this was to find definitions for the words that caused puzzlement and disagreement.

Socrates' questioning of those who made claims to wisdom showed up their lack of wisdom, and, not surprisingly, this aroused a good deal of resentment. Eventually, Socrates was brought to trial for questioning the religious ideas of his fellow citizens and for unsettling the minds of the young men who enjoyed arguing with him and seeing him argue with others. In the speech he made in his own defense he told the story we have just retold and explained that he believed it was his duty to continue questioning ideas and to make others question them. He compared the city-state of Athens, where he lived, to a magnificent horse that would be lazy and sluggish if it were not stirred up. He, Socrates, was the horsefly who kept the horse lively by nipping at it!

His fellow citizens voted the death penalty for Socrates, and he died as a martyr to his search for wisdom. But his spirit is embodied in the philosophical enterprise that was carried on by pupils of Socrates, such as Plato, and their pupils, such as Aristotle, for example. The quest for clear thinking about our concepts and for justification of our beliefs by looking at the arguments on both sides of the question has been carried on ever since in the spirit of Socrates and is an important part of what we mean by "philosophy." It is not the whole story, any more than the search for definitions is the whole story about clarifying our thinking. But Socratic questioning and the search for definitions is at least a good place, and perhaps the best place, to begin the study of philosophy and of logic as the method of philosophy.

SOCRATES AND EUTHYPHRO

When Socrates argued with his young friends or with those who had pretentions to wisdom, he often asked them to define a key term, then he examined the definition to see if it was adequate. Shortly before his trial, he met a man named Euthyphro, who regarded himself as a religious authority. Euthyphro was so sure of his own righteousness that he was prosecuting his own father for murder in a complicated case involving the death in captivity of one family servant who was being held because he had killed a fellow servant. Socrates began to question Euthyphro about what he meant by "righteousness" and "unrighteousness." (The Greek words mean "right" and "wrong" but also have a religious connotation. I have used the somewhat old-fashioned words "righteousness" and "unrighteousness" because no word in current usage has just those connotations of morality combined with religion.)

Socrates' motives in arguing with Euthyphro were probably somewhat mixed. Partly he wanted to make Euthyphro think about his own certainty that what he was doing was morally and religiously right. Partly he was exploring what religious Athenians like Euthyphro, some of whom were among his accusers, meant by "unrighteousness," since the word appeared in the accusations on which Socrates was being brought to trial. And partly perhaps Socrates thought he might have something to learn even from the opinionated Euthyphro.

At the beginning of the discussion Euthyphro tries to define "righteousness" by example; "righteousness is doing the sort of thing I am doing." But Socrates argues that this is like trying to define "bee" by talking about various kinds of bees; to define the word "bee" we need an account of what all bees have in common, and to define "righteousness" we need an account of what all righteous acts have in common.

Euthyphro eventually defines righteousness as "doing what the gods approve of" and unrighteousness as "doing what the gods disapprove of." Socrates agrees that this is the right *kind* of definition: It provides a characteristic that all such acts are supposed to have in common. However, is it a truly adequate definition? They must look at the pros and cons.

The first problem that arises is connected with ancient Greek religious belief: The ancient Greeks believed in many gods, and these gods were seen as very human, quarreling among themselves and having love affairs with each other and with mortals. How could the approval of such gods serve as a definition of righteousness and unrighteousness? For what one god approved, another might disapprove, making the same act both righteous and unrighteous.

Even if the gods were unanimous or if there were only one God as in the Jewish, Christian, and Islamic faiths, other problems remain. Is the approval and disapproval of the gods or of God purely arbitrary? If it is not then the gods or God must approve or disapprove actions for some *reason* or *reasons*. And should we not define righteousness and unrighteousness by giving those reasons, rather than by saying it is what the gods approve or disapprove?

Compare this question with the question of defining a "strike" in baseball. In one sense a strike is what the umpire says is a strike, because he is in the best position to know, and his decision is final in disputed cases. But the decision of the umpire is not arbitrary: He has certain standards by which he judges that a thrown ball is a strike. And in defining a strike in a rule book we describe these standards; we don't say "a strike is what the umpire calls a strike." If the pitcher is trying to throw a strike or the batter is trying to avoid a strike, that would be no help, whereas knowing where the strike zone is, its dimensions, etc., would be useful to both pitcher and batter.

Similarly, Euthyphro needs to think about whether his prosecution of his own father is really an act of righteousness, and Socrates needs to know what the Athenians think they are accusing him (Socrates) of. Euthyphro doesn't claim that a god has directly revealed his approval of Euthyphro's action: Socrates' accusers don't claim that the gods have directly revealed their disapproval of Socrates' actions. So what standards does Euthyphro appeal to that make him so sure the gods approve his action? What standards do Socrates' accusers appeal to that make them sure that the gods disapprove of what Socrates has been doing?

It is easy to sit back and enjoy Euthyphro's discomfort as Socrates presses his objections to each new attempt by Euthyphro, but it is much harder to come up with a definition of our own that would stand up to Socratic questioning. Eventually, Euthyphro makes an excuse to leave Socrates without ever having come up with a good definition. This should raise the question in his mind, "If I can't even define 'righteous' how can I be so sure that what I am doing is righteous?" When Socrates comes to trial his accusers cannot answer his questions about what their accusations mean either, but they are angered by this rather than stopping to think of how they can be so sure that what Socrates is doing is wrong.

Obviously the issues raised by Socrates go beyond questions of definition in a narrow sense; even if dictionaries had existed in Socrates' time, Euthyphro and Socrates could not have answered the questions at issue between them by looking up "righteousness." What is really at issue is clarifying a whole way of thinking about morality and its relation to religion. But getting as clear and general an account as possible of the meanings of key terms is a good start on this enterprise.

PROBLEMS OF DEFINITION

In the centuries since Socrates' death, philosophers have given a good deal of thought to the subject of definition. Different kinds of definition have been recognized, depending on the purpose for which the definition is needed. Sometimes it is allowable to simply lay down conditions for something to be called by a certain name or recognized as a member of a certain class. The laws define what an "eligible voter" is in a given election. A community trying to restrict access to parks or beaches to community residents only may have to lay down somewhat arbitrary conditions for what counts as a "resident." Such definitions do not explore or explain actual usage; they are what we call *stipulative* definitions. They have their uses, but they are seldom what we need in philosophical argument, where we need to clarify the concepts people actually use.

Another kind of definition is *persuasive* definition, which has some relation to actual usage but is slanted in a certain direction. In a time of dispute about national policy one group may define "good citizens" as ones who *always* defend their country's policy, whereas an opposing group may define "good citizens" as those who are prepared to criticize their country's policy. Probably a satisfactory analysis of "good citizen" would include the idea of supporting one's country's policy in some circumstances and criticizing it in others. To be convincing, persuasive definition must contain *some* of the truth; to persuade, it leaves out some of the truth also. Persuasive definitions are almost never useful in philosophy.

What we usually want and need in philosophical discussion is an *analytic* definition that gives a *clear, informative, and general* account of the way a word or phrase is *actually used*. The traditional "rules" for definition grow directly out of these requirements. Because a definition must be clear and informative, we do not want definitions that use obscure or unfamiliar terms, and we are not satisfied with a mere metaphor or comparison. We also want a positive account, for saying what something is *not* rarely gives us much information as to what it *is*. Nor will a definition be informative if it is *circular*, that is, if it uses in the definition the very word we were supposed to be defining or some synonym of that word or a word so closely linked with the original word that it will not be understood if the original word is not understood. We also want a definition to give an important characteristic of the thing defined, not some characteristic that only that thing happens to have, but which does not tell us anything about what makes that thing unique. (Human beings are two-legged creatures without feathers, but if a chicken lost all its feathers that would not make it a human being.)

These requirements give us our first four rules:

1. A definition must not be obscure or metaphorical.
2. A definition must not be negative if it can be positive.
3. A definition must not be circular.
4. A definition must not use a merely accidental characteristic of the thing defined.

The formal requirements for definition are merely expansions of what we mean by saying that definition must be *clear, informative, and general*. The generality requirement also shows that attempting to define something by merely giving examples is not satisfactory for analytic definition: The examples are not a definition but merely the raw material of definition.

The requirement that the definition reflect the way that a word is actually used give us two more rules.

5. A definition must not be too wide.
6. A definition must not be too narrow.

A definition is too wide if it covers *more* cases than the actual usage of the word covers (for example, "human beings are two-legged animals") and too narrow if it covers *fewer* cases than the actual usage of the word covers (for example, "human beings are tool-using animals").

The six rules provide us with ways in which a proposed definition can be *criticized*: A definition that fails any of these tests is for that very reason defective. A definition that satisfies all six rules may still not be ideal, but it is at least on the right track, and any defects it still has may be matters of degree; perhaps it could be clearer, more informative, more general, or fit the actual usage better than it does. A fairly good definition can often be refined in these respects until it becomes a very good one. A cooperative effort is often used here: A group of people can sometimes refine a definition more quickly and efficiently than a single person.

Even outside of philosophy, defining your terms well can often head off "verbal disputes" or "semantic disagreements" where the real issue is not facts or values but different understandings of a key term. Often we cannot get to the real issue *until* we clear up the semantic disagreement. An American and a Russian arguing about which country is more "democratic" no doubt will have many differences about facts and values, but they also probably have different understandings of the *word* "democratic"; perhaps the American thinks of it in terms of "electoral democracy," free elections, etc., whereas the Russian thinks of it in terms of "economic democracy," ownership by the people of the means of production. The American says to the Russian, "Look at your one-party elections; Russia isn't a democracy." The Russian counters, "Look at the small number of people who own your primary means of production; America is not a democracy." Both may have a point, but they are really "arguing past" each other; because of their different concepts of democracy the evidence they cite is not evidence against the other person's claim.

FINDING A GOOD DEFINITION

There is no infallible formula for finding a good analytic definition, but one traditional way of approaching the problem is still useful in many cases. This is the method of finding a general class into which the thing to be defined fits (a *genus*) and then giving some characteristics (*differentia*) that separate the thing to be defined from other things in the genus. Thus, an automobile falls into the genus *vehicles* and is differentiated from such vehicles as a trailer, a horse-drawn cart, etc., by being *self-propelled*. But because a motorcycle, for instance, is a self-propelled vehicle, we need to find further differentia that uniquely single out automobiles.

Sometimes a group of related terms can be defined systematically by showing a set of interrelations between them. In the exercises at the end of this chapter we look at two groups of definitions of emotions, one given by the seventeenth-century English philosopher Thomas Hobbes and the other by the seventeenth-century Jewish philosopher Baruch Spinoza. In each case the attempt is made to separate the emotions into positive and negative emotions ("desire" and "aversion" for Hobbes, "pleasure and pain" for Spinoza) and then define each emotion by its occasion or object (for example, "ambition is desire *for* honor or power").

The whole set of definitions could be arranged systematically as a sort of classification of emotions. Hobbes' definitions could be arranged as follows:

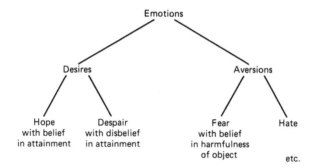

A very broad classification of general kinds of things, a sort of logical map of concepts, may help us to locate the proper genus in which to locate something we are trying to define. The broadest division is between *substances*, which *have* qualities or relations, and the qualities and relations which substances have.

The substances that almost any theory would acknowledge are persons and material objects. Many philosophers and nonphilosophers think that there are nonmaterial or *spiritual* substances, such as God, as well as material substances, such as rocks, trees, and automobiles. Even if we disagree that spiritual substances exist, it is worthwhile having them as part of our conceptual "map" because we have to define a concept clearly to be able to argue clearly about whether or not it exists.

CLASSIFYING SUBSTANCES

An ancient classification of substances, associated with the name of the logician and philosopher Porphyry, is the "tree of being" or "tree of Porphyry." Substances are divided into material substances that occupy space and have weight, and into spiritual substances that do not have location or weight, but which have knowledge and will. Material substances are divided into living and nonliving, and spiritual substances are divided into finite spirits and infinite spirit, which is God. Finite spirits are further divided into pure spirits, such as angels and souls, which are spirits that are normally and naturally embodied. A human person is regarded as a composite substance consisting of a soul united with a material body. Thus, we can ask of a human being what he or she knows and how much he or she weighs. Of an angel we can ask what it knows, but it makes no sense to ask how much it weighs, while of a rock it makes sense to ask what it weighs, but not to ask what it knows.

Dualism, the view that there are two *kinds* of substances, is deeply imbedded in ordinary language and ordinary thought. *Materialism* denies the existence of any spiritual substances, while *idealism* (in one of several senses of that philosophically overused word) denies that material substances are real: For the idealist, material objects can be reduced to ideas in minds. In Western philosophy the main argument has been between materialism and dualism, but some Western and many Eastern philosophers have given reasons for rejecting both materialism and the two-substance view in favor of philosophical idealism.

The arguments on each side are complex and continuing, but unless we have a clear idea of what each side *means* by matter and spirit, we have no hope of realizing any progress. For materialists, any properties or relations must be properties or relations of material substances, while for dualists some properties will be properties of material substances, some of spiritual substances. Relations may relate two or more spiritual substances, two or more material substances, or one or more material substances and one or more spiritual substances.

A very common move in arguments between materialists and nonmaterialists, even among philosophers, is for the materialist to claim that only material things exist, and for the nonmaterialist to cite things such as love or hope or knowledge as nonmaterial realities. But few nonmaterialists would claim that such things are *substances*. Thus, they must be properties or relations. But of what? If the materialist is right they must be properties or relations of material substances; there are no other kinds of substances. If the nonmaterialist is right there are nonmaterial substances, and such things as love or hope or knowledge will arguably be qualities or relations of such substances.

Of course, many ordinary definitions do not depend on solving such problems. For many purposes it will be more useful to explore the subdivisions of material substances: to divide living things into animals and plants; nonliving things into natural objects and artifacts, and so on. This may even clarify some issues between materialists and nonmaterialists, for if materialists are to reduce everything to the material, they must give some convincing account of just where in the area of the material to put each allegedly nonmaterial entity.

CLASSIFYING PROPERTIES

The oldest—and in many ways still the most interesting—classification of properties and relations was made by Aristotle. After distinguishing substances from what is possessed by substances, Aristotle listed *Quality* (shape, color), *Quantity* (dimensions, weight), and a number of things that are basically relations, although only a few relations are put into the category called *Relation* (for example, older than, taller than). In separate categories are put *Spatial Relations* (*where* a thing is in relation to other things), *Temporal Relations* (*when* a thing exists or acts), *Acting* (for example, running, hitting), *Being Acted on* (for instance, being hit). Finally, he gives two fairly minor relation categories: *Posture* (standing, sitting), which is basically the relation of parts of a thing to each other and to external things, and *Possession* (for example, having clothes on, having a stick in your hand).

Aristotle's categories are far from exhaustive, but they do provide a good starting point. We can define qualities as those properties of substances that can be understood without necessarily involving any other substance, and relations as properties of substances that can only be understood by reference to other substances. Thus, an object could be seen to be red or square even if it were the only object we had experienced. But a concept such as "larger than" requires the comparison of two substances.

This makes it clear that quantities are a special kind of relation: the relation of a substance or some aspect of a substance to some standard. This standard may itself be a substance, like the standard measures kept in certain government offices, but nowadays it is often a relation of a substance to a certain procedure that can be counted on to give the same result every time.

To return to definition, the first task is often to find the right category and subcategory. For example, an *inch* is a quantity, an *inchworm* a living substance, and *inching* is the action of moving in small increments. Neither an inch nor the action of inching are substances, and an inchworm is not a quality or relation of any substance.

What are the most basic substances? Are the parts of substances themselves to be considered substances? What about things that we normally think of in terms of a "mass" of material rather than one discrete object: sand, salt, wine, oil, gold, grain, and so on? All of these are fascinating questions, and in an extended sense even logical questions. But for present purposes we have probably said enough. The practical moral is that in giving an analytic definition we should first try to find an appropriate category, then narrow it down into the appropriate subcategory, then find differentia within the subcategory.

Some philosophers have thought that some early theories of meaning arose from confusion on this point. On this view Plato, when he tried to define such concepts as "justice," mistakenly looked for a *substance* instead of correctly looking for a relation or a kind of action. It has also been claimed that some later theories looked in the wrong category in attempting to define certain ideas. To explain a mind as a "bundle" of ideas is to mistakenly think of ideas as substances that can be meaningfully thought of as being put in bundles. Both Plato and the "bundle" theorists might well deny that their theories rest on mistakes about categories, however; my explanation may not do justice to their theories.

CLUSTER DEFINITIONS

Usually in a definition of this kind every part of the definition is a *necessary* condition (nothing without that characteristic fits the definition) and all the parts together are a *sufficient* condition (anything with all the characteristics fits the definition). However, some words seem to lack a definition of this kind, every part of which is a necessary condition. In such cases we may have to be content with a *cluster definition*.

A cluster definition is a set of conditions such that if anything has all *or most* of these characteristics it will be a thing of the kind being defined, but it can lack *some* of the characteristics and still be a thing of that kind. For instance, the word "game" has been given as an example of a word that cannot be given a definition of the noncluster kind. In general, games are activities with no practical purpose, which obey certain rules, which have some standard of success (winning or losing), and which are engaged in for amusement. But a gambling game might be played mainly for profit, a children's game of cops and robbers might have no standard of success (is there any standard way you win or lose?), and a game of catch may have no real rules though it has a standard of success (you "win" if you catch the ball; you "lose" if you miss it).

However, an activity that lacks too many of these characteristics is not a game. Strolling by the seashore, a friend and I may throw rocks in the water for amusement. This activity has no practical purpose and is engaged in for amusement, but it has no rules and no real way of winning or losing, so it would be odd to call it a game. Of course, I could make it into a game by making up rules and some sort of standard of success (for example, we each get ten rocks and the one who throws farthest or makes the biggest splash wins).

The rules for definition we have given would apply to both cluster and "strict" (noncluster) definitions. It is also usually possible to find a larger class (genus) and differences from other things within the class (differentia) for both strict and cluster definitions. The difference between the two kinds of definitions is that the differentia will be necessary conditions for the strict definition, but not in the case of the cluster definition.

Can philosophers be satisfied with cluster definitions? In some cases they may have to be. Some philosophers have argued, for instance, that in biology as opposed to mathematics and physics we must be content with cluster definitions of key concepts:

> . . . certain authorities are willing to accept something less than the deductive ideal in the organization of scientific theories. The laws in such theories might also be less than universal in form. Perhaps statistical laws, possibly even approximations, trend, and tendency statements might count as genuine scientific laws. Certain authorities are also willing to countenance definitions which depart from the traditional ideal of sets of conditions which are severally necessary and jointly sufficient. Perhaps definitions in terms of properties which occur together quite frequently but without the universality required by the traditional notion of definition might be good enough. For example, the names of biological species as temporally extended lineages can be defined only as cluster concepts. That is, no property which can be used to distinguish the species under investigation from all other species is universally distributed among the members of the species and vice versa. At best, membership in the species is determined by an individual possessing enough of the most important character listed in its definition.[1]

With regard to concepts that philosophers are especially interested in, such as knowledge and goodness, most philosophers would prefer a strict definition, but at least some philosophers think that such definitions may not be attainable. A good rule of thumb might be to try for a strict definition if possible, and if this is not possible to get the best cluster definition you can.

EXERCISES

A. Below are three more definitions that Euthyphro gives for righteousness. Criticize each in terms of the six rules for definition.

    1. Righteousness is that part of justice which has to do with the careful attention which ought to be paid to the gods; and that what has to do with

[1]David Hull, *Philosophy of Biological Science* (Englewood Cliffs, N.J.: Prentice-Hall, 1974), p. 47.

the careful attention which ought to be paid to men is the remaining part of justice.

2. Righteousness is the science of asking of the gods and giving to them.

3. Righteousness is the art of carrying on business between gods and men.

B. Criticize the following definitions in terms of the six rules for definition. (*Source:* Hobbes, *Leviathan.*)

1. Hope is the desire for something with a belief that we can attain it.
2. Despair is the desire for something with a belief that we cannot obtain it.
3. Fear is aversion from something with a belief that it may harm us.
4. Courage is fear with a hope of avoiding the harm by resistance.
5. Anger is sudden courage.
6. Self-confidence is constant hope.
7. Indignation is anger for an unjust injury to another.
8. Ambition is desire for honor or power.
9. Timidity is fear of things which can do us little harm.
10. Jealousy is love with fear that the love is not returned.

C. Criticize the following definitions in terms of the six rules for definition. (*Source:* Spinoza, *Ethics.*)

1. Desire is the actual essence of a man insofar as it is conceived as determined to a particular activity by some given modification of itself.
2. Pleasure is the transition of a person from a less perfect state to a more perfect state.
3. Pain is the transition of a person from a more perfect state to a less perfect state.
4. Wonder is the thought of anything which brings the mind to a standstill because the concept in question has no connection with other concepts.
5. Contempt is the conception of anything which touches the mind so little that its presence leads the mind to imagine these qualities which are not in it rather than those which are in it.
6. Love is pleasure accompanied by the idea of an external cause.
7. Hatred is pain accompanied by the idea of an external cause.
8. Derision is a pleasure, arising from our thinking of the presence of a quality which we despise in the presence of an object which we hate.
9. Hope is an inconstant pleasure, arising from the idea of something, past or future, about which we are uncertain.
10. Fear is an inconstant pain arising from the idea of something, past or future, about which we are uncertain.
11. Confidence is pleasure arising from the idea of something, past or future, of which we are certain.
12. Despair is pain arising from the idea of something, past or future, of which we are certain.
13. Joy is pleasure accompanied by the idea of something past which turned out to be better than hoped for.
14. Disappointment is pain accompanied by the idea of something past which turned out to be worse than we hoped for.
15. Pity is pain accompanied by the idea of an evil which has befallen someone else who we think is like ourselves.

16. Approval is love toward one who has done good to another.
17. Indignation is hatred toward one who has done evil to another.
18. Partiality is thinking too highly of anyone because of the love we bear him.
19. Disparagement is thinking too badly of anyone because we hate him.
20. Envy is hatred insofar as it induces a person to be pained by another's good fortune and to rejoice in another's evil fortune.
21. Empathy is love insofar as it induces a man to feel pleasure at another's good fortune and pain at his misfortune.
22. Self-esteem is pleasure arising from a man's contemplation of himself and his own power of action.
23. Humility is pain arising from a man's contemplation of his own weakness of body and mind.
24. Repentance is pain accompanied by the idea of some action which we believe we have performed by the free decision of our mind.
25. Pride is thinking too highly of oneself from self-love.
26. Honor is pleasure accompanied by the idea of some action of our own which we believe to be praised by others.
27. Shame is pain accompanied by the idea of some action of our own which we believe to be blamed by others.
28. Regret is the desire to possess something kept alive by the remembrance of that thing and at the same time held in check by the thought of other things which prevent our possessing it.
29. Gratitude is the desire to benefit one who has conferred a benefit on us.
30. Anger is the desire to injure someone whom we hate.
31. Cruelty is the desire to injure someone whom we love or pity.
32. Timidity is the desire to avoid a greater evil, which we dread, by undergoing a lesser evil.
33. Daring is the desire which sets us on to do something that our peers are afraid to do.
34. Cowardice is a fear which prevents us from risking some danger which our peers dare to meet.
35. Courtesy is the desire to act in a way which will please others and to refrain from actions which will displease them.

D. Attempt to give a better definition for one of the words in Exercises A–C.

2

Simple Arguments
in Plato's Dialogues

After Socrates was condemned to death he spent a comparatively long time in prison, for he could not be executed until the end of a religious festival, marked by the return of a ship from the holy island of Delos. During this time a man named Crito, who had been one of the young men who argued philosophical questions with Socrates, made an effort to persuade Socrates to escape from prison. Crito's motives were mixed. No doubt that genuine affection for Socrates played some part, but Crito was also concerned for his own reputation if he stood by and let Socrates be executed with no effort to save him. He may also have felt some guilt, for he had made many enemies during his political career and some of these enemies may have voted to condemn Socrates as a way of getting revenge on his friend Crito. (It was fairly common in Athenian politics to get at a man too powerful to be attacked himself by attacking his friends.)

Socrates listened patiently to Crito's arguments, but he laid down certain principles at the beginning of the discussion: If Crito could persuade him that it was morally right to escape from prison, Socrates would agree to do so, but if Socrates escaped it had to be because he was persuaded that it was right to escape. We might put these principles in a more formal way as follows:

If it is right to escape then Socrates should escape.

If Socrates should escape then it is right to escape.

We could also put this in *one* statement, "Socrates should escape if and only if it is right to escape," but the two separate statements are more useful in seeing the structure of the arguments used by Socrates and Crito.

We might picture Crito as trying to argue in the following way:

If it is right to escape then Socrates should escape.

It is right to escape.

Therefore Socrates should escape.

ARGUMENT PATTERNS

The first two of these three statements are what *logicians*, those who study logic, call the *premises* of the argument. The third statement is the *conclusion*. The premises and conclusion together make up an *argument* and this argument is *valid*; any reasonable person who agreed that the premises were true would admit that the conclusion must be true. Socrates has agreed that the first premise, "If it is right to escape then Socrates should escape," is true, so if Crito can persuade him that the second premise, "It is right to escape," is true then Socrates, being a reasonable person, will admit that the conclusion, "Socrates should escape," is true. Most of Crito's arguments are attempts to establish the truth of "It is right to escape."

Socrates, on the other hand, gives arguments to show that "It is not right to escape" is true. His argument can be set out in this way:

If Socrates should escape then it is right to escape.

It is not right to escape.

Therefore Socrates should not escape.

This argument is valid also, and Crito has agreed to the first premise. Therefore if Socrates can convince Crito that the second premise, "It is not right to escape," is true, then as a reasonable person Crito should admit the conclusion, namely that "Socrates should not escape."

The statements "It is right to escape" and "It is not right to escape" are what logicians call *contradictory*; they cannot both be true, and if one of them is false then the other is true. To see the structure of an argument it is often useful to let a single letter stand for a whole statement and express the contradictory of that statement by putting "not" in front of the letter.

Thus, "R" might stand for "It is right to escape" and "not R" for "It is not right to escape."

An "if" statement like the first premises of our arguments really consists of *two* statements linked together by the "if . . . then" form. So if "E" stands for "Socrates should escape" then we can express "If Socrates should escape then it is right to escape" as "If E then R," and "If it is right to escape then Socrates should escape" can be expressed as "If R then E." Another way of saying "If it is right to escape then Socrates should escape" is "Socrates should escape only if it is right to escape." In terms of our letters, this is "E only if R." The statement "Socrates should escape if and only if it is right to escape" can be expressed as "E if and only if R," or as the two "if" statements

If R then E

If E then R.

Now we can express the arguments of Crito and Socrates as

Crito:	If R then E	Socrates:	If E then R
	R		not R
	———		———
	E		not E

Instead of writing out the word "therefore" we draw a line after the premises and put the conclusion below the line, as in

7

5
—
12

where "7" and "5" are the numbers being added and "12" is the sum.

Unfortunately, there are bad arguments which look very much like these valid arguments and can mislead people who are trying to give valid arguments. If Crito had argued:

If Socrates should escape, it is right to escape.

It is right to escape.

Therefore Socrates should escape.

If E then R

R
———
E

this argument would *not* be valid: A reasonable person who accepted its premises could reject its conclusion. We can see this by looking at a parallel argument with the same basic pattern.

> **If I am Socrates then I am a philosopher.**
> **I am a philosopher.**
> _____
> **I am Socrates.**

$$\text{If S then P}$$
$$\frac{P}{S}$$

Both premises are true: If I were Socrates I would be a philosopher, and I am in fact a philosopher. But that does not mean that I am Socrates. So while any argument of the pattern

$$\text{If A then B}$$
$$\frac{A}{B}$$

is valid, arguments of the pattern

$$\text{If A then B}$$
$$\frac{B}{A}$$

are invalid.

Similarly, if Socrates had argued:

> **If it is right to escape then Socrates should escape.**
> **It is not right to escape.**
> _____
> **Socrates should not escape**

$$\text{If R then E}$$
$$\frac{\text{not R}}{\text{not E}}$$

this would be an invalid argument as we can see from the parallel case.

If I am Socrates I am a philosopher.

I am not Socrates.

I am not a philosopher.

If S then P

not S

not P

The premises are both true: If I were Socrates I would be a philosopher, and I am not Socrates, but the conclusion is false: It is not true that I am not a philosopher.

So we can see that though arguments of the form

If A then B

not B

not A

are valid, arguments of the form

If A then B

not A

not B

are invalid.

CANCELLATION AND VALIDITY

How do we distinguish valid arguments from invalid arguments? Since there are a limited number of valid patterns that are actually used in everyday arguments, one quite workable technique is simply to name and memorize the valid forms and their invalid "look-alikes." There are traditional names, some in Latin, for valid patterns, and traditional names for common fallacies. The patterns we have examined so far are as follows:

Valid		Invalid	
If A then B		If A then B	
A	*Modus Ponens*	B	Fallacy of Affirming
B	(M.P.)	A	the Consequent

Valid		Invalid	
If A then B		If A then B	
not B	*Modus Tollens*	Not A	Fallacy of Denying the
not A	(M.T.)	not B	Antecedent

(The letter abbreviations for *Modus Ponens* and *Modus Tollens* will come in handy later for certain purposes.)

There are many other techniques, some quite elaborate, for deciding whether arguments are valid or invalid. In this chapter I will introduce a very simple and useful technique for checking the validity of an argument, based on an analogy with the operation of cancellation in mathematics. Suppose I am summing up a column of figures with some debits and some credits:

$$+ \; \$5.00$$
$$+ \; \$8.00$$
$$- \; \underline{\$5.00}$$

Instead of adding $5.00 and $8.00 and then subtracting −$5.00, we can simply say that the $5.00 credit and the $5.00 debit *cancel out*, leaving the $8.00 credit:

$$(\$5.00 \; + \; \$8.00)$$

$$-\$5.00$$

leaves $8.00

To set up a similar operation in logic we make use of the fact that "If A then B" means at least "Either not A or B." If I say "If I am Socrates I am a philosopher," the one situation that cannot be compatible with this is my being Socrates but not being a philosopher. But if I am not Socrates I may or may not be a philosopher. This can be expressed as "Either I am not Socrates or I am a philosopher"; "Either not S or P."

We will now introduce a few simple symbols to help us write the structure of arguments more clearly. We will use "p" and "q" as stand-ins for any arbitrary statement, and symbolize

"If p then q" as "p > q"

"Not p" as "p̂"

"Either p or q" as "p ∨ q"

"Either not p or q" as "p̂ ∨ q"

We can express what we have just said about "If p then q" and "Either not p or q" as a *rule*:

$$\frac{p > q}{\hat{p} \vee q}$$

Consequence of Implication (C.I.)

The line between the two statements means that we can validly conclude the bottom line given the top line as a premise. Thus, any time we can write "p > q" we can write "$\hat{p} \vee q$" giving as our justification "C.I." ("Consequence of Implication").

We now need one more rule to deal with the arguments we have seen so far. The rule is:

p ∨ q

$\hat{p}$ Disjunctive
            Syllogism (D.S.)

_____

q

In this pattern we regard the "p" and "$\hat{p}$" as *cancelling out*, leaving the "q," just as the +$5.00 and the −$5.00 cancelled out, leaving the $8.00. But the order of the statements, or which one is negative, doesn't matter.

The patterns

p ∨ q	p ∨ q	$\hat{p}$ ∨ q	p ∨ $\hat{q}$
$\hat{p}$	$\hat{q}$	p	q
_____	_____	_____	_____
q	p	q	p

are *all* cases of Disjunctive Syllogism just as

$$\frac{\begin{array}{c}(\$5.00 + \$8.00) \\ -\$5.00\end{array}}{\$8.00}$$

$$\frac{\begin{array}{c}(\$5.00 + \$8.00) \\ -\$8.00\end{array}}{\$5.00}$$

$$\frac{\begin{array}{c}(\$5.00 - \$8.00) \\ +\$8.00\end{array}}{\$5.00}$$

$$\frac{\begin{array}{c}(\$8.00 - \$5.00) \\ +\$5.00\end{array}}{\$8.00}$$

are all cases of mathematical cancellation.

Let us look at our valid and invalid patterns in this way. *Modus Ponens*

$$\frac{\begin{array}{l}\text{If p then q}\\ \text{p}\end{array}}{\text{q}}$$

becomes

$$\frac{\begin{array}{l} p > q \\ p \end{array}}{q}$$

and we replace "p > q" by "p̂ ∨ q" to get

$$\frac{\begin{array}{l} \hat{p} \vee q \\ p \end{array}}{q}$$

which is obviously a case of cancellation. Similarly with *Modus Tollens*

$$\frac{\begin{array}{l}\text{If p then q}\\ \text{not q}\end{array}}{\text{not p}} \quad \text{becomes} \quad \frac{\begin{array}{l} p > q \\ \hat{q} \end{array}}{\hat{p}} \quad \begin{array}{l}\text{which}\\ \text{becomes}\end{array} \quad \frac{\begin{array}{l} \hat{p} \vee q \\ \hat{q} \end{array}}{\hat{p}}$$

and the righthand form is another case of cancellation.

On the other hand, an invalid argument "won't cancel." Consider the Fallacy of Affirming the Consequent:

$$\frac{\begin{array}{l}\text{If p then q}\\ \text{q}\end{array}}{\text{p}}$$

becomes

$$\frac{\begin{array}{l} p > q \\ q \end{array}}{p}$$

Substituting "$\hat{p} \vee q$" for "$p > q$" we get

$$\hat{p} \vee q$$

$$\frac{q}{p}$$

and we can see that the "q's" will not cancel out, and even if they did we would have "$\hat{p}$" left instead of "p."

Similarly with Denying the Antecedent:

If p then q		p > q		$\hat{p} \vee q$
$\dfrac{\text{not } p}{\text{not } q}$	becomes	$\dfrac{\hat{p}}{\hat{q}}$	which becomes	$\dfrac{\hat{p}}{\hat{q}}$

and obviously the two "$\hat{p}$'s" don't cancel, and if they did would yield "q" rather than "$\hat{q}$."

Once we have grasped the principle involved we can simply "cancel" a letter standing alone and a letter which is the antecedent of an "if . . . then" statement or a negated letter standing alone and the consequent of an "if . . . then" statement. It may help to think of a statement to the left of the ">" we use for "if . . . then" as "inside" the angle and a letter under the "hat" we use for negation as also "inside" an angle. The general principle will be that letters "inside" an angle cancel letters "outside" an angle. If a letter is inside an angle, it must stay inside; if a letter is outside an angle, it must stay outside. In *Modus Ponens*:

$$p > q$$

$$\frac{p}{q}$$

we can see that "p >" and "p" cancel, leaving "q," which was outside an angle, as a simple letter. In *Modus Tollens*:

$$p > q$$

$$\frac{\hat{q}}{\hat{p}}$$

"q̂" and "q" cancel leaving "p >." But since "p >" by itself means nothing, we move the angle above the letter to give us "p̂." If we keep in mind the principles that letters inside an angle cancel letters outside, a letter inside an angle must stay inside, and a letter outside an angle must stay outside, then we can see a pattern that will be a key to many argument patterns.

A letter that is *both* under a "hat" and to the left of a ">" is the same as a simple letter: The two angles cancel *each other* out. This amounts to a *two-way* rule:

$$\frac{\hat{p} >}{p} \quad \text{or} \quad \frac{\hat{\hat{p}}}{p} \qquad \begin{array}{l}\text{Double} \\ \text{Negation (D.N.)}\end{array}$$

That is, a letter within two angles may be replaced by a letter inside none, and a letter inside no angles may be replaced by a letter inside two. The argument

$$\frac{\hat{p} > \hat{q}}{\quad q \quad} \\ p$$

which is an instance of *Modus Tollens*, uses this principle: "q" cancels "q̂" and "p̂ >" reduces to "p." The general principles also hold for simple applications of Disjunctive Syllogism without any "if . . . then" statements.

In the arguments

$$\frac{p \vee \hat{q}}{\hat{p}} \qquad \frac{\hat{p} \vee q}{\hat{q}} \qquad \frac{\hat{p} \vee \hat{q}}{p} \qquad \frac{\hat{p} \vee \hat{q}}{q}$$
$$\hat{q} \qquad\qquad \hat{p} \qquad\qquad \hat{q} \qquad\qquad \hat{p}$$

which are all instances of Disjunctive Syllogism, the letters with "hats" cancel the same letters without "hats," and the remaining letter is left, retaining its "hat" if it had one.

For instance, Socrates and Crito agree on the argument

Either we will follow the opinions of the uninformed majority or the opinions of the wise.

We will not follow the opinions of the uninformed majority.

Therefore we will follow the opinions of the wise.

Using "M" for "We will follow the opinions of the uninformed majority" and "W" for "We will follow the opinions of the wise" this becomes:

M or W

not M
_____

W

which becomes

$M \lor W$

$\hat{M}$
_____

W

which is obviously a case of Disjunctive Syllogism.

But sometimes the majority might agree with the wise, so it is not safe to argue

Either we will follow the opinions of the uninformed majority or we will follow the opinions of the wise.

We will follow the opinions of the wise.

Therefore we will not follow the opinions of the majority.

This becomes

M or W		$M \lor W$
M	or	M
___		___
not W		$\hat{W}$

which does not cancel out. This form

p or q		$p \lor q$	False Disjunctive
p		p	Syllogism
___		___	
not q		$\hat{q}$	

is misleading because sometimes in everyday speech "Either p or q" means "Either p or q *and not both*." But for logical purposes we will assume that

"Either p or q" means "One or the other and possibly both" and express "one or the other but not both" in a different way.

SOME NEW ARGUMENT FORMS

So far we have four valid forms of argument: Consequence of Implication, *Modus Ponens, Modus Tollens,* Disjunctive Syllogism, and invalid variants for each. We could probably analyze most arguments with a list of a dozen or so valid arguments and a few two-way rules like Double Negation. Or we could use cancellation methods to analyze arguments and decide validity by whether or not an argument cancels out to leave the conclusion. Both ways are effective, and both have some problems. There is an argument form involving two conditional statements as premises:

If p then q	or in symbols	$p > q$	Hypothetical
If q then r		$q > r$	Syllogism (H.S.)
If p then r		$p > r$	

We could convert this using Consequence of Implication (C.I.) to the form:

$$\hat{p} \vee q$$
$$\hat{q} \vee r$$
$$\hat{p} \vee r$$

However, there are two problems. First, we need a new rule, *Cancel and Collect*, to justify arguments of the forms:

$p \vee q$	$p \vee \hat{q}$	$\hat{p} \vee \hat{q}$	$\hat{p} \vee q$	$p \vee q$
$\hat{q} \vee r$	$q \vee r$	$q \vee r$	$\hat{q} \vee r$	$\hat{q} \vee \hat{r}$
$p \vee r$	$p \vee r$	$\hat{p} \vee r$	$\hat{p} \vee r$	$p \vee \hat{r}$ etc.

All of these are cases of Cancel and Collect (C.C.) and all are valid arguments.

However, the conclusion of Hypothetical Syllogism is *not* "$\hat{p} \vee r$" but the *stronger* statement "$p > r$." By saying "$p > r$" is stronger than "$\hat{p} \vee r$" we mean that we have a rule for going from "$p > r$" to "$\hat{p} \vee r$" but no rule for going from "$\hat{p} \vee r$" to "$p > r$."

We could solve this problem by interpreting "$p > r$" as meaning the *same* as "p̂ ∨ r" so we would have a *two-way* rule linking "p > r" and "p̂ ∨ r." But for reasons we will explain later we will *not* do this: Where we need a conclusion of the form "p > r" we will *not* use Consequence of Implication to change "p > q" to "p̂ ∨ q" and "q > r" to "q̂ ∨ r" and then cancel. Instead we will regard the "q" in "p > q" and the "q" in "q > r" as cancelling each other out in accordance with our general rule that a letter inside an angle cancels the same letter outside of an angle. We then "collect" the "p >" and "> r" into "p > r," so "p" stays inside an angle and "r" outside.

But we can collect the results of cancellation into an "if . . . then" statement only if both statements we cancelled were "if . . . then" statements. In the argument

$$p > q$$
$$\hat{q} \lor r$$
$$\overline{\hat{p} \lor r}$$

which is an instance of Cancel and Collect, the conclusion *must* be "p̂ ∨ r" and *cannot* be "p > r," since both statements involved in the cancellation were not "if . . . then" statements. (This is a *restriction* on H.S. and C.C. forbidding certain steps.)

(It is perfectly all right to insert negative statements into a pattern as long as the negative statement is inserted *every* time. Thus

$$p > \hat{q}$$
$$\hat{q} > r$$
$$\overline{p > r}$$

is a variant of Hypothetical Syllogism (H.S.), but

$$p > \hat{q}$$
$$q > r$$
$$\overline{p > r}$$

is not, because we did not put "q̂" instead of "q" in both occurrences of "q.")

We have now covered almost all of the common argument patterns and have shown how all of them can be treated as cases of cancellation. The arguments are:

If p then q	Consequence	$p > q$
——————	of Implication	——————
not p or q	(C.I.)	$\hat{p} \vee q$

If p then q	*Modus*	$p > q$
p	*Ponens*	p
——————	(M.P.)	——————
q		q

If p then q	*Modus*	$p > q$
not q	*Tollens*	$\hat{q}$
——————	(M.T.)	——————
not p		$\hat{p}$

Either p or q	Disjunctive	$p \vee q$
not p	Syllogism	$\hat{p}$
——————	(D.S.)	——————
q		q

Either p or q	Cancel	$p \vee q$
Either not q or r	and	$\hat{q} \vee r$
——————	Collect	——————
Either p or r	(C.C.)	$p \vee r$

If p then q	Hypothetical	$p > q$
If q then r	Syllogism	$q > r$
——————	(H.S.)	——————
If p then r		$p > r$

We also had a two-way rule useful in transforming statements

$$\frac{\hat{\hat{p}} >}{p} \quad \text{or} \quad \frac{\hat{\hat{p}}}{p} \quad \text{Double Negation (D.N.)}$$

We will now consider a useful but rather puzzling two-way rule:

$$\frac{p \vee p}{p} \quad \text{or} \quad \begin{array}{c} p \\ p \\ \hline p \end{array} \quad \begin{array}{l} \text{Repetition} \\ \text{(Rep.)} \end{array}$$

This rule says that you neither add nor take away anything by expressing "p" as "p or p," or by saying it twice. This is quite unlike mathematics where 5 is certainly *not* the same as 5 + 5. It means that in the logical case we can use the *same* statement to make *two* cancellations; for example:

> If we follow the opinion of the wise, it is not right to escape.
>
> If we follow the opinion of the wise, Socrates should not escape.
>
> We will follow the opinion of the wise.
> _____
> It is not right to escape.
>
> Socrates should not escape.

In cancellation form:

$$\begin{array}{c} W > R \\ W > E \\ W \\ \hline R \\ E \end{array}$$

where the one "W" cancels *both* "W's."

1	W > R	Premise
2	W > E	Premise
3	W	Premise
4	R	1,3 M.P.
5	E	2,3 M.P.

(Note that we simply cite line numbers, instead of "Premise 1," "Line 4," etc., from now on.)

This is perfectly legitimate and this argument *is* valid.

The reason for this is that, whereas with money we can only spend the money once and then it is gone, with information we do not "use up" an item of information by using it in an argument. If I draw money from the bank and spend it, the money is gone. If I look up a fact in the encyclopedia and use it, the information remains there to be used again.

SETTING UP ARGUMENTS

To write out a complex argument we *number* the premises. Each line that is a premise has Premise (or "P") written to the right of it.

Example	1 p $\lor$ q	Premise
	2 $\hat{p}$	Premise

Each line that is not a premise must be *justified* by writing the number of the lines that are used to get this line and the rule that justifies getting this line.

$$3 \quad q \qquad\qquad 1,2 \text{ D.S.}$$

Usually we will take two premises at a time, get a conclusion from them, and then use that conclusion with one of the other premises to get a further conclusion.

Example	1 p $\lor$ q	P	(We write "P" as an
	2 p > r	P	abbreviation for "Premise.")
	3 $\hat{q}$	P	
	4 p	1,3 D.S.	
	5 r	2,4 M.P.	

Sometimes we may not know which will follow from given premises. If we do, we can write it to the right of the premises.

Example	1 p	P	
	2 p > $\hat{r}$	P	Conclusion: s
	3 r $\lor$ s	P	

If we do not, we write out a question mark to the right of the premises:

    1 p ∨ q   P
    2 p > r   P   Conclusion?
    3 r̂   P

If we think the *opposite* of a given statement may be true we can write it out with a question mark:

    1 p   P
    2 p > r̂   P   Conclusion q?
    3 q̂ ∨ r   P

If the opposite of the proposed conclusion *does* turn out to be true, we say we have *refuted* the conclusion.

Sometimes an implication or disjunction may be *part* of another statement, as "If either p or q then r." To avoid ambiguity in such cases we will use parentheses for punctuation. Thus, "If either p or q then r" would be "(p ∨ q) > r" and "Either p or if q then r" would be "p ∨ (q > r)." "If p then q is true then r is true" would be "(p > q) > r," while "If p is true then if q is true then r is true" would be "p > (q > r)."

Given these new logical techniques we can now return to the arguments of the *Crito* and do them more justice. Crito's major argument for his conclusion "It is right for Socrates to escape" can be put as follows:

If Socrates does not escape he will leave his children without a father.

If he leaves his children without a father he will injure his children.

If he injures his children he does something unjust.

If it is true that if Socrates does not escape then he does something unjust, then it is right to escape.

We symbolize this argument using the symbol "#" as short for "stands for" when we give letter abbreviations for statements.

    1 Ê > W   E # Socrates escapes
    2 W > I   W # Socrates will leave his children without a father
    3 I > U   I # Socrates injures his children
    4 (Ê > U) > R   U # Socrates does something unjust
    ─────────
       R   R # It is right for Socrates to escape

The argument cancels to the conclusion:

1 $\hat{E} > W$ (1−3 cancel to $\hat{E} > U$, and this cancels the

2 $W > I$ $\hat{E} > U$ in the antecedent of 4.)

3 $I > U$

4 $(\hat{E} > U) > R$

Notice that we cannot cancel the "$\hat{E} > U$" in the antecedent of the last premise by simply using single letters. Even if we regarded the "E" as being inside three angles (the cap, the ">" between "E" and "U" and the ">" between "$\hat{E} > U$" and "R"), and the "U" as being inside one angle (the ">" between "$\hat{E} > U$" and "R"), we have no rule to cancel the "E" and "U" individually: We must cancel the whole expression "$\hat{E} > U$" which is inside the ">" between it and "R" with the "$\hat{E} > U$" which results from lines 1−3. This cancellation will be an example of *Modus Ponens*, with the whole expression "$\hat{E} > U$" substituted for the "p" in the pattern.

We can prove the conclusion as follows:

1 $\hat{E} > W$

2 $W > I$

3 $I > U$

4 $(\hat{E} > U) > R$

5 $\hat{E} > I$ 1,2 H.S.

6 $\hat{E} > U$ 3,5 H.S.

7 R 4,6 M.P.

Socrates both gives positive arguments for "It is not right to escape" and refutes Crito's argument. His counterargument can be represented as follows:

If I do not escape, my friends will take care of my children.

If my friends take care of my children, I will not injure my children.

If I will not injure my children, I will not be doing something unjust.

If it is true that if I don't escape then I will not be doing something unjust, then it is not right to escape.

Therefore it is not right to escape.

In symbols:

$\hat{E} > F$ F # Socrates' friends will look after his children.

$F > \hat{I}$ I,U,R, as above

$\hat{I} > \hat{U}$

$(\hat{E} > \hat{U}) > \hat{R}$

This cancels to the conclusion:

$\hat{E} > F$ $> F$ cancels F

$F > \hat{I}$ $> \hat{I}$ cancels $\hat{I} >$

$\hat{I} > \hat{U}$ This leaves $\hat{E} > \hat{U}$, which cancels $\hat{E} > \hat{U}$

$(\hat{E} > \hat{U}) > \hat{R}$ in the last premise.

The argument can be proved as follows:

1 $\hat{E} > F$

2 $F > \hat{I}$

3 $\hat{I} > \hat{U}$

4 $(\hat{E} > \hat{U}) > R$

5 $\hat{E} > \hat{I}$ 1,2 H.S.

6 $\hat{E} > \hat{U}$ 3,5 H.S.

7 $\hat{R}$ 4,6 M.P.

Socrates also gives another argument:

If I escape and take my children with me then we will live in some country less free than Athens.

If we live in some country less free than Athens, this will be bad for my children.

If this will be bad for my children, then I will have injured them.

If I injure my children, I do something unjust.

If it is true that if I escape and take my children then I do something unjust, then it is not right to escape.

Therefore it is not right to escape.

In symbols:

T > L	T # Socrates escapes and takes his children
L > A	L # They will live in a place less free
A > I	than Athens
I > U	A # Living in a place less free than
(T > U) > R̂	Athens will be bad for Socrates'
	children

R̂

This cancels as follows:

T > L	> L cancels L >
L > A	> A cancels A >
A > I	> I cancels I >
I > U	This cancels to T > U, which cancels
(T > U) > R̂	T > U in the last premise

R̂

The conclusion can be proved as follows:

1	T > L	
2	L > A	
3	A > I	
4	I > U	
5	(T > U) > R̂	
6	T > A	1,2 H.S.
7	T > I	6,3 H.S.
8	T > U	7,4 H.S.
9	R̂	8,5 M.P.

Socrates' positive arguments for not escaping, as opposed to his rebuttal of Crito's argument, can be put as follows:

If I break an agreement I do something unjust.

If I have been content with Athenian laws all my life then I have agreed to keep those laws.

If I have agreed to keep those laws then if I do something forbidden by Athenian laws, I break an agreement.

If I escape I do something forbidden by Athenian laws.

I have been content with Athenian laws all my life.

If it is true that if I escape I do something unjust, then it is not right to escape.

Therefore it is not right to escape.

In symbols:

$B > U$	B # Socrates breaks an agreement
$C > A$	C # Socrates has been content with Athenian laws all his life
$A > (F > B)$	
$E > F$	A # Socrates has agreed to keep Athenian laws
C	F # Socrates does something forbidden by Athenian law
$(E > U) > \hat{R}$	

$\hat{R}$

This cancels as follows:

$B > U$	C cancels $C >$
$C > A$	$> A$ cancels $A >$
$A > (F > B)$	$B >$ cancels $> B$
$E > F$	$F >$ cancels $> F$
C	leaving $E > U$, which cancels
$(E > U) > \hat{R}$	$E > U$ in the last premise

$\hat{R}$

In proof form:

$$1\ \ B > U$$
$$2\ \ C > A$$
$$3\ \ A > (F > B)$$
$$4\ \ E > F$$
$$5\ \ C$$
$$6\ \ (E > U) > \hat{R}$$

7 A	2,5 M.P.
8 F > B	3,7 M.P.
9 F > U	8,1 H.S.
10 E > U	9,4 H.S.
11 $\hat{R}$	10,6 M.P.

Socrates also gives another argument:

If I perform an act of ingratitude I act unjustly.

If the Laws of Athens have benefited me then if I do something forbidden by these laws I perform an act of ingratitude.

If the Laws of Athens enabled me to be born and brought up in freedom, then they have benefited me.

The Laws of Athens have enabled me to be born and brought up in freedom.

If I escape I do something forbidden by the Laws of Athens.

If it is true that if I escape I act unjustly then it is not right to escape.

Therefore it is not right to escape.

We can symbolize this argument as follows:

$P > U$	P # Socrates is performing an act of ingratitude
$B > (F > P)$	B # The Laws of Athens have benefited Socrates
$L > B$	F # Socrates does something forbidden by the Laws
L	L # The Laws of Athens have enabled Socrates to be
$E > F$	born and brought up in freedom
$(E > U) > \hat{R}$	
$\overline{\hat{R}}$	

The argument cancels to the conclusion:

P > U	L cancels L >
B > (F > P)	B > cancels > B
L > B	> F cancels F >
L	> P cancels P > leaving E > U, which cancels
E > F	E > U in the last premise
(E > U) > $\hat{R}$	
$\overline{}$	
$\hat{R}$	

As a matter of fact, Crito does not put up much argument against these premises, but it is worth noting that the premises which Socrates uses would be difficult for Crito to argue with. Crito represents himself, and perhaps really thinks of himself, as a patriotic Athenian indignant at the injustice done to Socrates and grateful to Socrates for his teaching. Thus, it would be hard for him to say, "Ingratitude is not unjust" or "Athenian Law does not benefit its citizens." Similarly, Crito, a somewhat conventional man, will find it difficult to deny seeming truisms such as "If Socrates leaves his children without a father he injures them" or "If Socrates injures his children he does something unjust." As a patriotic Athenian he will find it hard to deny that the Laws of Athens have enabled Socrates to be born and brought up in freedom, thus that the Laws have benefited Socrates. Nor will he want to deny that it would disadvantage Socrates' children to be brought up away from Athens.

If Crito were a little more intelligent he might try to argue that exile for the children with Socrates still alive and able to teach and inspire them might be better than being left to the care of those who are not family, even if they are friends of Socrates. Or he might challenge the last premise of Socrates' rebuttal: that if it is true that Socrates does not escape he does not do something unjust, then it is not right to escape. But by and large Crito argues with platitudes himself and is unable to challenge the platitudes that Socrates uses in return. As often in the dialogues, Socrates argues with his opponent very much in the opponent's own terms.

There are a great many arguments in Plato's dialogues about Socrates that can be better understood by being broken down into simple propositions and set up as arguments in the system of logic given in this chapter. In many cases we may want to challenge the premises of the arguments, but usually they are valid: They cancel to their conclusions and can be proved by the rules.

However, in arguments by less able philosophers, and even sometimes in Plato's dialogues, we find arguments that are invalid, and thus will not cancel to the indicated conclusion. In the exercises at the end of this chapter, both valid and invalid arguments are presented to give you practice in detecting invalid arguments and establishing valid ones.

When you encounter an invalid argument it is often good practice to see if any reasonable alteration of the premises would give a valid argument to the conclusion indicated. When the argument seems to be valid a "double check" system is a good idea: First see if the argument cancels to its conclusion and then try to construct a proof.

APPENDIX TO CHAPTER 2

The argument patterns we have given so far will handle most arguments we are likely to encounter in ordinary philosophical contexts. But more complex arguments do occur, and to handle them we need a more complete system of statement logic. To begin with, we need a new symbol to express the idea of "and"; we will write "p and q" as "p $\wedge$ q." The basic rule for this new connective is:

$$\frac{p \wedge q}{} \quad \text{Conjunction}$$

p

q

That is, from "p" and "q" separately we can conclude "Both p and q" and from "Both p and q" we can conclude "p" and "q" separately.

But now we have a problem distinguishing "Not both p and q" from "Both not p and q" in our symbolic language. It looks as if "$\hat{p} \wedge q$" might mean either one. To get over the ambiguity we must introduce a larger hat over a larger statement. Thus, "$\hat{p} \wedge q$" will be "Both not p and q" while $\overline{p \wedge q}$ will be "Not both p and q."

We can now state an argument form using "not both A and B":

$$
\begin{array}{ccc}
\text{Not both p and q} & & \overline{p \wedge q} \\
\underline{p } & \text{which} & \underline{p } \\
\text{not q} & \text{becomes} & \hat{q}
\end{array}
$$

To get this in form for cancellation we make use of a fact about "not" combined with "and" which can be expressed as a *two-way* rule:

$$
\begin{array}{ccc}
\underline{\text{not (p and q)}} & \text{DeMorgan's} & \overline{p \wedge q} \\
\text{not p or not q} & \begin{array}{l} \text{Rule} \\ \text{(De.M.)} \end{array} & \hat{p} \vee \hat{q}
\end{array}
$$

where the double line means we can go from $\overline{p \wedge q}$ to "p $\vee$ q" *or* from "$\hat{p} \vee \hat{q}$" to "$\overline{p \wedge q}$." Given this two-way rule we can go from

$$\overline{p \wedge q} \qquad \hat{p} \vee \hat{q}$$

$$p \qquad \text{to} \quad p$$

$$\overline{} \qquad\qquad \overline{}$$

$$\hat{q} \qquad\qquad \hat{q}$$

which is plainly a case of Disjunctive Syllogism.

On the other hand, a fallacy that looks like the argument we have just seen is:

> Not both p and q
>
> Not p
>
> ―――――――――
>
> Not q

For example:

> **I am not both Socrates and a philosopher.**
>
> **I am not Socrates.**
>
> **Therefore I am not a philosopher.**

which becomes

> Not Both S and P
>
> Not S
>
> ―――――――――
>
> Not P

In symbols this is

$$\overline{S \wedge P}$$

$$\hat{S}$$

$$\overline{}$$

$$\hat{P}$$

which can be transformed by DeMorgan's Rule (De.M.) to

$$\hat{S} \vee \hat{P}$$

$$\hat{S}$$

$$\overline{}$$

$$\hat{P}$$

where plainly the two "$\hat{S}$'s" don't cancel.

So if Socrates argued:

I can't both follow the opinion of the wise and the opinion of the un-informed multitude.

I won't follow the opinion of the uninformed multitude.

I won't follow the opinion of the wise.

This would be a fallacy:

Not both W and M		$\overline{W \wedge M}$		$\hat{W} \vee \hat{M}$
Not M	which becomes	$\hat{M}$	which becomes	$\hat{M}$
Not W		$\hat{W}$		$\hat{W}$

because the two "M's" don't cancel out.
    There are other invalid variants of this argument:

$\overline{p \wedge q}$	$\overline{p \wedge q}$	$\overline{p \wedge q}$	$\overline{p \wedge q}$
$\hat{p}$	$\hat{q}$	p	q
$\hat{q}$	$\hat{p}$	q	p

none of which cancel out to the conclusion

$\hat{p} \vee \hat{q}$	$\hat{p} \vee \hat{q}$	$\hat{p} \vee \hat{q}$	$\hat{p} \vee \hat{q}$
$\hat{p}$	$\hat{q}$	p	q
$\hat{q}$	$\hat{p}$	q	p

Certain traditional argument patterns can be handled by our techniques.

If p then q	
If r then s	Constructive
p or r	Dilemma (C.D.)
q or s	

If p then q

If r then s   Destructive

Not q or not s   Dilemma (D.D.)

Not p or not r

In symbols these are

p > q   Constructive   p > q   Destructive

r > s   Dilemma (C.D.)   r > s   Dilemma (D.D.)

p ∨ r   q̂ ∨ ŝ

---

q ∨ s   p̂ ∨ r̂

and they work out very well by *two* applications of Cancel and Collect:

1 p > q   Premise

2 r > s   Premise

3 p ∨ r   Premise

4 q ∨ r   1, 3, C.C.

5 q ∨ s   2, 4, C.C.

1 p > q   Premise

2 r > s   Premise

3 q̂ ∨ ŝ   Premise

4 p̂ ∨ ŝ   1, 3, C.C.

5 p̂ ∨ r̂   2, 4, C.C.

Because the conclusion of these two arguments is of the "Either . . . or" form, there is no problem about "p̂ ∨ q" being weaker than "p > q."

Moreover, because we sometimes need to change the *order* of a line we will sometimes need the two-way rules.

p ∨ q   Commutation   p ∧ q
=====   (Com.)   =====
q ∨ p   q ∧ p

There are no explicit examples of Constructive Dilemma or Destructive Dilemma in Socrates' argument with Crito, but we could reconstruct some of their reasoning as follows:

If we follow the opinion of the uninformed majority it is right for Socrates to escape.

If we follow the opinion of the wise, Socrates should not escape.

Either we follow the opinion of the uninformed majority or we follow the opinion of the wise.

It is right for Socrates to escape or Socrates should not escape.

which in symbols is:

If M then R		$M > R$
If W then not E		$W > \hat{E}$
M or W	or	$M \lor W$
R or not E		$R \lor \hat{E}$

As we can see, this is a case of Constructive Dilemma, and it cancels out.
   Alternatively they might argue:

If we follow the opinion of the uninformed majority it is right to escape.

If we follow the opinion of the wise, Socrates should not escape.

Either it is not right for Socrates to escape or it is not true that Socrates should not escape.

Therefore either we do not follow the opinion of the uninformed majority or we do not follow the opinion of the wise.

In symbols:

If M then R	$M > R$
If W then not S	$W > \hat{S}$
not R or not not S	$\hat{R} \lor \hat{\hat{S}}$
Not M or not W	$\hat{M} \lor \hat{W}$

Parentheses for grouping will enable us to mix "or" with "and" while avoiding ambiguity, to distinguish between

Either Socrates should escape and follow the opinion of the wise or follow the opinion of the uninformed majority.

$$(E \wedge W) \vee M$$

and

Socrates should escape and either follow the opinion of the wise or follow the opinion of the uninformed majority.

$$E \wedge (W \vee M)$$

For the sake of completeness we need rules to tell us what to do when we need to untangle a complex statement of this kind; the rules:

$$\frac{p \wedge q}{p \vee q} \qquad \text{And to Or (A.O.)}$$

$$\frac{p \vee (q \wedge r)}{(p \vee q) \wedge (p \vee r)} \qquad \text{Distribution (Dist.)}$$

$$\frac{p \wedge (q \vee r)}{(p \wedge q) \vee (p \wedge r)} \qquad \text{Distribution (Dist.)}$$

$$\frac{p > q}{p > (p \wedge q)} \qquad \text{Absorption (Abs.)}$$

$$\frac{p > (q > r)}{(p \wedge q) > r} \qquad \text{Exportation (Exp.)}$$

But these rules will seldom be used. However, one fairly useful two-way rule tells us that

$$\frac{p > q}{\hat{q} > \hat{p}} \qquad \text{Transposition (Transp.)}$$

For example, "If we follow the opinions of the uninformed multitude it is right to escape" means the same as "If it is not right to escape then it is not right to follow the opinions of the uninformed multitude." (Warning: "p > q" is *not* the same as "q > p.")

It is also useful to have a special symbol for "if and only if" and a rule that tells us that "p if and only if q" can be broken down into two "if" statements. We will write "p if and only if q" as "p <> q" and give the rules

p <> q	Definition	p <> q	Commutation
――――――	of Equivalence	――――――	(Com.)
p > q	(D.E.)	q <> p	
q > p			

Finally, we need a few rules dealing with combinations of ">" and other connectives:

(p ∨ q) > r	p > (q r)	p ∧ q̂
―――――――	―――――――	―――――――
p > r	p > q	‾p > q‾
q > r	p > r	
Implication	Implication of And	Negation of
of Or (I.O.)	(I.A.)	Implication (N.I.)

We now have enough rules to handle almost any argument by rule technique, and enough transformation rules to handle almost any argument by cancellation techniques. The exercises contain arguments from the debate between Crito and Socrates as well as from other arguments Socrates had with other opponents, as reported by Plato in his dialogues. The more complicated rules in the Appendix will be used only in the later sets of exercises.

EXERCISES

Symbolize,* show valid or invalid by cancellation, and if valid give a proof.
A. (*Source:* Plato, *Euthyphro, Apology.*)
    1. If righteousness meant "what is pleasing to the gods," an action could be both righteous and unrighteous. An action cannot be both righteous and

―――――――

*When you symbolize, always give a "dictionary" showing which letter you use to abbreviate which sentence or phrase.

unrighteous. Therefore, righteousness does not mean "what is pleasing to the gods."

2. If the gods love courage it is righteous. Courage is righteous. Therefore, the gods love it.

3. If the gods love courage it is always good. Courage is not always good. Therefore, the gods don't love it.

4. If Euthyphro is righteous, he is just. If he is just he is pleasing to the gods. Therefore, if Euthyphro is pleasing to the gods he is righteous.

5. If the service which we pay to the gods is like the service the trainer pays to his horses, then we will improve and benefit the gods of our service. But, if we improve and benefit the gods by our service, the gods stand in need of us. However, the gods do not stand in need of us. Therefore, the service we pay to the gods is not like that the trainer pays to his horses.

6. If our services to the gods are like those services a slave does for his master, the gods profit in some way from our services. If they profit from our services, they owe us something. But our services to the gods are not like those a slave does for his master. Therefore, the gods owe us nothing.

7. If our worship of the gods is like a business transaction, then the gods must gain something. But, if the gods gain something, they are benefited by us. But we cannot benefit the gods. Therefore, our worship is not like a business transaction.

8. If Socrates were like the philosophers described by the comic poets, he would speculate about the heavens and try to make the weaker case appear stronger. But Socrates neither speculates about the heavens nor tries to make the weaker case stronger. Therefore, he is not like the philosophers described by the comic poets.

9. If prejudices have risen against Socrates, then if he has not been doing what the comic poets describe, then he must have been doing something out of the ordinary. But he has not been doing what the comic poets describe. Therefore, he must have been doing something out of the ordinary.

10. If no one is wiser than Socrates, then Socrates must be very wise or others must not be as wise as they appear. But Socrates is not very wise. Therefore, others must not be as wise as they appear.

B.   Source: Plato, *Meno*

1. If Socrates did not believe that when he dies he will be in the company of gods and good men, he would do wrong in not objecting to death. If he does believe this, he would not do wrong in not objecting to death. He does believe it. Therefore, he would do wrong in not objecting to death.

2. If death is the separation of the soul from the body, then, if the soul can exist apart from the body, the soul becomes free of the body through death. It is not true that the soul becomes free of the body through death. Therefore, either death is not the separation of the soul from the body or else the soul cannot exist apart from the body.

3. If the body is a hindrance to the soul, then it is good for the soul to be free of the body. If this is true, then death is not to be feared. But, if in the knowledge of the highest things the soul is deceived by the body, the

body is a hindrance to the soul. But the soul is deceived by the body in this way. Therefore, death is not to be feared.

4. If it is impossible in company with the body to know anything purely, one of two things follows: Either true knowledge is possible nowhere or only after death. But, if partial knowledge can be had in this life, then true knowledge is possible somewhere. But we can have partial knowledge in this life. Therefore, either true knowledge was not possible after death, or it would not be impossible in company with the body to know anything purely.

5. If death is a freeing of the soul and if philosophy seeks to free the soul, then, if you are truly a philosopher, you will not fear death. But death *is* a freeing of the soul, and this *is* what philosophy seeks. Therefore, if you fear death you are not truly a philosopher.

6. If the soul is destroyed when the body is destroyed, then death is to be feared, but, if the soul is not destroyed when the body dies, there is hope. So it follows that, if there is no hope, death is to be feared.

7. If people are questioned properly, then they show knowledge not acquired during this life. They could not do this if they had not acquired their knowledge in a previous life. If they acquired their knowledge in a previous life, it can be proved that the soul can exist independent of the body. Thus, if people are questioned properly, then it can be proved that the soul can exist independent of the body.

8. If we recognize some things as equal and some as unequal, then we must know what equality itself is. But, if nothing in our sense experience is the same as equality itself, either we don't know what equality itself is or we don't acquire this knowledge by sense experience. If we don't acquire this knowledge through sense experience, then we were born having some knowledge. Since we do recognize some things as equal and some as unequal, and, since nothing in our sense experience is the same as equality itself, it follows that we were born having some knowledge.

9. If the soul is like a tune played on a musical instrument, then it could not exist before the body existed. But, if the argument from recollection is a good one, then the soul did exist before the body existed. If the soul did exist before the body existed, it could exist before the body existed. Therefore, either the argument from recollection is not a good one or the soul is not like a tune played on a musical instrument.

10. If the soul is immortal, fear of death is out of place. But, if the soul outwears many bodies but at last wears out itself, the soul is not immortal. If the soul is like the eternal Ideas, however, it is immortal. But the soul is like the eternal Ideas. So, therefore, it is not true that the soul outwears many bodies but at last wears out itself, and fear of death is out of place.

C. (*Source*: Plato, *Crito* and *Apology*) Ignore phrases in parentheses.

1. (Crito is practicing athletics.) He will either pay attention to the trainer's opinion or to the opinion of the multitude, but not to both. If he pays attention to the opinion of the trainer, he will not fear the multitude's blame, and welcome their praise. If he pays attention to the multitude, he will fear the blame and welcome the praise of the multitude. If he does not pay attention to the trainer's opinion, he does harm to himself.

Therefore, if he pays attention to the opinion of the multitude, he has done harm to himself and has feared the blame and welcomed the praise of the multitude.

2. Socrates will not do what is wrong. if he returns evil for evil, he will do wrong. If he breaks an agreement with the state because he has been unjustly condemned, he will return evil for evil. If he makes his escape he will be breaking an agreement. Therefore, he will not make his escape.

3. If the Laws of Athens enabled Socrates' parents to marry and to raise and educate Socrates, then the Laws are even more to be respected than his parents. If they are, then if he attempts to destroy the Laws, this would be as bad as attempting to destroy his parents. The Laws of Athens did enable Socrates' parents to marry and to raise and educate Socrates. If Socrates attempts to escape, he will disobey the Law. Disobeying the Law means destroying the Law. Therefore, if Socrates attempts to escape, this would be as bad as attempting to destroy his parents.

4. If Socrates did not approve of the Laws of Athens, he could have either emigrated from Athens or tried to have the Laws changed. If he neither emigrated nor tried to have the Laws changed, then Socrates agreed to obey the Laws. It is not true that Socrates emigrated from Athens. He did not try to have the Laws changed. Therefore, he approved of the Laws and agreed to obey them.

5. If Socrates escapes, then his friends will suffer. If he escapes, he will be regarded as an enemy if he is a lawbreaker. Escaping is breaking the Law. Therefore, if Socrates escapes, he will be regarded as an enemy, and his friends will suffer.

6. If Socrates avoids well-governed cities, his life will not be worth living. If he goes to Thessaly, he will become a laughing stock and will not be able to bring up his children well. Escaping means that Socrates will go to Thessaly or will avoid well-governed cities, so either his life is not worth living, or his children will not be well brought up.

7. If Socrates escapes, then things will not be better for him in this world, and, when he comes to the next world, he will come as a lawbreaker. If Socrates is pursued by Crito, he will escape. If things will not be better for him in this world, he will not be happy in this world, and, if he comes to the next world as a lawbreaker, he will not be happy in the next world. Therefore, if Socrates is persuaded by Crito, he will be unhappy both in this world and in the next.

8. Either the dead man feels nothing, or death is a change and migration for the soul from this place to another place. If the dead man feels nothing, then eternity is like a night of dreamless sleep, and death is a blessing. If death is a change and migration from this place to another, then we shall be with the great men of the past, and death is a blessing. Thus, death is a blessing.

9. If Socrates meets the souls of the great after death, he will cross-examine them. If he cross-examines them, then, he cannot be put to death for cross-examining them. If he cannot be put to death for it, he can spend eternity cross-examining the souls of the great and will be eternally happy.

Thus, if Socrates meets the souls of the great after death, he will be eternally happy.

10. If no evil can happen to a good man either living or dead, then Socrates' death is not an evil. If his death is not an evil, his "signal" would not have warned him to act differently at his trial, and he would have no reason to be angry with his accusers. Thus, if Socrates did have reason to be angry with his accusers, this would mean that it was false that no evil can happen to a good man, either living or dead.

D. 1. Take one of the invalid arguments in exercises A–C and change *one* premise to make it a valid argument. If this is not possible, explain why.

2. Take one of the invalid arguments in exercises A–C and make it valid by *adding* one premise.

3. Take one of the valid arguments in exercises A–C and argue for or against its premises.

3

Arguments
in Medieval Philosophy

We now make a historical jump from the beginning of philosophy in Greece to the middle of the next great period of philosophy. After the death of Socrates his pupil Plato founded a philosophical school known as the Academy. One of the students at the Academy, who later founded a school of his own, was Aristotle, the first philosopher to study logic systematically. After Aristotle the center of philosophical interest moved away from Athens and also to some extent away from the theoretical questions that interested Socrates, Plato, and Aristotle. As the empire of Alexander the Great broke up and the Roman Empire began to emerge, philosophers were mainly interested in questions about how to live the most satisfactory life in a world of change and danger. Later, when barbarian invaders overwhelmed the Roman Empire, there was a period in which intellectual activities of all kinds—science, mathematics, philosophy—were largely neglected in the struggle to survive.

At the end of the classical period, however, Christian philosophers such as Boethius in Rome and Augustine in Roman Africa had incorporated a great deal of Greek philosophy into their thinking about Christianity. During the Dark Ages the works of Boethius and Augustine and many works of the Greek philosophers were preserved and copied in Christian monastaries, leading to the great revival of philosophical activity in the

Middle Ages. In the thirteenth century there was vigorous philosophical activity, spurred by the rediscovery and translation of manuscripts of Aristotle's work and also by the intellectual clashes among Christianity, Judaism, and Islam.

The Christian, Jewish, and Moslem philosophers of the Middle Ages were beset with the problem of relating their religious beliefs both to the classical culture that was becoming increasingly known to scholars and to rival religious systems. This led to an intellectual culture that was very much aware of alternative views and very argumentative, in sharp contrast to the stereotype of the Middle Ages as monolithic and completely subject to faith and authority.

AQUINAS AND THE *SUMMA*

One towering figure in the medieval philosophy was Thomas Aquinas, an Italian who defied the objections of his noble family to become a Dominican friar, a member of a religious order dedicated to spreading and defending Christianity by preaching and teaching. (The official name of this order, founded by Saint Dominic, a Spaniard, is "The Order of Preachers" and its motto is "Truth.")

Aquinas was a student of the German Dominican Albert the Great and was later a teacher himself at the University of Paris. He absorbed the works of Aristotle, which were just being translated into Latin by another Dominican. Aquinas was familiar with the works of such great Jewish medieval philosophers as Maimonides and such great Moslem philosophers as Avicenna. Aquinas' encyclopedic work, the *Summa Theologica*, discusses a great many philosophical topics as well as many theological ones. For Aquinas, theology itself was the application of philosophical methods to the truths revealed in both the Old and New Testaments. Thus, in arguing with Islamic and Jewish philosophers, he had as common ground with them the philosophical methods developed from the study of Greek philosophy and the Old Testament, which was accepted by both Moslems and Jews.

The form of the *Summa Theologica* is very typical of medieval philosophy. Each problem and topic is divided into subproblems, and nothing is taken for granted. The topic of the first part of the *Summa* is God, and Aquinas begins by asking whether the existence of God can even be argued about; he then considers arguments for *and against* the existence of God.

The structural form of the *Summa* consists of "articles" in which each subtopic is written as a question; for example, "Can it be proved that God exists?" There are then a series of "objections," which are *negative* answers to the question posed. The objections are followed by a "counterclaim," frequently a quotation from some authoritative source, which gives reason to think that the answer to the question should be positive. Then in the "body" of the article Aquinas gives reasons for *either* a positive answer to the question *or* for suspending judgment because there are strong considerations on each side. He then goes on to answer the objections raised at the beginning of the article.

There are obvious advantages to this procedure. By considering objections first, you make sure that you are aware of both sides of the question—and with almost any philosophical question there is something to be said on both sides. The counterclaim says in effect, "But wait a minute: Here is a reason to consider a positive answer to the question." The body of the question gives reasons for a positive answer, assesses the balance of evidence, and finally the objections are answered.

Consider, for example, the article headed "Whether the existence of God can be proved." Aquinas cites three objections. The first can be rendered in modern English as follows, "The existence of God is a matter of faith. What is a matter of faith cannot be proved. Thus the existence of God cannot be proved." We can put this in the form of a deductive argument:

If the existence of God is a matter of faith, it cannot be proved.

The existence of God is a matter of faith.

Therefore the existence of God cannot be proved.

In symbols, the argument is:

$$F > \hat{E} \qquad \text{F \# The existence of God is a matter of faith}$$

$$\underline{F} \qquad\qquad \text{E \# The existence of God can be proved}$$

$$\hat{E}$$

It cancels to the indicated conclusion:

$$F > \hat{E}$$

$$\underline{F} \qquad\qquad F > \text{cancels } F$$

$$\hat{E}$$

This is an obviously valid argument, an instance of *Modus Ponens*. So if Aquinas wants to reject the conclusion, he must reject one of the premises. In the reply to this objection, this is in fact what he does. He says that the existence of God is not a matter of faith, but is a "preliminary" or "preamble" to faith, something that must be known before the question of faith can arise.

Some philosophers today would agree with Aquinas about this, but others would disagree, and it is important to see that some of those who agree will be people who believe that God does exist and some of those who disagree will be people who reject the existence of God. Those who come to such questions for the first time often come to them with assumptions or presuppositions, which need to be examined and challenged. It is often assumed both by religious believers and nonbelievers that *of course* the existence of God is a matter of faith and thus cannot be proved. But Aquinas, one of the greatest Christian philosophers, specifically rejects this idea, and so do many contemporary Christian philosophers.

This brings out one of the great advantages of Aquinas' method. By making arguments and objections clear it forces us to examine our assumptions and preconceptions. If we think that the existence of God is a matter of faith, *why* do we think so? If we think it is not, *why* not? Let us look at a few possible reasons. Someone might claim that "everybody knows" that the existence of God is a matter of faith. But the fact that Aquinas and many other Christian, Jewish, and Moslem philosophers have rejected this idea is a powerful piece of counterevidence. Someone might say, "It is a matter of faith for *me*." That may indeed be true, but it does not mean that everyone would agree. Aquinas specifically allows for the possibility that for *some* people, the existence of God is taken on faith, but this does not settle the question as to whether it is or should be taken on faith by other people.

FAITH, ARGUMENT, AND GOD

Those who deny that the existence of God is a matter of faith might begin by giving an informal definition of faith: "By faith we mean trusting God, or believing certain things are true because God has said them." One might then counter, "But how can we trust God or believe things because God has said them unless we first know that there *is* a God?" Some religious believers might give the following reply: "We must hear about God and what God has said before we can have faith. But when we do hear about God and God's word, then God moves our hearts and minds to belief; and unless we resist God's action on us, we will come to have faith simply by hearing God's word preached to us and accepting it."

This is a perfectly understandable view, which many religious believers would agree with. But here Aquinas' counterclaim is relevant. He quotes a passage from St. Paul's Epistle to the Romans in which Paul says that the pagans should have been able to know that God exists from seeing the universe created by God, even without any direct revelation from God, such as was given to the Jewish people.

Of course, the Jewish or Islamic religious believer can reject the authority of Paul's Epistle, but it seems that the Christian religious believer who claims that God is known *only* by faith has a problem: God's word is to be believed; the New Testament is part of God's word; the Epistle to the Romans is part of the New Testament, and it seems that the Epistle to the Romans says that God can be known without revelation.

Without trying to settle the complex philosophical and theological issues involved, we can draw a logical moral. When an argument pro or con on a question is set up in deductive form we can see if the argument is valid or invalid. If it is invalid we can reject it or try to put it into a valid form. If the argument is valid we can then ask about the truth or falsity of the premises. If we accept all the premises of a valid argument, then if we are reasonable people, we will accept the conclusion. If we reject the conclusion we must reject one or more of the premises. And we must not do this arbitrarily if we are to be reasonable: We must give *reasons* for accepting or rejecting the premise or premises. These reasons can themselves be put in the form of arguments, and the process of evaluating these arguments is the same as for the original argument: Is the argument valid? Are the premises true? Why or why not?

This process of evaluating deductive arguments is not the only tool of philosophy. We have already seen that definition can be an important step in solving philosophical problems, and we will later look at nondeductive arguments. Some philosophy seems to consist of bringing us face to face with our experiences in a way that makes us realize certain things about those experiences, and sometimes nonargumentative methods seem best for these purposes. But argument is one important part of philosophy, and until we thoroughly understand it we cannot even contrast other philosophical methods with it. Until we can make implicit arguments explicit and see whether apparently nonargumentative philosophical discourse can be put in argument form, we cannot be sure that we have an instance of discourse that is both nonargumentative and philosophically important. If there are important parts of philosophy that are not argumentative, we can ask how these relate to argument. Do we, for example, sometimes appeal to "intuition" of some sort in philosophy? If so, do these intuitions provide us with premises for arguments or do they somehow conflict with argumentation?

To return to Aquinas, his second objection to the idea that God's existence can be proved is that to prove the existence of God we would have to understand the nature of God. Because we do not know the nature of God, we cannot prove God's existence. In symbolic form this is:

$$E > K$$
$$\hat{K}$$
___
$$\hat{E}$$

E # The existence of God is provable

K # We know the nature of God

It cancels as follows:

$$E > K \quad \hat{K} \text{ cancels} > K$$
$$\hat{K} \qquad E > \text{becomes } \hat{E}$$
___
$$\hat{E}$$

The form is *Modus Tollens*, and in cancellation form it cancels to the conclusion, so we know the argument is valid. Aquinas rejects the conclusion: Which premise does he reject? In this case Aquinas grants the second premise, that we do not know the nature of God, but rejects the first premise. He argues that in many cases where we argue from an effect to the cause we can know that a cause *exists* and know *something* about the cause without fully understanding the nature of the cause. For instance, you can be quite sure that damage to a certain tree was caused by lightning without understanding fully the nature of lightning.

Interestingly enough, the third objection can be taken as a sort of reply to this reply, even though in the arrangement of the *Summa* the reply to Objection 2 comes considerably after Objection 3. In this third objection, Aquinas says that if we argue from effect to cause, the effect must be "proportional" to the cause. If we find a broken twig on the ground, we do not need to postulate an elephant stepping on it to explain what has occurred: A human being or a small animal stepping on the twig could have broken it. But because God is infinite and the physical universe is infinite, God is not "proportional" to the universe, and thus we cannot argue from a finite effect to an infinite cause, God. Interestingly, this argument does not have the conclusion "God cannot be proven to exist," but only "God cannot be proven to exist *by a causal argument*." In symbols the argument is:

$$E > P$$

E # The existence of God can be proven by a causal argument

$$I > \hat{P}$$

P # There is a proportionality between God and the universe

$$I$$
___
$$\hat{E}$$

I # God is infinite and the universe is finite

The argument cancels as:

E > P
I > $\hat{P}$ > P cancels > $\hat{P}$

I   I > cancels I

——   E > becomes $\hat{E}$

$\hat{E}$

and can be proven as follows:

1 E > P   P

2 I > $\hat{P}$ P

3 I   P

4 $\hat{P}$ 2,3 M.P.

5 $\hat{E}$ 1,4 M.T.

Which premise does Aquinas reject, since he wants to maintain "E"? He certainly does not want to deny that God is infinite, nor does he deny that the universe is finite. Thus he cannot deny that there is a lack of proportion between God and the universe. What he must deny then, and does deny, is that there cannot be an argument from cause to effect when effect and cause are "disproportionate." The pros and cons of this require rather thorough discussion, which we will give in a later chapter when we discuss causal arguments in general.

We have already seen that Aquinas' counterclaim is a quotation from the New Testament. It is important to realize that Aquinas does not treat this as *settling* the philosophical question, only as giving a reason to look at the other side. We can now look at Aquinas's positive reasons for thinking God's existence is provable.

This is basically an elaboration of a point we have already looked at in examining Aquinas' reply to one of the objections. Sometimes we know of the existence of something because of direct experience; sometimes we can show that something exists by reasoning from basic principles, as we do in mathematics. But often we are convinced that something exists because it provides the best explanation of something that we experience directly. This kind of reasoning from a state of affairs to the cause or explanation of that state of affairs is the kind of reasoning that Aquinas thinks we are using when we argue for the existence of God. The universe as we experience it is in need of explanation: God provides the best explanation.

Reasoning of this kind is now called *inductive* reasoning, and because science characteristically uses this kind of reasoning, it has been increasingly reflected on as science has become more prominent. We now understand this kind of reasoning better than it would have been understood in Aquinas' day, and we will return to the idea of arguments for the existence of God as inductive arguments in a later chapter. But for now we will look at arguments for the existence of God as Aquinas understood them. Because deductive logic was better understood in Aquinas' time than inductive reasoning, the arguments are put in a deductive form, which raises some problems of interpretation.

OBJECTIONS TO GOD'S EXISTENCE

Before giving his positive arguments for the existence of God, however, Aquinas considers two objections to the idea of God's existence. The first is the argument from evil: Good and evil are incompatible; thus, if good has unlimited power, evil should not exist. But if God exists, then good has unlimited power, for by definition God is all-powerful and all good. Hence, because evil does exist, God does not exist. Put formally, the argument is:

> If good has unlimited power, evil would not exist.
>
> If God exists then good has unlimited power.
>
> Evil exists.
>
> Therefore God does not exist.

In symbols this is:

$$U > \hat{E} \qquad U \text{ \# Good is unlimited}$$
$$G > U \qquad E \text{ \# Evil exists}$$
$$\underline{E} \qquad \quad G \text{ \# God exists}$$
$$\hat{G}$$

It cancels as follows:

$$U > \hat{E} \qquad U > \text{cancels} > U$$
$$G > U \qquad > \hat{E} \text{ cancels } E$$
$$\underline{E} \qquad \quad G > \text{becomes } \hat{G}$$
$$\hat{G}$$

We can show validity by the rules as follows:

$$
\begin{array}{lll}
1 & U > \hat{E} & P \\
2 & G > U & P \\
3 & E & P \\
4 & G > \hat{E} & 1,2 \text{ H.S.} \\
5 & \hat{E} & 3 \text{ D.N.} \\
6 & \hat{G} & 4,5 \text{ M.T.}
\end{array}
$$

Because the argument is valid, if Aquinas wishes to deny the conclusion he must reject at least one premise. The premise he rejects is the premise that if good has unlimited power, then evil would not exist. In his reply to this objection Aquinas argues that evil can produce good: that evil can be a necessary condition for some good things. Thus, a good God can allow evil in order to bring about greater goods, goods that would not be possible without the evils which are their necessary conditions. In his brief answer to the objection, Aquinas does not elaborate on this point, but elsewhere in the *Summa* he draws out the implications of the answer. It is impossible, he argues, to have moral good without freedom, and if created beings are free they may misuse their freedom to commit sin, as we have in fact done. Once sin is committed the only way in which sin can be healed is by suffering. Thus, moral evil is allowed in order to allow the greater good of free will, and suffering is allowed in order to deal with the problems to which sin gives rise.

Whether these kinds of answers are satisfactory is a major problem in the philosophy of religion. Some people would argue that the suffering in the world is too high a price to pay for freedom: In effect, these people deny that freedom is a *greater* good. Some philosophers have argued that God could have given us freedom without allowing the possibility of sin and suffering. Other philosophers claim that freedom would not be genuine unless it could be misused. The debate still rages among philosophers today.

Aquinas' second objection is not precisely an objection to the existence of God. The second objection argues that explanations can be found for everything that does not involve God. Thus, we do not need the idea of God to explain any part of our experience. This of course doesn't show that God doesn't exist: God might exist even if God is not the explanation of the universe. But if we add the assumed premise "if God exists then the universe cannot be explained without God," then we do get an argument, the conclusion of which is "God does not exist." We can reconstruct Aquinas' argument as follows:

If everything can be explained as the result of natural forces or human will, then God is not necessary to explain the universe.

Everything can be explained as the result of natural forces or human will.

If God exists, God is necessary to explain the universe.

Therefore God does not exist.

We can put this in symbols as follows:

$N > \hat{G}$ N # Everything can be explained by natural forces or human will

N

$E > G$ E # God exists

$\hat{E}$ G # God is necessary to explain the universe

It cancels as follows:

$N > \hat{G}$ N cancels N >

N $> \hat{G}$ cancels > G

$E > G$ E > becomes $\hat{E}$

$\hat{E}$

And is provable as follows:

$$1 \ N > \hat{G} \quad P$$
$$2 \ N \qquad\quad P$$
$$3 \ E > G \quad\ P$$
$$4 \ \hat{G} \qquad\quad 1,2 \ M.P.$$
$$5 \ \hat{E} \qquad\quad 3,4 \ M.T.$$

Of course the premise that Aquinas wishes to deny is the assertion that everything can be explained by natural forces or human will. In the body of the article, Aquinas points out five features of the universe that he thinks can only be explained by God. The five features are change, causality, contingency, the moral order, and the apparent order and under-standability of the universe. Each of these arguments has features that we can analyze better further on in the book. For now, we will take a prelim-inary look at several of the arguments.

AQUINAS' ARGUMENTS FOR GOD'S EXISTENCE

The first three arguments all have a common structure that is in many ways best seen in the third argument. This is an argument from *contingency* and *necessity*. By a *contingent* thing, Aquinas means a thing that (1) does not always exist, and (2) the existence of which is caused by something outside of itself, that is, it would not exist unless it was brought into existence by something else. By a *necessary* thing, Aquinas means something that (1) always exists and (2) is causally independent, that is, it exists without being brought into existence by anything other than itself; it would exist whether or not anything else existed.

Using these ideas Aquinas argues as follows:

Contingent things exist (for example, ourselves and most of the things we ordinarily experience, such as mice, mountains, and the moon).

If contingent things exist they must be brought into existence (by the definition of "contingent").

If contingent things are brought into existence, either there is a nec-essary being which brings some of them into existence or they have been brought into existence only by other contingent things.

If contingent things have been brought into existence only by other contingent things, there is a dependent infinite regress of contingent things.

There cannot be a dependent infinite regress of contingent things.

If contingent things were brought into existence by a necessary thing, a necessary thing exists.

If a necessary thing exists, God exists.

In symbols this is:

C   C # Contingent things exist

C > B   B # Contingent things are brought into existence

B > (N ∨ O)   N # A necessary being brings them into existence

O > I   O # Only contingent things bring contingent things

Î   into existence

N > E   I # There is a dependent infinite regress

E > G   E # A necessary being exists
─────   G # God exists

G

The argument cancels to the indicated conclusion:

C

C > B   C cancels C >

B > (N ∨ O)   > B cancels B >

O > I   > I cancels Î

Î   O > cancels O

N > E   N cancels N >

E > G   > E cancels E >
─────

G

It can be worked out step by step as follows:

1	C	P
2	C > B	P
3	B > (N ∨ O)	P
4	O > I	P
5	Î	P
6	N > E	P
7	E > G	P
8	B	1,2 M.P.
9	N ∨ O	8,3 M.P.
10	Ô	4,5 M.T.

11 N	9,10 D.S.
12 E	11,6 M.P.
13 G	12,7 M.P.

This is the most complex argument we have seen so far, and because it has seven premises, there are many ways in which the conclusion could be avoided. We will discuss each premise in turn.

1. We might deny that contingent things exist by denying part of the definition. Obviously, many things we experience don't always exist, but we might deny that things that don't always exist need something to bring them into existence. But this seems to run contrary to both experience and reason: We never see something begin to exist without a cause, and it seems unreasonable that such a thing could happen.

2. Unless we challenge the definition of contingent things, this premise is simply true by definition.

3. We might try to find some third possibility for contingent things being brought into existence, or deny one of the two possibilities. Neither alternative seems very promising; "contingent" and "necessary" are so defined that they seem mutually exclusive and seem to cover all the possibilities.

4. A dependent infinite regress is a series in which a member of the series cannot have a certain characteristic unless an infinite number of preceding items have this characteristic. Why would a situation in which only contingent things brought other contingent things into existence be a situation of this kind? The characteristic in question, of course, is existence. By definition a contingent thing cannot have existence unless it received existence from something else. If only contingent things bring other contingent things into existence, then each thing that brought something else into existence would need to be brought into existence itself. If there were any finite number of contingent things, then we would arrive at a contingent thing that had nothing to bring it into existence. But then, by the definition of contingent, it would not exist; and so nothing that depended on it for existence would exist, that is, nothing at all would exist, which, as Aquinas says, is absurd. So if only contingent things exist, there must be an infinite number of them.

Consider for example a case in which there are five contingent things, *A, B, C, D, and E*. *A* is brought into existence by *B*, *B* is brought into existence by *C*, *C* is brought into existence by *D*, and *D* is brought into existence by *E*. But what brings *E* into existence? If nothing does, *E* does not exist and neither does *D*, since without *E*, *D* won't exist. But if *D* doesn't exist, *C* won't; if *C* doesn't, *B* won't, and if *B* doesn't, *A* won't, so nothing will exist. On the other hand, if we have an *F* to cause *E*, a *G* to cause *F* and so on, we have something to bring each thing into existence, it seems.

The only way to avoid a dependent infinite regress is to allow circular causation, to say that *E* is brought into existence by *A* in our example. But this seems absurd; *A* didn't exist when *E* was brought into existence, so how could *A* bring *B* into existence when it didn't exist itself? However, circular causation is a *possible* though not a very plausible way to deny infinite regress.

5. Aquinas denies that infinite regress is possible, not because he thinks causal circles are possible, but in order to conclude to a necessary being. The denial that infinite regress is possible is the most controversial premise in Aquinas' argument, and most philosophers who deny Aquinas' conclusion deny this premise. They argue that in a dependent infinite regress there is a cause of existence for every contingent thing. True, every cause of existence itself needs a cause, but because we have an infinite number of contingent things, every contingent thing has another contingent thing to be its cause. As a later philosopher, David Hume, was to observe, "What is the difficulty? Each thing you say requires a cause. But for each thing which requires a cause there is a thing to cause it."

Those who agree with Aquinas find this reply unsatisfactory. They agree that if we look at dependent regresses in general, we find that members of the regress only have the characteristic in question if something has it without having to receive it. If we imagine the regress going to infinity it seems that we would get no result. Thus, for example, if I can only get a typewriter by borrowing if from you, and you can only get a typewriter by borrowing it from someone else, and the someone else can only get one by borrowing it from another person, and so on, it seems that we either reach someone who has a typewriter without borrowing it or I never get a typewriter. If we were told in advance that every person in the chain of borrowers could only get a typewriter by borrowing it from someone else, we might say that there's no use even starting the chain; we can be sure that I'd never get a typewriter. Similarly, if each thing had to "borrow" existence from something else, it is argued, we could be sure that nothing would have existence now, which is absurd.

Arguments and counterarguments along these lines still go on, and some, involving the nature of infinity and what might happen in other infinite cases, are quite complex and deep. But at any rate, premise 5 is still being hotly debated.

6. If a necessary being brings contingent things into existence, then it would seem that such a necessary being must have existed when the

things were being brought into existence. And if a necessary being exists at all, then by definition it always exists, so it would exist now. A being which caused other things and then went out of existence would be contingent by our definitions. So again the choice seems to be to challenge the definitions or accept the premise.

7. Aquinas seems to assume that any necessary being would be God. But other philosophers have argued that perhaps the physical universe itself could be a necessary being, always existing and existing whether anything else exists or not. In one sense of "the physical universe" there seem to be serious objections to this. If the physical universe is just the sum total of all contingent things, then it would seem that a collection of contingent things would still be contingent. But if we mean the basic "stuff" of the universe, "matter-energy," then perhaps this has always existed and exists whether anything else exists. So someone could agree that Aquinas' argument proves that *a* necessary being must exist, but deny that Aquinas has shown that God exists.

One could argue that only God could be a necessary being, or one could argue that even if the physical universe had always existed and existed independently of anything else, there might be important features of the universe that were still unexplained. Aquinas' fourth and fifth arguments bring up two such features: Argument 4 argues that God is necessary to explain the existence of objective value, and Argument 5 argues that God is necessary to explain the apparent order and understandability of the universe.

Argument 4 is put in Aristotelian terms, which are hard to understand without a good deal of background in philosophy. In modern terms the argument can be stated as follows:

Objective differences in value (good and bad) exist.

If objective differences in value exist, then a standard of value must exist.

If a standard of value exists, God must exist.

Therefore, God exists.

In symbols the argument is:

$$O \qquad\qquad O \text{ \# Objective differences in value exist}$$

$$O > S \qquad S \text{ \# A standard of value exists}$$

$$S > G \qquad G \text{ \# God exists}$$

$$\overline{}$$

$$G$$

The argument is valid by cancellation:

O

O > S   O cancels O >

S > G   > S cancels S >
_____

G

It can be worked out in steps as follows:

1 O   P

2 O > S   P

3 S > G   P

4 S   1,2 M.P.

5 G   4,3 M.P.

Any of the three premises can be challenged, but each challenge has its consequences. If we deny the existence of objective differences in value, then we are taking a "relativist" or "subjectivist" position in ethics. This seems attractive to some people, but there is a price to pay. If all values are relative or subjective, then we cannot say that any action is objectively right or wrong. But almost anyone feels that there are some actions that are truly right or wrong. Someone may be very permissive about sexual ethics, for example, but very indignant about apartheid, sexual discrimination, pollution, or governmental dishonesty. Furthermore, if nothing is objectively wrong, then the argument from evil against the existence of God loses much or all of its force. If what is right or wrong for someone is simply what that individual believes is right or wrong, then if God believes it is right to cause innocent people great suffering, then it is right for God to do so.

In short, by giving up the objectivity of values, we give up the right to make judgments that anything is genuinely wrong. This may seem to some too high a price to pay, but the issue is a highly complex and controversial one, requiring a thorough discussion of ethics and moral theories. Logically speaking we can only insist that people be consistent: We cannot give up the objectivity of value and then treat some things as objectively wrong.

Even if we grant the objectivity of value, however, we might deny that we need an existing standard of value. We might, for instance, know directly that things were good or bad, right or wrong, without the need of any standard. Good and bad, right and wrong, might be simple qualities that we perceive directly, as colors are perceived. We don't need to know some external standard to know whether any object is red; we simply see that it is. Perhaps we can know that things are good and bad, right and wrong, in a direct way also.

The greatest objection to this theory is the widespread disagreement on matters of value. People rarely disagree on what color things are; if values are directly perceived, like colors, why do we so often disagree on good and bad, right and wrong? If you and I disagree on a question of value, is one of us simply wrong, or perhaps "value-blind" in the way some people are color-blind? Again, we are involved in deep and complex ethical issues.

Even if we agree that there must be some objective standard of moral value, must this standard be God? And what is it about God that constitutes the standard? If good and right are what God approves of and bad and wrong are what God disapproves of, is God's approval and disapproval purely arbitrary or does God have some *reason* for approving of some things and disapproving of others? And if God has such a reason why cannot this be used as a standard, independently of God?

In general, this fourth argument of Aquinas, which is a version of what is called the "moral argument" for the existence of God, involves us in a whole range of ethical questions. The challenge of moral arguments for God can be put as follows: If there is a loving being who created the universe, the "God the Father Almighty, Creator of Heaven and Earth" mentioned in the Christian creeds, then this would seem to make sense of the demands of morality. Can any alternative explanation of morality be found that does not explain *away* morality, does not rob it of its force? If not we must either reject morality or accept God as the source of morality. Many nontheists agree with this: They accept the premise "If morality is objective then God exists" and argue "God does not exist; therefore morality is not objective." Theists argue from the same first premise but argue "God does exist; therefore morality is objective." Both arguments are valid and share the same first premise:

$$M > G \qquad M > G \qquad M \text{ \# Morality is objective}$$
$$\underline{\hat{G}} \qquad \quad \underline{M} \qquad \quad G \text{ \# God exists}$$
$$\hat{M} \qquad \quad G$$

The first is *Modus Tollens*. The second is *Modus Ponens*. But some philosophers, as we have seen, reject the first premise and try to find an objective foundation for morality other than God, or deny that morality needs a foundation.

We have presented Aquinas' argument from morality to God as a deductive argument, but as we will see in later chapters it can also be regarded as an inductive argument. This is also true of the argument from order and understandability, Aquinas' fifth argument. Aquinas' argument can be presented in modern terms as follows:

The universe is orderly and understandable.

If there was not an intelligent Designer of the universe, then the universe would not be orderly and understandable.

If there is an intelligent Designer of the universe, then God exists.

Therefore, God exists.

The argument can be put in symbols as:

$$U \qquad U \,\#\text{ The universe is orderly and understandable}$$
$$\hat{D} > \hat{U} \qquad D \,\#\text{ There is an intelligent Designer}$$
$$\underline{D > G} \qquad G \,\#\text{ God exists}$$
$$G$$

The argument cancels out:

$$U$$
$$\hat{D} > \hat{U} \qquad U \text{ cancels} > \hat{U}$$
$$\underline{D > G} \qquad \hat{D} > \text{ cancels } D >$$
$$G$$

and it can be reconstructed as follows:

$$
\begin{array}{lll}
1 & U & P \\
2 & \hat{D} > \hat{U} & P \\
3 & D > G & P \\
4 & U > D & 2 \text{ Transp.} \\
5 & D & 1,4 \text{ M.P.} \\
6 & G & 5,3 \text{ M.P.}
\end{array}
$$

Although the universe certainly seems to be orderly and understandable, we might think that such order and understandability was merely an illusion created by chance, and that the universe is in fact neither orderly nor understandable. If we take this position then we could reject premise 1, but we would also have to reject science, for science claims to help us understand a universe by understanding the laws that give it order.

We might, on the other hand, grant that the universe was genuinely orderly and understandable but deny that such order and understandability require a designer, thus rejecting premise 2. Or we might grant that order and understandability require a designer, but deny that such a designer need be the same as the traditional God: all-powerful, all knowing, perfectly good. In his criticisms of the traditional "Design" argument, David Hume suggested several alternative views: Perhaps the universe developed by some internal laws of development, as a plant or animal develops. Perhaps the universe was designed, but by a being less than the traditional God, even a contingent being who has ceased to exist, or a group of beings who united their efforts to create the universe as it now is. Hume suggests that these hypotheses are possibilities and that they are just as probable as the idea the universe was created by a God of the traditional kind. If we regard the Design argument as a deductive argument we would have to reject these alternatives as even possible. If we regard it as an inductive argument, we can grant that these alternatives are possible, but argue that the hypothesis that the universe was created by a God of the traditional kind is very much more probable on the evidence.

In general, Aquinas' five arguments are an impressive demonstration of the possibility of giving deductive arguments for the existence of God, which are valid arguments and whose premises are at least highly plausible. Even if we eventually decide that the arguments are best regarded as inductive arguments, we will still have learned a great deal from the effort to put them into deductive form. To someone who thinks that the existence of God cannot be argued, Aquinas provides a powerful counterexample. If someone thinks that Aquinas' arguments do not succeed in proving the existence of God, it is up to that person to give reasons for rejecting the premises of Aquinas' arguments. He or she must be prepared to live with the consequences of rejecting the premises rejected; not, for example, to reject objective morality as a premise of the moral argument and yet declare that the suffering in the world is objectively wrong. Or to give another example, anyone who rejects the idea that the universe is orderly and understandable cannot then appeal to science.

Since a powerful and persuasive theory is not usually destroyed merely by criticism, but by being replaced by a better theory, the critic might also ask what alternate explanation he or she gives of the data cited by Aquinas. Why do contingent things exist? Why does the universe at least seem to be orderly and understandable? If anything is objectively good or bad, right or wrong, what is the basis of this goodness or badness, rightness or wrongness? Many great minds have been convinced by arguments like those of Aquinas that God exists. If the arguments are rejected there should be good reasons for the rejection and a reasonable alternative view should be presented.

EXERCISES

A. The following arguments are suggested by Thomas Aquinas' *Summa Theologica*, Question 2, Article 2. Do the following:
  a. Symbolize each argument.
  b. Check the argument by cancellation to see if it is a valid proof or a valid refutation of the statement "God exists."
  c. If the argument is not valid, see if you can supply any plausible premise or premises to make it a valid proof or refutation.
  d. If the argument is valid, discuss whether it is sound (that is, the premises are true.
  e. If you think the argument is sound, discuss how the premises might be established.

  1. Does God exist? It would seem not, for if God existed a perfectly good being would exist. But if a perfectly good being existed, no evil could exist. But evil does exist.

  2. Does God exist? It would seem not, for the Universe could be explained perfectly well if God doesn't exist.

  3. Whatever comes into existence has a cause for its existence. Nothing causes itself. It cannot be the case that everything is caused by something else. Thus something exists that is a cause but is not caused. Something that is a cause but is not caused would be the same as God.

  4. Whatever changes is changed by something. Nothing changes itself. It cannot be true that everything that changes is changed by something else. Thus something exists that changes things but is not itself changed. Such a being would be the same as God.

  5. Either something exists at all times whether or not anything else exists, or else everything does not exist at some time and exists because something else exists. If everything did not exist at some time, then there would have been a time at which nothing existed. But if there was ever a time when nothing existed, nothing would exist now. Something exists now. Therefore, something exists that exists at all times and exists whether or not anything else exists. This something would be the same as God.

  6. If there is a designer of the Universe, then God exists. If there were not a designer of the Universe, unintelligent things would not behave in an orderly and understandable way. But unintelligent things do behave in an orderly and understandable way.

  7. If there are real differences in goodness between things, then there must be a Supreme Good. A Supreme Good would be the same as God. But there are real differences in goodness between things.

  8. If someone is perfectly good, then if permitting evil to exist brings about greater good, that person will permit evil to exist. If some perfectly good person will permit evil, then the greatest objection to God's existence is overcome and God exists.

9.   If the Universe cannot be explained without God, then God exists. If causation, change, and existence cannot be explained without God then the Universe cannot be explained without God. But causation, change, and existence cannot be explained without God.

10.   If the existence of God is the best explanation of causation, change, existence, goodness, and the order of the Universe, then God exists. There is no better explanation of these things than God.

B.   The following arguments are suggested by arguments given by David Hume in his *Dialogues on Natural Religion*. Symbolize the arguments. If a conclusion is given as a statement, check to see if the argument is a valid proof. If the conclusion is a question, see if it is a valid proof or refutation. If no conclusion is given, find the conclusion.

1.   If you are a sincere skeptic, you will not trust either your senses or your experience. If you do not trust your senses or your experience, you will not believe that your body can be injured by a fall. If you do not believe that your body can be injured by a fall, you will leave the room by the window rather than the door. Therefore, if you leave by the door, you are not a sincere skeptic.

2.   If your skeptical arguments are effective, you would not rely on accepted rules of behavior. If your arguments are not effective, I do not need to answer them. So, either you rely on accepted rules of behavior, or I do not need to answer your arguments.

3.   If we have no experience of God, we have no idea of God. If we have no idea of God, we cannot say whether God is like human beings in any respect. We have no experience of God. Therefore. . . .

4.   If the existence of anything is demonstrable, its nonexistence implies a contradiction. If anything can be thought of as existing, it can also be thought of as not existing. If it can be thought of as not existing, its nonexistence does not imply a contradiction. Can we say that the existence of anything thought of as existing is not demonstrable?

5.   If there is a necessarily existing being, it may have qualities that, if known, would make its nonexistence contradictory. The Universe may have qualities that, if known, would make its nonexistence contradictory. Therefore, the Universe is a necessarily existing being.

6.   If every part of the Universe has a different cause, the Universe as a whole does not need a cause. If the Universe as a whole does not need a cause, then God is not needed to explain the Universe. Therefore. . . .

7.   Even if happiness outweighs unhappiness, unhappiness exists. If a perfectly good, all-powerful God existed, unhappiness would not exist. Can a perfectly good, all-powerful God exist?

8.   If God exists, then evil is not what we would expect. If evil is what we would expect if God does not exist, then there can be no argument from the world as it is to the existence of God. Therefore. . . .

9.   If there is a good God and an evil God, both good and evil would exist

in the world. But if there were a good God and an evil God, the world would not be orderly and uniform. Both good and evil exist, but the world is orderly and uniform. So can a good God and an evil God both exist?

10. The causes of the Universe are either perfectly good, perfectly evil, are both good and evil, or are neither good nor evil. If the causes of the Universe were perfectly good, there would be no evil. If they were perfectly evil, there would be no good. There is both good and evil. Therefore. . . .

C. Symbolize and check for validity by the cancellation method. If valid, give a proof. (*Source*: Spinoza, *The Ethics*.)

1. If substance is conceived through itself, then a conception of it can be formed independently of any other conception.
   If a conception of substance can be formed independently of any other conception, then substance is prior to its modifications.

   If substance is prior to its modifications, it is conceived through itself.

2. Either substance is produced by something internal or by something external.
   It is not produced by anything external, and if it is produced by something internal, it is its own cause.

   Substance is its own cause.

3. Either substance is finite or it is infinite.
   If it were limited by something else, it would be finite.
   It is not limited by something else.

   Substance is infinite.

4. If substance can be divided into parts, then either the parts would retain the nature of substance or they would lose the nature of substance.
   The parts would not retain the nature of substance.
   The parts would not lose the nature of substance.

   Substance cannot be divided into parts.

5. If the parts of a divided substance were substances, they would retain the nature of substance.
   If the parts of a divided substance were substances, a substance could be made up of other substances.
   It is false that a substance could be made up of other substances.

   It is false that the parts of a divided substance would retain the nature of substance.

6. If the parts of a divided substance were not substances, they would not retain the nature of substance.
   If the parts of a divided substance were substances, a substance could be made up of other substances.
   It is false that a substance could be made up of other substances.

It is false that the parts of a divided substance would retain the nature of substance.

7. If the parts of a divided substance would lose the nature of substance, then, if a substance were divided, a substance could be destroyed.
    It is false that a substance could be destroyed.

    ───

    It is false that the parts of a divided substance would lose the nature of substance.

8. If the parts of a divided substance would lose the nature of substance and a substance could be divided, then a substance could be destroyed.
    A substance could not be destroyed.

    ───

    A substance could not be divided.

9. If the parts of a divided substance would lose the nature of substance, then, if a substance were divided, a substance could be destroyed.
    It is false that a substance could be destroyed.

    ───

    Either it is false that the parts of a divided substance would retain the nature of substance, or it is false that substance could be divided.

10. If a substance could be divided, either the parts would retain the nature of substance or they would lose the nature of substance.
    It is false that the parts would retain the nature of substance.
    Either it is false that the parts would lose the nature of substance, or it is false that a substance could be divided.

    ───

    A substance could not be divided.

D. 1. Take one invalid argument from exercises A–C and make it valid by changing *one* premise. If this is not possible, explain why.
    2. Take one invalid argument from exercises A–C and make it into a valid argument by *adding* a premise.
    3. Defend the premises or criticize the premise of a valid argument from exercises A–C.

4

Syllogistic Arguments and Assumptions

In analyzing Aquinas' arguments, we were able to use the *statement logic* that we introduced in Chapter 2. But the standard system of logic in the Middle Ages was *syllogistic logic*, a way of analyzing and formalizing arguments developed by Aristotle during the fourth century before Christ. Aristotle developed all the essentials of this kind of logic, but in his non-logical works he did not make a great deal of *use* of syllogistic logic—scholars have commented on the fact that it is surprisingly difficult to find arguments of this kind in Aristotle except in the book in which he develops his logical system. However, Aristotle's logic began to be developed, simplified, and taught by later philosophers, and by the medieval period almost every European university curriculum had a course in Aristotelian logic as part of its "general education" courses, which preceded more specialized studies such as philosophy, law, or theology.

After the medieval period, reaction set in against the technical hair-splitting that later medieval philosophy had fallen into, and even against Aristotelian logic. But even many of the critics of medieval philosophy assumed that logic was more or less synonymous with Aristotelian logic. It was not until the late nineteenth century that the domination of Aristotle's system of logic was seriously challenged. Now the pendulum has swung in the other direction, and modern logic texts often neglect Aristotelian logic.

This is a pity because Aristotelian logic is useful both in itself and for helping to understand arguments given by philosophers and others during the many centuries during which Aristotelian logic was the common logical system.

In the statement logic developed in Chapter 2 and used in Chapter 3, we had symbols and rules for logically important ideas such as "not," "or," "and," "if . . . then." With these we could do justice to many arguments. But a major logical distinction that cannot be made in statement logic is that between "every" and "some," "no" and "some . . . not." This has already led to some oversimplification in our presentation of Aquinas' arguments. We represented one of Aquinas' objections to the existence of God as saying "If good and evil are incompatible, then if good has infinite power then evil will not exist." But what Aquinas more nearly says is, "If *any* two things are incompatible, then if one is infinite, the other will not exist." In one of Aquinas' arguments against the provability of God, we represented his argument as "If the existence of God is a matter of faith it is not provable." But his argument is better represented as "*No* matter of faith is provable; the existence of God is a matter of faith; therefore, the existence of God is not provable."

Both of these are cases where a general principle (about incompatible things, about the provability of matters of faith) is applied to particular cases; good and evil in one argument, the existence of God in the other. A common pattern in such arguments is:

Every M is P

Every S is M

―――――――――

Every S is P

For example:

Every matter of faith is unprovable.

Every statement about God is a matter of faith.

―――――――――――――――――――

Every statement about God is unprovable.

CATEGORICAL SYLLOGISMS

This pattern of argument is what is known as a *categorical syllogism*; we will usually call it a syllogism for short where no confusion arises with Disjunctive Syllogism or Hypothetical Syllogism. In a categorial syllogism there are three *terms*. In our example the terms were "matter of faith," "unprovable," and "statement about God." These three terms are divided among three *statements* in such a way that one term, called the *major* term, appears in one premise and is the predicate of the conclusion ("unprovable" in the example); one term, called the *minor* term, appears in the other premise and is the subject of the conclusion ("statement about God" in our example); and one term, called the *middle* term, appears in both premises and *not* in the conclusion ("matter of faith" in our example). In the pattern with letters:

Every M is P

Every S is M
_____

Every S is P

The major term is represented by "P" (for "predicate"), the minor term by "S" (for "subject"), and the middle term by "M" (for "middle").

Each of the three statements in a syllogism—the two premises and the conclusion—must be in one of six *standard forms*:

A Every S is P

E No S is P

I Some S is P

O Some S is not P

U *N* is P

Y *N* is not P

The letters A,E,I and O are traditional labels for the first four statements, "U" and "Y" have been added for the last two statements for reasons which we will explain shortly. An "A" statement of the form

Every S is P

is a *universal affirmative* statement, because it gives us *positive* information about *everything* of a certain kind. An "E" statement

No S is P

is a *universal negative* statement, because it gives us *negative* information about everything of a certain kind. Our earlier example, "Every matter of faith is unprovable," could also be put in negative form as "No matter of faith is provable." In fact, that might be a better form for it, because "unprovable" is a negative idea. If we put the premise in that form we could give another syllogism:

> No matter of faith is provable.
>
> Every statement about God is a matter of faith.
> _____
> No statement about God is provable.

This has the same three terms, but it is a different syllogism of the form:

> No M is P
>
> Every S is M
> _____
> No S is P

Notice that this syllogism also meets the conditions we have laid down: It has a major term, minor term, and middle term, and each statement is in standard form.

The third standard-form statement is *particular affirmative* because it gives us *limited positive* information. If we went back to the first form of our first premise and limited the second premise to a more cautious statement we could have the syllogism:

> Every matter of faith is unprovable.
>
> Some statement about God is a matter of faith.
> _____
> Some statement about God is unprovable.

The form is:

> Every M is P
>
> Some S is M
> _____
> Some S is P

and it also meets all the conditions for a syllogism. But while our first two syllogisms are two different ways of putting the same argument, this syllogism has a more limited conclusion because one of the premises is more limited.

If we use the universal negative form of our first premise, we get the argument:

No matter of faith is provable.

Some statement about God is a matter of faith.

No statement about God is not provable.

This has the form:

No M is P

Some S is M

Some S is not P

Again, this meets all the conditions for a syllogism, and its conclusion is negative because one premise is negative and limited because one premise is limited.

The fourth standard-form statement is:

Some S is not P

This gives us limited negative information and is thus a *particular negative.* We could substitute for the second premise in our sample argument "Some statement about God is not a matter of faith," keep the positive form of the first premise, and get the argument.

Every matter of faith is unprovable.

Some statement about God is not a matter of faith.

Some statement about God is not unprovable.

This is just as much a syllogism as our first four examples, but whereas they were valid arguments, this one is invalid. Its pattern is

Every M is P

Some S is not M

Some S is not P

Another argument of this pattern is:

> Every student of mine is a human being.
>
> Some child of mine is not a student of mine.
> _____
> Some child of mine is not a human being.

where the premises are true and the conclusion is false. Because a valid argument pattern cannot have instances where the premises are true and the conclusion is false, we can see that the syllogism form

> Every M is P
>
> Some S is not M
> _____
> Some S is not P

is an invalid form.

To get a valid form with *A* and *O* premises and an *O* conclusion we have to go to one of the two following forms:

> Every P is M
>
> Some S is not M
> _____
> Some S is not P
>
> or
>
> Some M is not P
>
> Every M is S
> _____
> Some S is not P

For example:

> Every provable statement is scientific
>
> Some statement about God is not scientific.
> _____
> Some statement about God is not provable.

or

> Some account of mystical experience is not provable.
>
> Every account of mystical experience is a statement about God.
> _____
> Some statement about God is not provable.

There are many ways of deciding whether syllogisms are valid or invalid. Because there are hundreds of patterns that meet the conditions of being a syllogism and comparatively few that are valid, one way that is quite feasible and that was used for centuries is simply to memorize the valid patterns. A variety of ingenious techniques were used to help memorize the patterns, including the technique of giving each valid pattern a name that gave clues to the structure of the syllogism and putting the names into a little verse that could be memorized. The traditional names of our first six valid patterns are:

	Every M is P			No M is P	
Barbara	Every S is M	Celarent		Every S is M	
	Every S is P			No S is P	
	Every M is P			No M is P	
Darii	Some S is M	Ferio		Some S is M	
	Some S is P			Some S is not P	
	Every P is M			Some M is not P	
Baroco	Some S is not M	Bocardo		Every M is S	
	Some S is not P			Some S is not P	

Notice that the vowels in these names tell which standard-form statements make up the pattern. "Barbara" is "AAA," three universal affirmatives; "Celarent" consists of a universal negative, a universal affirmative, and a universal negative conclusion, "EAE"; and so on.

In this system, statements about individuals are treated as universal affirmative or negative. Thus, the syllogism

> **Every matter of faith is unprovable.**
>
> **God is a matter of faith.**
> _____
> **God is unprovable.**

would be treated as a "Barbara" syllogism and

> **No matter of faith is provable.**
>
> **God is a matter of faith.**
> _____
> **God is not provable.**

would be treated as a "Celarent" syllogism. Because there are some important differences between universals and statements about individuals, we can use our additional letters and name these two patterns:

Every M is P

Barburu   *N* is M

N is P

No M is P

Celurynt   *N* is M

N is not P

Both "Barburu" and "Celurynt" are valid patterns.

CANCELLATION FOR SYLLOGISMS

We will now introduce a symbolic technique for checking the validity of syllogistic arguments, similar to the cancellation system of Chapter 2. First we introduce a way of writing the six standard-form statements:

A Every S is P	S))P
E No S is P	S)(P
I Some S is P	S()P
O Some S is not P	S((P
U *N* is P	*N*))P
Y *N* is not P	*N*)(P

Notice that of the two "curves" which are written between the letters, the left curve represents universal/particular and the right curve represents affirmative/negative. The two universal statements, A and E, and the statements about individuals U and Y all have a "concave" left curve: The letter next to the curve is "inside" the curve. The two particular statements, I and O, have a "convex" left curve: The letter next to the curve is "outside" the curve. The three negative statements, E, O, and Y, all have concave right curves: The letter next to the curve is "inside" the curve. The three positive statements, A, I, and U, all have convex right curves: The letter next to them is "outside" the curve. A and U, and E and Y have the same curve pattern: They are distinguished by the italic *N* in the subject position of the individual statement. This marks the similarity between A and U, E and Y recognized by traditional Aristotelian logic, and also the differences we wish to make note of.

When we symbolize specific arguments we will use capital letters for *terms* and italic capital letters for *proper names*. Thus, the sample arguments we have seen so far can be symbolized:

Barbara	Every F is U	F))U	
	Every S is F	S))F	F # Matter of faith
	Every S is U	S))U	U # Unprovable thing
			P # Provable thing
Celarent	No F is P	F)(P	S # Statement about God
	Every S is F	S))F	G # God
	No S is P	S)(P	
Darii	Every F is U	F))U	
	Some S is F	S()F	
	Some S is U	S()U	
Ferio	No F is P	F)(P	
	Some S is F	S()F	
	Some S is not P	S((P	
Baroco	Every F is U	F))U	
	Some S is not U	S((U	
	Some S is not F	S((F	
Bocardo	Some U is not S	U((S	
	Every U is F	U))F	
	Some F is not S	F((S	
Barburu	Every F is U	F))U	
	G is F	*G*))F	
	G is U	*G*))U	

	No F is P	F)(P
Celurynt	*G* is F	*G*))F
	G is not P	*G*)(P

The technique for deciding the validity of a syllogism is a new kind of cancellation: *Curve* cancellation. A term *inside* a curve cancels with the same term *outside* a curve, and in a valid argument the terms that do not cancel stay inside a curve if they are inside and outside a curve if they are outside. Thus, all the valid forms we have seen so far curve-cancel in this way:

Barbara	F))U S))F ─── S))U	F)cancels)F	Barburu	F))U G))F ─── G))U	F)cancels)F
Celarent	F)(P S))F ─── S)(P	F)cancels)F	Celurynt	F)(P G))F ─── G)(P	F)cancels)F
Darii	F))U S()F ─── S()U	F)cancels)F	Ferio	F)(P S()F ─── S((F	F)cancels)F
Baroco	F))U S((U ─── S((F	)Ucancels(U	Bocardo	U(((S U))F ─── F((S	U(cancelsU)

But in the invalid argument:

F))U

S((F

───

S((U

the middle term does not cancel, and even if it did, "U" would be left on the wrong side of a curve.

In addition to cancellation we need two supplementary rules:

R1   If no premise is universal, no conclusion follows.

This eliminates such misleading cancellations as:

> M()P   Some students are male.
>
> S((M   Some females are not students.
> _____
> S()P   Some females are male.

R2   A conclusion is negative if and only if one premise is negative.

This prevents misleading cancellations such as

> M)(P   No human is four-legged.
>
> M((S   Some human is not a cat.
> _____
> S)(P   No cat is four-legged.

which obviously has true premises and a false conclusion.

A principle similar to the combination of Rule 1 and Rule 2 was called by the medievals the rule of *Nullo et Omni*, that is, "none and all." For convenience we will call the combination of Rules 1 and 2 the Rule NO, and if we find a syllogism that violates it we will write "NO—Invalid."

In general, however, we will rarely need to invoke Rule NO: Almost every naturally occurring syllogistic argument (as opposed to artificial examples) that is met with will be invalid either because the middle term does not cancel or because the terms are not in proper relation to their curves after cancellation.

There are also arguments that are invalid by cancellation but that can be made valid by limiting one premise; for example:

> Every child of mine is a boy.
>
> Every child of mine is a child of my wife.
> _____
> Some child of my wife is a boy.

This does not cancel

> C))B
>
> C))W
> _____
> W()B

but it seems intuitively valid. We can make the argument valid by limiting the second premise:

> Every child of mine is a boy.
>
> Some child of mine is a child of my wife.
> _____
>
> Some child of my wife is a boy.

$$M))B$$
$$M()W$$
$$\overline{}$$
$$W()B$$

Syllogisms such as this with "weakened" conclusions were allowed by Aristotle and the medievals: The original syllogism with the universal premises and a particular conclusion was given the name "Darapti" and recognized as valid.

Modern logicians have become more cautious about syllogisms with universal premises and a particular conclusion, for a particular conclusion seems to say that something of a certain kind *exists* whereas some universals are merely hypothetical. Suppose I have a foolproof method of detecting cheating on tests and I tell my students:

> Every student who cheats is a cheater who will be caught.
>
> Every cheater who will be caught is a student who will lose credit.
> _____
>
> Some student who cheats is a student who will lose credit.

Now both premises could be true; my system might be foolproof and I might be determined to punish every cheater. But if my students believe this, probably none of them would cheat. Yet the conclusion sounds as if some existing student *will* lose credit for cheating.

Some logicians still think that hypothetical cases like this are fairly rare and can be handled in other ways, and therefore want to allow syllogisms with weakened premises, as Aristotle and the medievals did. But because of cases like this most logicians today reject such syllogisms, and our system follows this course.

Three variant forms which do not differ in an important way from forms we have examined are:

	Every P is M		Some M is P
Camestres	No S is M	Disamis	Every M is S
	No S is P		Some S is P

$$\text{Camystrys} \quad \frac{\begin{array}{l} \text{Every P is M} \\ N \text{ is M} \end{array}}{N \text{ is not P}}$$

We include these because order of particular or negative premises are different than in earlier forms, leading to possible confusion. All other variations of valid syllogisms are different only in the order of subject and predicate in E or I premises.

NEGATIVE TERMS

We can put a curve over a letter to symbolize the opposite of a term; for example, if "P" stands for "provable," "$\hat{P}$" can stand for "unprovable." Thus, the premise "Every matter of faith is unprovable" could be written:

$$F))\hat{P}$$

As we saw, this is the same as "No matter of faith is provable," suggesting a two-way rule:

$$\frac{S)(P}{S))\hat{P}}$$

In fact, given this new notation we can provide three more rules:

$$\frac{S))P}{S)(\hat{P}} \qquad \frac{S()P}{S((\hat{P}} \qquad \frac{S((P}{S()\hat{P}}$$

These four rules are collectively called "Obversion" in traditional logic. The first and last rules simply express a negative predicate term in a different way, whereas the two middle rules get a positive from two negatives, as in our Double Negation Rule in statement logic.

There are also analogs of Transposition and Commutation:

$$\frac{S))P}{\hat{P}))\hat{S}} \qquad \frac{S((P}{\hat{P}((\hat{S}} \qquad \frac{S)(P}{P)(S} \qquad \frac{S()P}{P()S}$$

The first two rules are traditionally called "Contraposition" and the second two "Conversion."

Such rules are very useful in traditional logic to put nonstandard syllogisms in standard form. For example:

> Every provable thing is not a matter of faith.
>
> No statement about God is not a matter of faith.
> _____
> No statement about God is provable.

$$P))\hat{F}$$
$$S)(\hat{F}$$
$$\overline{}$$
$$S)(P$$

can be "reduced" to our earlier Celarent syllogism

$$P)(F$$
$$S))F$$
$$\overline{}$$
$$S)(P$$

by obverting both premises in the curve system; however, we can simply cancel:

$$P))\hat{F} \qquad (\hat{F} \text{ cancels })\hat{F}$$
$$S)(\hat{F}$$
$$\overline{}$$
$$S)(P$$

using the idea that a letter with a curve above it is "inside" a curve, and a letter with a curve above it and also inside an adjoining concave curve is the same as a letter outside any curve. We can thus give such arguments as:

$$M))P \qquad \hat{P})(M$$
$$S)(\hat{M} \qquad S)(\hat{M}$$
$$\overline{} \qquad \overline{}$$
$$S))P \qquad S))P \qquad \text{etc.}$$

The rules we now have enable us to check any syllogism for validity and do all the traditional transformations of statements discussed in traditional Aristotelian logic. (Obversion, Conversion, and Contraposition are traditionally called *Immediate Inferences*, "Immediate" means "not needing a middle term" rather than "instant.") However, traditional Aristotelian logic also investigated two other topics: *enthymemes* and *sorites*.

ENTHYMEMES

An *enthymeme* is a syllogism with either one premise or the conclusion missing. Because the syllogistic form is very specific we can always tell what premise, if any, can be supplied to make a valid syllogism out of an enthymeme and what conclusion, if any, can be validly inferred from two standard-form premises. Thus, given the premises

Every F is non P

Every S is F
_____
_____

we can see that the only valid conclusion is

Every S is non P

In cancellation form this is especially easy, for we simply cancel the middle term and collect the remaining terms, leaving inside terms inside and outside terms outside:

F))$\hat{P}$

S))F
_____

S))$\hat{P}$

If one premise is missing, the cancellation system helps, because we need a premise that will cancel the middle term and leave the remaining terms in the right relation to their curves.

For example, in the enthymeme

_____
S))F
_____

S))P

we need a premise in which F is inside a curve (so it will cancel) and P is outside a curve, as it is in the conclusion. Only "F))P" will do the job:

F))P

S))F
_____

S))P

Enthymemes are especially useful in philosophy, because often a philosophical argument has premises that are left unexpressed because they seemed obvious to the philosopher giving the argument. But these premises are often not at all obvious to critics of that philosopher, and it helps to bring out just what premise is needed to make a valid argument. For example, Duns Scotus, the great medieval Franciscan philosopher, gave a number of arguments about God that used Aristotelian assumptions that seem highly questionable to later philosophers. For instance, Scotus argued "The First Being (God) has infinite power because it can cause endless motion."

The conclusion is expressed first and the word "because" signals that the second statement is a premise from which it is to be derived. The argument is thus:

The First Being can cause endless motion.

The First Being has infinite power.

or in symbols:

$$\overline{F))E}$$
$$\overline{F))I}$$

F # The First Being

E # Being that can cause endless motion

I # Being with infinite power

It is clear that the missing premise is

$$E))I$$

"Every Being which can cause endless motion has infinite power," since only "E))I" will cancel the "E" in the expressed premise and put "I" in the right relation to its curve.

In Aristotelian science it was believed that the motion in the universe was endless and that infinite power was necessary to cause such motion. However, modern scientific cosmology would challenge both assumptions. One plausible scientific model of the universe is one in which the universe eventually "runs down," stops expanding, and gradually reaches a state where nothing moves. Another possible scientific scenario for the universe is an endless series of expansions and contractions, but on such theories only a finite amount of energy or "power" is involved. Thus, when we make Duns Scotus' argument explicit we see that the assumed premise is highly questionable. (In general, the weakest arguments in ancient and medieval philosophy were those based on the science of the day, because science has changed dramatically since that time. This may be a warning against basing philosophy on current science.)

In more everyday arguments it is also important to bring out assumptions and make them explicit. As we have seen, many people argue

No matter of faith is provable.

———————————

No statements about God are provable.

In symbols:

$$F)(P$$

———————————

$$S)(P$$

The only possible premise to make a valid argument is

$$S))F$$

"Every statement about God is a matter of faith."

The statement may be questionable. Suppose an atheist *denies* that God exists. This is a "statement about God," but the atheist would want to deny that it is a matter of *faith* for him or her that God does not exist. Such an atheist might at least want to weaken the premise to "Every positive statement about God is a matter of faith."

Expressions of prejudice are often put in enthymeme form; for example, "She's Scandinavian so she has no sense of humor" or "He's Polish so he's dumb." Put as enthymemes, these are:

———————————

She is Scandinavian.

———————————

She has no sense of humor.

and

———————————

He is Polish.

———————————

He is dumb.

But the only possible premises that will make these arguments valid are "No Scandinavian has a sense of humor" and "Every Polish person is dumb":

No Scandinavian has a sense of humor.

She is a Scandinavian.

———————————

She does not have a sense of humor.

No S is H	S)(H
S is S	S))S

| S is not H | S)(H |

Every Polish person is dumb.

He is Polish.

He is dumb.

Every P is D	P))D
H is P	H))P

| *H* is D | H))D |

But when these premises are brought out into the open, they are obviously false. Do *no* Scandinavians have a sense of humor? What about Victor Borge, the great Danish comedian? Are *all* Polish people dumb? What about Nicolaus Copernicus, the great Polish astronomer? And, of course, particular premises in place of the universals will not give us valid conclusions:

Some Scandinavians don't have a sense of humor.

She is Scandinavian.

She doesn't have a sense of humor.

Some S is not H	S((H
S is S	S()S

| S is not H | S))H |

is invalid and so is:

Some Polish person is dumb.

He is Polish

He is dumb.

Some P is D	P()D
H is P	H))P

| *H* is D | H))D |

Neither argument cancels out.

SORITES ARGUMENTS

Another kind of syllogistic argument is a *sorites*, a group of more than two premises from which a conclusion can be derived by syllogistic means. For example, Duns Scotus gives the argument

> No absolutely perfect being can be excelled in perfection.
>
> Every finite being can be excelled in perfection.
>
> God is an absolutely perfect being.
> _____
>
> Therefore, etc.

where "Therefore, etc." means that Scotus thought the conclusion was so obvious it didn't need to be expressed.

To find the conclusion we treat the premises as premises for a *series* of enthymemes with missing conclusions. When we have reconstructed the argument, we will have a *chain* of syllogisms such that the conclusion of the first syllogism is one of the premises of the next, and if this does not exhaust the premises, the conclusion of that syllogism is one of the premises of the third, and so on.

Symbolizing Scotus' argument:

> No A is E   A # Absolutely perfect being
>
> Every F is E   E # Can be excelled in perfection
>
> G is A   G # God
>
> A)(E
>
> F))E
>
> G))A

From the first two premises we can get the conclusion "No A is F" or "A)(F." Putting this together with the third premise we get "God is not finite," "G)(F." The argument would look like this:

No A is E	A)(E
Every F is E	F))E
No A is F	A)(F
G is A	G))A
G is not F	G)(F

We could also cancel directly to the conclusion by cancelling twice

A)(E	A) cancels A)
F))E	)E cancels E)
G))A	
———	
G)(F	

Sorites arguments are not very common, but they do provide good practice at using syllogistic techniques. The nineteenth-century Oxford mathematician Charles Lutwidge Dodgson, author of *Alice in Wonderland* (under the pen name Lewis Carroll), invented a number of tricky and ingenious sorites arguments. (He preferred to use *soriteses* as the plural, and we will follow him in this.) The Carroll soriteses are intended to give a good workout in using such rules as Obversion, Contraposition, etc., as well as finding conclusions for pairs of premises. Carroll soriteses can be solved directly by cancellation methods, but it is illuminating to reconstruct the chain of syllogisms to see the steps in the argument. So for soriteses and other complex arguments we will use a "double-check" system; cancel to find the conclusion, then reconstruct the chain of syllogisms that leads to that conclusion.

Consider the following Carroll sorites:

All writers who understand human nature are clever.

No one is a true poet unless he can stir the hearts of men.

Shakespeare wrote *Hamlet*.

No writer who does not understand human nature can stir the hearts of men.

None but a true poet could have written *Hamlet*.

We must now find the conclusion and reconstruct the chain of syllogisms. We symbolize the argument as follows, numbering the premises:

1	U))C	U # Understands human nature
2	M̂))T̂	C # Clever
3	S))W	M # Can stir people's hearts
4	Û)(M	T # True poet
5	T̂)(W	W # Writer of *Hamlet*

Of the premises, 1 and 3 are very easy to symbolize, and 4 and 5 are fairly straightforward. Premise 2 is tricky because it contains the word "unless," which needs careful translation. In general, "No A unless B" means "Every non B is non A" or "Every A is B"; for example, No one is a mother unless she is female" means "Every nonfemale is a nonmother" or Every mother is female." Using the general cancellation rule we can cancel every letter but "S" and "C":

U))C	U) cancels Û)
M̂))T̂	M) cancels (M
S))W	)T̂ cancels T̂)
Û)(M	)W cancels (W
T̂)(W	

Since "S" must be inside a curve and "C" outside, the only possible conclusion is "S))C." (The conclusion "C((S" would violate NO.) Thus, the conclusion is "Shakespeare was clever."

We can reconstruct the chain of syllogisms:

1	U))C	
2	M̂))T̂	
3	S))W	
4	Û)(M	
5	T̂)(W	
6	T))M	2 Contrap.
7	M)(Û	4 Conv.
8	M))U	7 Obv.
9	T))U	6,8 Barbara
10	W)(T̂	5 Conv.
11	W))T	10 Obv.
12	W))U	9,11 Barbara
13	W))C	1,12 Barbara
14	S))C	3,13 Barbara

We can now see that what Carroll did was to begin with a very simple chain of Barbara syllogisms:

$$\text{(2) T))M}$$
$$\text{(4) M))U}$$
$$\overline{}$$
$$\text{T))U}$$
$$\text{(5) W))T}$$
$$\overline{}$$
$$\text{W))U}$$
$$\text{(1) U))C}$$
$$\overline{}$$
$$\text{W))C}$$
$$\text{(3) S))W}$$
$$\overline{}$$
$$\text{S))C}$$

He complicated a number of premises by obversion, conversion, and contraposition, then scrambled the order of the premises.

What we do in reconstructing the chain of syllogisms is uncomplicate all the complications and display the original simple structure. This seems like building up a barrier only to unbuild it, but the practice in using all of the techniques used in this chapter is very useful. Therefore, in the set of exercises at the end of the chapter I will give some Carroll soriteses as well as some more realistic examples.

EXERCISES

A. Put the following syllogisms in standard form, symbolize them, and check for validity by cancellation. If valid, name the pattern which the syllogism seems closest to (Barbara, Celerant, etc.). If invalid, give an example of a syllogism of the same form with true premises and a false conclusion.

1. Every simple substance is imperishable.
The soul is a simple substance.
Therefore the soul is imperishable.

2. Every composite substance is perishable.
The soul is not a composite substance.
Therefore the soul is not perishable.

3. What is good is perfect, and sufficient to its possessor.
Pleasure is not perfect, nor sufficient to its possessor.
Therefore pleasure is not what is good.

4. What is good is perfect and sufficient to its possessor.

Wisdom is perfect and sufficient to whoever possesses it.
Therefore wisdom is what is good.

5. Every human being is a rational animal.
   Every woman is a human being.
   Every woman is a rational animal.

6. Every human being has free will.
   Some animal is a human being.
   Some animal has free will.

7. No stone is intelligent.
   Some substance is a stone.
   Not every substance is intelligent.

8. Every virtue is beneficial.
   No vice is beneficial.
   No vice is a virtue.

9. Everyone that reasons is a human being.
   Not every animal is a human being.
   Not every animal reasons.

10. No stone is sentient.
    Every animal is sentient.
    No animal is a stone.

11. No horse is winged.
    Some animal is winged.
    Not every animal is a horse.

12. No beneficial thing is a vice.
    Every virtue is beneficial.
    No virtue is a vice.

13. Every human being is an animal.
    Some reasoner is a human being.
    Some animal reasons.

14. No sentient thing is a stone.
    Every animal is sentient.
    No animal is a stone.

15. No winged thing is a horse.
    Some animal is winged.
    Not every animal is a horse.

16. Every human being is intelligent.
    Every human being is an animal.
    Some animal is intelligent.

17. Every evil is to be shunned.
    Some evil is pleasurable.
    Something pleasurable is to be shunned.

18. Some human being is foolish.
    Every human being is intelligent.
    Some intelligent being is foolish.

19. No circle is rectilinear.
    Every circle is a figure.
    Not every figure is rectilinear.

20. No liar is praiseworthy.
    Some liar is a human being.
    Not every human being is praiseworthy.

21. Not every human being is a geometrician.
    Every human being is intelligent.
    Not every intelligent being is a geometrician.

22. Every human being is an animal.
    Every animal is sentient.
    Some sentient being is a human being.

23. Every envious person is delighted by the troubles of others.
    No person delighted by the troubles of others is good.
    No good person is envious.

24. No avaricious person is a philosopher.
    Every philosopher is a human being.
    Not every human being is avaricious.

25. No illiterate person is a scientist.
    Some scientist is a barbarian.
    Not every barbarian is illiterate.

B. Find the conclusions of the following soriteses, and reconstruct the chain of syllogisms. (*Source*: Lewis Carroll, *Symbolic Logic*).

Note: Several things about these Carroll soriteses need explaining. The term "Univ." stands for "Universe of Discourse." For present purposes you need know only that "Univ." indicates a class of which all the terms of the sorites are subclasses or members. Thus in the dictionary for 1 below, "E" stands for "easy logic examples worked by me," "M" stands for "logic examples worked by me which make my head ache," and so on.

Carroll is also fond of using complicated exceptive forms, which make standardizing difficult. In some cases your only recourse is to take the two terms in a sentence and try them in various standard-form statements, asking yourself if the standard-form statement gives you the meaning of the original. However, to aid you I give below a few typical Carrollisms with corresponding standard forms. These cannot be applied mechanically, however, since context can alter meaning. Use your knowledge of English and your common sense. "Nothing except A is B" usually means "Every B is A." "No A fails to be B" is usually equivalent to "Every A is B." "Nothing is A unless it is B" usually means "Every A is B." Be careful also of Carroll's habit of inverting subject and predicate by using clauses and of the way in which the "Univ." term is sometimes stressed, sometimes omitted.

Note: These exercises are quoted directly from Carroll's *Symbolic Logic* and preserve Carroll's spelling and punctuation.

1. When I work a Logic-example without grumbling, you may be sure it is one that I can understand;

These soriteses are not arranged in regular order, like the examples I am used to;

No easy example ever makes my head ache;

I can't understand examples that are not arranged in regular order, like those I am used to:

I never grumble at an example, unless it gives me a headache.

Univ. "Logic-examples worked by me"; A # arranged in regular order, like the example I am used to; E # easy; G # grumbled at by me; M # making my head ache; T # these Soriteses, U # understood by me.

2. Every idea of mine, that cannot be expressed as a Syllogism, is really ridiculous;

None of my ideas about Bath-buns are worth writing down;

No idea of mine, that fails to come true, can be expressed as a Syllogism;

I never have any really ridiculous idea, that I do not at once refer to my solicitor;

My dreams are all about Bath-buns;

I never refer any idea of mine to my solicitor, unless it is worth writing down.

Univ. "my ideas"; A # able to be expressed as a Syllogism; B # about Bath-buns; C # coming true; D # dreams; R # really ridiculous; S # referred to my solicitor; W # worth writing down.

3. None of the pictures here, except the battle-pieces, are valuable;

None of the unframed ones are varnished;

All the battle-pieces are painted in oils;

All those that have been sold are valuable;

All the English ones are varnished;

All those in frames have been sold.

Univ. "the pictures here"; B # battle-pieces; E # English; F # framed; O # oil-paintings; S # sold; V # valuable; D # varnished.

4. Animals, that do not kick, are always unexcitable;

Donkeys have no horns;

A buffalo can always toss one over a gate;

No animals that kick are easy to swallow;

No hornless animal can toss one over a gate;

All animals are excitable, except buffaloes.

Univ. "animals"; A # able to toss one over a gate; B # buffaloes; D # donkeys; E # easy to swallow; X # excitable; H # horned; K # kicking.

5. No one, who is going to a party, ever fails to brush his hair;

No one looks fascinating, if he is untidy;

Opium eaters have no self-command;

Every one, who has brushed his hair, looks fascinating;

No one wears white kid gloves, unless he is going to a party;

A man is always untidy, if he has no self-command.

Univ. "persons"; G # going to a party; H # having brushed one's hair; S # having self-command; L # looking fascinating; O # opium eaters; T # tidy; W # wearing white kid gloves.

6. A plum-pudding, that is not really solid, is mere porridge;
Every plum-pudding, served at my table, has been boiled in a cloth;
A plum-pudding that is mere porridge is indistinguishable from soup;
No plum-puddings are really solid, except what are served at *my* table.
Univ. "plum-puddings"; B # boiled in a cloth; D # distinguishable from soup; M # mere porridge; R # really solid; S # served at my table.

7. No interesting poems are unpopular among people of real taste;
No modern poetry is free from affectation;
All *your* poems are on the subject of soap-bubbles;
No affected poetry is popular among people of real taste;
No ancient poem is on the subject of soap-bubbles.
Univ. "poems"; A # affected; N # ancient; I # interesting; S # on the subject of soap-bubbles; P # popular among people of real taste; W # written by you.

8. All the fruit at this Show, that fails to get a prize, is the property of the Committee;
None of my peaches have got prizes.
None of the fruit, sold off in the evening, is unripe;
None of the ripe fruit has been grown in a hot-house;
All fruit, that belongs to the Committee, is sold off in the evening.
Univ. "fruit at this Show"; B # belonging to the Committee; G # getting prizes; H # grown in a hot-house; P # my peaches; R # ripe; S # sold off in the evening.

9. Promise-breakers are untrustworthy;
Wine-drinkers are very communicative;
A man who keeps his promises is honest;
No teetotalers are pawnbrokers;
One can always trust a very communicative person.
Univ. "persons"; H # honest; P # pawnbrokers; B # promise-breakers; T # trustworthy; V # very communicative; W # wine-drinkers.

10. No kitten, that loves fish, is unteachable;
No kitten without a tail will play with a gorilla;
Kittens with whiskers always love fish;
No teachable kitten has green eyes;
No kittens have tails unless they have whiskers.
Univ. "kittens"; G # green-eyed; L # loving fish; T # tailed; E # teachable; W # whiskered; P # willing to play with a gorilla.

C. Put the following enthymemes and sorites from Duns Scotus' *Ordinatio* into standard syllogistic form, supplying missing elements where necessary. Ignore phrases in parentheses.

1. (The philosopher argues that) the First Being has infinite power because it moves with an endless movement.

2. (One can argue equally well that) the First Being has infinite power since it can cause endless motion.

3. (Now it is clear that) since the First Being exists in virtue of itself, it has the ability to cause endless motion.

4. The First Being has an infinite effect in its power, but whatever has an infinite effect in its power is infinite; therefore, etc.

5. Any being that possesses all causal power is infinite, but (Avicenna assumes) the First Being does possess all causal power; therefore, etc.

6. (Some argue that) the First Cause has infinite power, because any being that can bridge a gap between infinite extremes has infinite power. But a being that can create something from nothing can bridge a gap between infinite extremes (being and nothingness) and the First Cause can do this.

7. The First Being after God depends on Him totally and is made from no material; thus it is created from nothing.

8. The things that can be known are infinite in number, but they are all known by God. Therefore, the mind of God is infinite.

9. We can always love and seek something greater than any finite being. We cannot love or seek anything greater than God; therefore, etc.

10. An absolutely perfect being cannot be excelled in perfection. But any finite being can be excelled in perfection. God is an absolutely perfect being; therefore, etc.

D. 1. Take one invalid syllogism from exercises A–C and make it valid by changing *one* premise. If this is not possible explain why.

2. Take one invalid syllogism from exercises A–C and make it into a valid sorites by *adding* a premise.

3. Defend the premises or criticize the premises of a valid syllogism from exercises A–C.

5

Mixed Arguments in Descartes and Leibniz

We now move on to the beginning of what is usually called "modern" philosophy, a period often regarded as beginning with Thomas Hobbes in England and with René Descartes on the continent of Europe. As we said in the last chapter there are several things to remember about the end of medieval philosophy. First, late-medieval philosophy was seen by many as degenerating into hairsplitting arguments over minor points. Second, a great deal of medieval logic and medieval philosophy was in fact carried over into the next period. As a result, the early "modern" philosophers were often very critical of medieval philosophy but often shared assumptions and preconceptions with the medieval philosophers.

René Descartes (1596–1650) made a serious effort to rebuild philosophy "from scratch" without making any assumptions. But as we will see, certain assumptions crept into his discussions. Descartes describes his project as follows.

> Several years have now elapsed since I first became aware that I had accepted, even from my youth, many false opinions for true, and that consequently what I afterwards based on such principles was highly doubtful; and from that time I was convinced of the necessity of undertaking once in my life to rid myself of all the opinions I had adopted, and of commencing anew the work of building from the foundation, if I desired to establish a

firm and abiding superstructure in the sciences. But as this enterprise appeared to me to be one of great magnitude, I waited until I had attained an age so mature as to leave me no hope that at any stage of life more advanced I should be better able to execute my design. On this account, I have delayed so long that I should henceforth consider I was doing wrong were I still to consume in deliberation any of the time that now remains for action. To-day, then, since I have opportunely freed my mind from all cares (and am happily disturbed by no passions), and since I am in the secure possession of leisure in a peaceable retirement, I will at length apply myself earnestly and freely to the general overthrow of all my former opinions. But, to this end, it will not be necessary for me to show that the whole of these are false—a point, perhaps, which I shall never reach; but as even now my reason convinces me that I ought not the less carefully to withhold belief from what is not entirely certain and indubitable, than from what is manifestly false, it will be sufficient to justify the rejection of the whole if I shall find in each some ground for doubt. Nor for this purpose will it be necessary even to deal with each belief individually, which would be truly an endless labour; but, as the removal from below of the foundation necessarily involves the downfall of the whole edifice, I will at once approach the criticism of the principles on which all my former beliefs rested.[1]

DESCARTES' SKEPTICAL ARGUMENTS

Plainly, Descartes had a very strict idea of certainty, which might be defined as follows:

certainty = having no reasons for doubt.

Given this definition of certainty, Descartes' procedure was to ask about each of his beliefs if he had any reason to doubt it. If he did, he rejected that belief. Only when he reached some belief that he could find no reason to doubt would Descartes accept the belief and use it as a starting point for his investigation.

He begins, in the first of his *Meditations*, to examine all the beliefs that he had previously accepted on the evidence of his senses: sight, hearing, touch, etc. For a very large class of these beliefs he was able to use the following argument:

Every ordinary belief based on the senses is sometimes mistaken.

Every belief which is sometimes mistaken is a belief I have reason to doubt.

Every belief I have reason to doubt is not certain.

Every belief which is not certain is a belief I should reject.

[1] Rene Descartes, *Meditations on the First Philosophy* (Paris, 1641). Meditation I, paragraph 1. (Passages from philosophical works which appear in many editions will be referred to by chapter or section where available and by paragraph within such subdivisions.)

Therefore every ordinary belief based on the senses is a belief I should reject.

We could put the argument in symbols as follows:

O))S	O # Ordinary beliefs based on the senses
S))D	S # Beliefs sometimes mistaken
D))Ĉ	D # Beliefs I have reason to doubt
Ĉ))R	C # Certain beliefs
——	
O))R	R # Beliefs that should be rejected

The argument cancels to its conclusion:

O))S	)S cancels S)
S))D	)D cancels D)
D))Ĉ	)Ĉ cancels Ĉ)
Ĉ))R	
——	
O))R	

We can prove the conclusion as follows:

1 O))S
2 S))D
3 D))Ĉ
4 Ĉ))R
5 O))D   1,2 Barbara
6 O))Ĉ   5,3 Barbara
7 O))R   4,6 Barbara

So for a large class of beliefs Descartes found reason to reject them because they were sometimes mistaken, and thus dubious, and thus not certain. The rejection of beliefs that were not absolutely certain is the method which Descartes employed to get down to a firm foundation for knowledge. Given his definition of certainty and this method, Descartes' argument seems convincing.

However, Descartes granted that some of our beliefs are not ever mistaken. Descartes' examples are that he is in a given place, wearing clothing, holding a piece of paper in his hands. It seems insane to doubt such obvious facts. For such apparently obvious beliefs Descartes employs a new argument:

Every apparently obvious sensory belief is a belief based on the senses I could have if I were dreaming.

Every belief based on the senses which I could have if I were dreaming is a belief I have reason to doubt.

Every belief I have reason to doubt is not certain.

Every belief which is not certain is a belief which ought to be rejected.

Every apparently obvious sensory belief ought to be rejected.

In symbols:

A))M	A # Apparently obvious sensory beliefs
M))D	M # Beliefs based on the senses that could be had in
D))Ĉ	a dream
Ĉ))R	(D,C,R, as above)
————	
A))R	

The argument cancels to its conclusion:

A))M	)M cancels M)
M))D	)D cancels D)
D))Ĉ	)Ĉ cancels Ĉ)
Ĉ))R	
————	
A))R	

It can be proved as follows:

1 A))M

2 M))D

3 D))Ĉ

4 Ĉ))R

$$5 \quad A))D \quad 1,2 \text{ Barbara}$$

$$6 \quad A))\hat{C} \quad 3,5 \text{ Barbara}$$

$$7 \quad A))R \quad 4,6 \text{ Barbara}$$

Premises 3 and 4 are consequences of Descartes' definition and method. If we wish to reject premise 2 we would have to show that these beliefs *couldn't* be held in a dream: In other words, establish that we *can't* be dreaming now. This could be possible, but it seems quite difficult. To reject premise 2 it seems that we would have to say that even if we were dreaming such apparently obvious beliefs would not be dubious, which seems implausible. So again, granted Descartes' method and his definition, we seem to have a convincing argument.

But what about theoretical beliefs? Surely if I believe that $7 + 5 = 12$, this is certain whether I am believing this is a dream or not. Against such cases Descartes employs the argument:

Every theoretical belief is a belief I might hold because some powerful evil demon is deceiving me.

Every belief which I might hold because some powerful evil demon is deceiving me is a belief I have reason to doubt.

Every belief I have reason to doubt is not certain.

Every belief which is not certain is a belief I should reject.

Therefore every theoretical belief is a belief I should reject.

In symbols:

T))M	T # Theoretical beliefs
M))D	M # Beliefs I might hold because a powerful evil
D))Ĉ	demon is deceiving me
Ĉ))R	(D,C,R as above)
——	
T))R	

The argument cancels to its conclusion:

T))M	)M cancels M)
M))D	)D cancels D)
D))Ĉ	)Ĉ cancels Ĉ)
Ĉ))R	
——	
T))R	

The conclusion can be proved as follows:

1 T))M

2 M))D

3 D))Ĉ

4 Ĉ))R

5 T))D   1,2 Barbara

6 T))Ĉ   3,5 Barbara

7 T))R   4,6 Barbara

Again, Descartes would challenge us to show that such a deceptive demon, clouding our theoretical reasoning, *could* not exist. And surely if a powerful demon was deceiving us we might make all kinds of theoretical mistakes.

Hence, for each of three kinds of beliefs—ordinary beliefs based on the senses, apparently certain sensory beliefs, and theoretical beliefs—we have found reason to doubt each type of belief and therefore to conclude that they are not certain and therefore to reject them:

O))R

A))R

T))R

Is there *any* belief we cannot doubt? Descartes believed that we can find one such belief, our belief that we ourselves exist. As he says in Meditation Three:

> I am conscious that I exist, and I who know that I exist inquire into what I am. It is, however, perfectly certain that the knowledge of my existence, thus precisely taken, is not dependent on things, the existence of which is as yet unknown to me. . . .

Descartes' argument seems to be:

The belief that I exist cannot be doubted.

Every belief that cannot be doubted is certain.

No certain belief should be rejected.

Therefore the belief that I exist should not be rejected.

In symbols:

I))D̂	*I* # The belief that I myself exist
D̂))C	(D,C,R as above)
C)(R	

$$\frac{}{I)(R}$$

The argument cancels to its conclusion:

I))D̂	)D̂ cancels D̂)
D̂))C	)C cancels C)
C)(R	

$$\frac{}{I)(R}$$

The proof is simple:

1 *I*))D̂

2 D̂))C

3 C)(R

4 *I*))C   1,2 Barburu

5 *I*)(R   3,4 Celurynt

But now we notice something rather curious. The common pattern of our first three arguments involved the steps:

$$D))\hat{C}$$

$$\hat{C}))R$$

But our new argument involves *different* steps:

$$D̂))C$$

$$C)(R$$

and these are not equivalent to the similar statements found in our first three arguments, because in general "D̂))C" is not the same as "D))Ĉ" and

"C))R" is not the same as "C)(R." So Descartes has *added* to his previous assumptions a *new* set:

> If a belief is *not* dubious it *is* certain.

> If a belief *is* certain it should *not* be rejected.

The first new assumption might reasonably be said to follow from the definition of certainty implicit in Descartes' discussion:

certainty = having no reason for doubt.

The second new assumption may be regarded as an expansion of his methodological principle:

> If a belief is not certain, reject it *and* if a belief is certain, accept it.

DESCARTES' ARGUMENTS FOR GOD'S EXISTENCE

Descartes now turns to a proof for the existence of something other than himself: that is, the existence of God. To do justice to Descartes' arguments on this point we change over to statement logic. Descartes argues as follows:

If I have an idea of God, I have the idea of an infinite being.

If I have an idea of an infinite being, it must have an adequate explanation.

If I am a finite being, my own experience cannot be an adequate explanation of the idea of infinite being.

If my own experience is not an adequate explanation of my idea of an infinite being, the idea must have been put into my mind by an infinite being.

If the idea of an infinite being was put into my mind by an infinite being, such a being exists.

If an infinite being exists, God exists.

I am finite.

I do have the idea of God.

Therefore God exists.

In symbols:

H > I   H # I have an idea of God

I > A   I # I have the idea of an infinite being

F > [M > Â]   A # I have an adequate explanation of my idea

M̂ > P   M # My own experience is the explanation of my idea

P > E   P # Idea put into my mind by infinite being

E > G   E # Infinite being exists

H

F _____   F # I am finite

G   G # God exists

The argument cancels to its conclusion:

H > I   H cancels H >

I > A   > I cancels I >

F > [M > Â]   F cancels F >

M̂ > P   > A cancels > Â

P > E   M > cancels M̂>

E > G   > P cancels P >

H   > E cancels E >

F

The proof is as follows:

1 H > I

2 I > A

3 F > [M > Â]

4 M̂ > P

5 P > E

6 E > G

7 H

8 F

9 I   1,7 MP

10 A   2,9 MP

11 M > Â 8,3 MP

12 M̂   10,11 MT

13 P   12,4 MP

14 E   5,13 MP

15 G   14,6 MP

Premise 8, that we are finite beings, seems obviously true. Let us grant that we have an idea of God, premise 7. Premise 1 follows from Descartes' definition of God as an infinite being. Premise 2 seems reasonable: Surely if I have an idea it is reasonable to ask for an adequate explanation of why I have that idea. Since we have granted the antecedent of premise 3, we can deduce "M > Â" from premise 4.

But "M > Â" and most of the remaining premises seem open to question. *Why* couldn't some operation of a finite mind be an adequate explanation of the idea of an infinite being? Even if it was not, is the *only* adequate explanation of my idea of God that the idea was put into my mind by an infinite being? Perhaps such a being would have to exist in order to put things into my mind, but would the being who put the idea into my mind have to be God?

Once Descartes has proved to his own satisfaction the existence of God, he uses this to dismiss some of his previous grounds for doubt. If God exists, then God would not permit an evil demon to systematically disturb our theoretical knowledge. Therefore, we can trust our theoretical reasoning if it is based on principles that seem as "clear and distinct" as our certainty of our own existence. For Descartes these "clear and distinct" theoretical principles included the principles of mathematics and logic, but as Descartes continues his arguments, we find him assuming that a number of metaphysical and philosophical truths are "clear and distinct" in the same way. By and large these are metaphysical and philosophical principles that are part of the medieval philosophical synthesis. They probably reached Descartes through his reading and through his education at Jesuit schools before he began his own philosophical reflections. Later philosophers were to challenge these medieval principles and therefore to challenge those parts of Descartes' philosophy based on them.

DESCARTES' ONTOLOGICAL ARGUMENT

Thus, in his further discussion of the idea of God, Descartes presents the following argument:

> There only remains, therefore, the idea of God, in which I must consider whether there is anything that cannot be supposed to originate with myself. By the name God, I understand a substance infinite [eternal, immutable], independent, all-knowing, all-powerful, and by which I myself, and every

other thing that exists, if any such there be, were created. But these properties are so great and excellent, that the more attentively I consider them the less I feel persuaded that the idea I have of them owes its origin to myself alone. And thus it is absolutely necessary to conclude, from all that I have before said, that God exists: for though the idea of substance be in my mind owing to this, that I myself am a substance, I should not, however, have the idea of an infinite substance, seeing I am a finite being, unless it were given me by some substance in reality infinite. . . . The idea, I say, of a being supremely perfect, and infinite, is in the highest degree true; for although, perhaps, we may imagine that such a being does not exist, we cannot, nevertheless, suppose that his idea represents nothing real, as I have already said of the idea of cold. It is likewise clear and distinct in the highest degree, since whatever the mind clearly and distinctly conceives as real or true, and as implying any perfection, is contained entire in this idea. And this is true, nevertheless, although I do not comprehend the infinite, and although there may be in God an infinity of things that I cannot comprehend, nor perhaps even compass by thought in any way; for it is of the nature of the infinite that it should not be comprehended by the finite; and it is enough that I rightly understand this, and judge that all which I clearly perceive, and in which I know there is some perfection, and perhaps also an infinity of properties of which I am ignorant, are formally or eminently in God, in order that the idea I have of him may become the most true, clear, and distinct of all the ideas in my mind.[2]

We might reconstruct the argument as follows:

> **God is a perfect being.**
>
> **A perfect being has all perfections.**
>
> **Reality is a perfection.**
>
> **Therefore a perfect being is real.**

Put in syllogistic form this seems plausible:

$G))P$	G # God
$P))H$	P # Perfect being
$H))R$	H # Being having every perfection
$\overline{\quad\quad}$	R # Being having reality
$G))R$	

The argument cancels

$G))P$	)P cancels P)
$P))H$	)H cancels H)
$H))R$	
$\overline{\quad\quad}$	
$G))R$	

[2]Descartes *Meditations*, Meditation III. Paragraph 22.

and is provable as follows:

1 $G))$P

2 $P))$H

3 $H))$R

4 $G))$H   1,2 Barburu

5 $G))$R   4,3 Barburu

This has seemed to some people to be another plausible "ontological" argument for the existence of God. (An ontological argument is one that attempts to move from a definition of God to the reality or existence of God.)

Put in statement logic, the argument has a somewhat different aspect:

$G > P$ G # God exists

$P > H$ P # God is a perfect being

$\underline{H > R}$ H # God has all perfections

$G > R$ R # God has reality

In this form the argument cancels to its conclusion

$G > P$ $> P$ cancels $P >$

$P > H$ $> H$ cancels $H >$

$H > R$

$\overline{G > R}$

and is easily proved:

1 $G > P$

2 $P > H$

3 $H > R$

4 $G > H$ 1,2 HS

5 $G > R$ 3,4 HS

But the argument only shows that *if* God exists, God has reality. If we tried to derive the conclusion "God has reality" from these premises, the argument would be invalid. If we add "God exists" as a premise, the argument becomes trivial; it would be accepted only by those who already believe in the reality of God.

Why does the syllogistic argument seem convincing? It can easily appear that its first premise, "God is an absolutely perfect being," and its second premise, "An absolutely perfect being possesses every perfection," are simply true by definition. Therefore, many critics of the argument have focused on the third premise: "A being which possesses every perfection would possess reality." Philosophers have argued that existence is not a perfection, not even a property of things.

But in fact the issue is both simpler and deeper than this. If we reflect on the way in which the concept of existence or reality functions in our language, we will see that to assert *any* property of a thing is to assert that it exists. If my watch is black, my watch exists. If my cat is furry, my cat exists. To say that a given thing exists is just to say that it has some properties. In this respect it is parallel to indefinite pronouns like "someone" or "something." If I say "Something is red," you are being told that some individual has a property but not which individual. If I say "My cat exists," you are being told that my cat has some properties, but you are not being told which properties.

Thus, as soon as I make the categorical assertion "God is an absolutely perfect being," I have *already* asserted that God exists. As soon as I make the assertion "An absolutely perfect being has every perfection," I have asserted that an absolutely perfect being exists. Therefore these are the controversial premises, which a nontheist should reject. "A being which has every perfection has reality" is merely a grammatical or logical remark about the way in which concepts like "real" and "existing" function in our language.

The medieval view was that only affirmative, categorical statements imply reality or existence in this way. If I say "God didn't create the world" or "*If* God created the world God created matter," I am not asserting the existence of God.

Of course there will be problems of interpretation on the medieval view. Apparently positive statements may really be negative; apparently categorical statements may turn out to be hypothetical; apparently simple statements may turn out to be compound. (For example, "Sherlock Holmes was a detective" may turn out to be literally false but true if regarded as an elliptical form of "In the stories by Arthur Conan Doyle, Sherlock Holmes was a detective.") A full exploration of these problems is beyond the scope of this chapter. But we can make the general point about Descartes' argument and similar ones that a definition will only give you a hypothetical truth; God is *defined* as a perfect being so *if* anything is God, that is a perfect being. But this gives us no information as to whether anything satisfies the definition.

Probably the medieval assumption that is most questioned by later philosophers is that existing things could be divided into "matter" and "spirit." As we saw in Chapter 1, Matter was defined as that which occupies space and has weight. Spirit was defined as that which neither occupies space nor has weight, but which has knowledge and will. (Both matter and spirit were said to have *duration*: that is, they exist over a period of time.)

Descartes argued that, because we are most directly aware of ourselves as thinking beings, this is what we essentially are. And thinking beings can be purely spiritual in the medieval view. So Descartes thought of humans as essentially spiritual beings united with a material body but not essentially united. This "Cartesian dualism" has been the object of many attacks, some of which we will examine in later chapters.

One interesting argument for dualism that is implicit in Descartes may be presented as follows:

Every quality of material objects is inconceivable apart from material objects.

Some qualities of minds are not inconceivable apart from material objects.

Therefore some qualities of minds are not qualities of material objects.

This is obviously valid; a simple syllogism that cancels as follows:

O))I	)I cancels I)
M((I	O # Quality of material objects
M((O	I # Inconceivable apart from material objects
	M # Qualities of mind

But if some qualities of minds are not qualities of material objects, then it would seem that minds are not material objects. This is best represented in statement logic:

If some qualities of minds are not qualities of material objects, then minds are not material objects.

Some qualities of minds are not qualities of material objects.

Therefore minds are not material objects.

In symbols:

$\hat{Q} > \hat{A}$	Q # Every quality of mind is a quality of material objects
$\hat{Q}$	
$\hat{A}$	A # Minds are material objects

This is a simple *Modus Ponens* argument, $\hat{Q}>$ cancels $\hat{Q}$, leaving $\hat{A}$.

Arguments of this kind could be handled as mixed arguments in the following way: We write out all of our statements in curve notation, but join some curve-notation statements with statement logic connecting as follows:

1 O))I   (O,I,M as above)

2 M((I

3 M((O > D)(M

4 M((O   1,2 Baroco

5 I)(M   3,4 M.P.

It would be a little confusing, though possible, to do this by cancellation:

O))I   )I cancels I)
                                  yielding M((O
M((I   which cancels

M((O >D)(M   M((O>

———————————

D)(M

There are richer and more complex systems, such as modern predicate logic in which we have a unified system that can handle both statement-logic arguments and syllogistic arguments. However, a great many philosophical arguments can be handled by statement logic, syllogistic logic, or a combination of the two.

MIXED ARGUMENTS IN LEIBNIZ

Such a combination was, in fact, common in the period of which we are writing. Gottfried Wilhelm Leibniz (1646–1716), who was born shortly before Descartes' death, often mixed syllogistic arguments with such statement-logic forms as Hypothetical Syllogism. One of his major works was the *Theodicy*, in which he examined and tried to refute various objections to the existence of God. He later wrote a "syllogistic abridgement" of the *Theodicy* in which he gave his arguments in a strict logical form and commented on the truth of the premises much as we have been doing. He would present a syllogism, then offer a *prosyllogism*, which was another syllogism whose conclusion was one of the premises of the first syllogism. The prosyllogism was often an imaginary or real opponent's argument for a premise that Leibniz wished to reject. A typical passage is as follows:

I. *Objection*. Whoever does not choose the best is lacking in power, or in knowledge, or in goodness.

God did not choose the best in creating this world.

Therefore, God has been lacking in power, or in knowledge, or in goodness.

Answer. I deny the minor, that is, the second premise of this syllogism; and our opponent proves it by this

Prosyllogism. Whoever makes things in which there is evil, which could have been made without any evil, or the making of which could have been omitted, does not choose the best.

God has made a world in which there is evil; a world, I say, which could have been made without any evil, or the making of which could have been omitted altogether.

Therefore, God has not chosen the best.[3]

Notice several interesting things about this passage. The second premise (the *minor* premise because it contains the *minor* term, that is, the subject of the conclusion) is *not* just the antecedent of the major premise (major because it contains the *major* term, the consequent of the conclusion). It has what could be regarded as a parenthetical remark, "in creating the world." We could ignore this and symbolize as follows:

B))L   G # God

G))B   B # One who does not choose the best
———
G))L   L # One lacking in power, knowledge, or goodness

and we would have a simple Barburu syllogism. But we could also symbolize as follows:

G))C   C # Creator of the world

C))B   (G, B, L as above)

B))L
———
G))L

<hr>

[3]Leibniz: *The Theodicy, Abridgement of the Argument to Syllogistic Form* (Berlin, 1710.) Objection I.

This is a simple sorites with two Barburu parts, which cancels as follows:

G))C   )C cancels C)

C))B   )B cancels B)

B))L

——————

G))L

The expanded version has the advantage of separating what a theist would wish to affirm (God created the world) from what a theist would want to deny (the Creator did not choose the best).

Leibniz's "prosyllogism" could be symbolized as follows:

A))B   A # A maker of avoidable evil

G))A   (G, B, as above)

——————

G))B

This is a simple Barburu syllogism again, but it could be expanded as follows:

G))C

C))A

A))B

——————

G))B

Again we have a simple sorites that cancels as follows:

G))C   )C cancels C)

C))A   )A cancels A)

A))B

——————

G))B

(We could also break down the predicate of the first premise of the first argument and the first premise of this argument into ". . . lacking in power," ". . . lacking in knowledge," ". . . lacking in goodness" and "which could have been made without evil," "the making of which could be omitted." But since these parts of the predicates are never separated, there seems no point in complicating the argument.)

Thus we see that although Leibniz thinks of his arguments as simple syllogisms, they need to be somewhat expanded—at least into sorites to take into account all the terms that Leibniz introduces.

Leibniz's reply to the objections he raises is interesting both philosophically and logically. He grants that there is evil in the world, but he denies that this means that the maker of the world did not choose the best. Part of his reasons for this position are traditional ones: It is reasonable to allow evil to bring about a greater good. But Leibniz also takes the view that this *is* the best of all possible worlds:

> I have followed the opinion of St. Augustine, who has said a hundred times, that God has permitted evil in order to bring about good, that is, a greater good; and that of Thomas Aquinas (in libr. II. sent. dist. 32, qu. I, art. 1), that the permitting of evil tends to the good of the universe. I have shown that the ancients called Adam's fall *felix culpa*, a happy sin, because it had been retrieved with immense advantage by the incarnation of the Son of God, who has given to the universe something nobler than anything that ever would have been among creatures except for it. For the sake of a clearer understanding, I have added, following many good authors, that it was in accordance with order and the general good that God allowed to certain creatures the opportunity of exercising their liberty, even when he foresaw that they would turn to evil, but which he could so well rectify; because it was not fitting that, in order to hinder sin, God should always act in an extraordinary manner. To overthrow this objection, therefore, it is sufficient to show that a world with evil might be better than a world without evil; but I have gone even farther, in the work, and have even proved that this universe must be in reality better than every other possible universe.[4]

Many philosophers and nonphilosophers have found the idea that this is the best possible world absurd: Voltaire's *Candide* is a savage literary attack on the idea. But some philosophers also argue that the concept of a best *possible* world has no meaning if we are talking in terms of an infinitely powerful being, for an infinite power could always improve on *any* world. So just as there can be no largest number, since we can always add to it, there can be no best possible world, for a God could always improve on it.

Turning to the next objection, we find Leibniz shifting easily into statement-logic forms:

II. *Objection.* If there is more evil than good in intelligent creatures, then there is more evil than good in the whole work of God.

Now, there is more evil than good in intelligent creatures.

Therefore, there is more evil than good in the whole work of God.

---

[4]*Theodicy, Abridgement* Answer to Objection I.

What Leibniz calls a "conditional syllogism" here is an example of what we call *Modus Ponens*:

M > W   M # There is more evil than good in intelligent
                creatures
M
———   W # There is more evil than good in the whole
W   work of God

Of course the argument cancels and is valid. Leibniz denies both premises, for reasons too complex to analyze quickly here. In the third Objection, the main argument is in statement-logic form, and the two prosyllogisms that Leibniz gives are best analyzed using syllogistic logic:

III. *Objection*. If it is always impossible not to sin, it is always unjust to punish.

Now, it is always impossible not to sin; or, in other words, every sin is necessary.

Therefore, it is always unjust to punish.

The minor of this is proved thus:

1. *Prosyllogism*. All that is predetermined is necessary. Every event is predetermined.

Therefore, every event (and consequently sin also) is necessary. Again this second minor is proved thus:

2. *Prosyllogism*. That which is future, that which is foreseen, that which is involved in the causes, is predetermined.

Every event is such.

Therefore, every event is predetermined.[5]

The first argument can be symbolized:

S))N > P)(J   S # Sin

S))N   N # Necessary events
————
P)(J   P # Punishments

                   J # Just acts

This is a simple *Modus Ponens* argument with complete standard form subject-predicate statements instead of statement letters. Leibniz regards

[5]*Theodicy, Abridgement* Objection III.

"It is impossible not to sin" and "Sin is necessary" as the *same* statement, for reasons we will examine in due course.

The first prosyllogism is in fact an enthymatic sorites:

$$
\begin{array}{ll}
\text{P))N} & \text{P \# Predetermined events} \\
\text{E))P} & \text{E \# Events} \\
* \quad \text{S))E} & \text{(S,N as above)} \\
\hline
\text{S))N}
\end{array}
$$

The resulting argument is a simple sorites chain of two Barbara syllogisms, but without the assumed premise "Every sin is an event," it would not yield the conclusion needed, the antecedent of the first argument.

The second premise of this prosyllogism is proved by another argument:

$$
\begin{array}{ll}
\text{F))P} & \text{F \# Events which are future, foreseen, and} \\
\text{E))F} & \qquad \text{involved in causes} \\
\hline
\text{E))P} & \text{(P,E as above)}
\end{array}
$$

The form is a simple Barbara syllogism, and is of course valid.

The remaining arguments in the abridgement of the *Theodicy* will be left as exercises for the end of this chapter. Some of them can be dealt with purely by statement logic, some purely by syllogistic logic, but the majority will be best handled in a mixed system.

When dealing with mixed statement-logic and syllogistic arguments, the following principles should be kept in mind:

1. Standard form subject-predicate statements from the syllogistic system of Chapter 4 may be substituted for the statement variables in the argument forms given in Chapter 2.

2. If such statements are cancelled, they must cancel another statement that is identical or equivalent.

3. Equivalent statements may be substituted for each other in *part* of a complex statement, but argument forms may not be applied to the antecedents of conditionals. Thus:

$$[A \wedge B] > C$$

may be replaced by

$$[B \wedge A] > C$$

but not by $[A \lor B] > C$

$$[[A \land B] \lor [B \land C]] > [D > F]$$

may be replaced by

$$[[B \land A] \lor [C \land B]] > [\hat{F} > \hat{D}]$$

but not by $[A \lor C] > [D > F]$

4. Although statement negation and statement connections may be applied to the standard-form statements from Chapter 3, there is no way of joining statements or negating statements with the curve connectives and curve negation of Chapter 3 to statements from Chapter 2 for these apply only to *terms* not to statements. Thus:

$$\overline{A))B} \land A)(B$$

is meaningful, but

$$\hat{p} \text{ or } p)) q \text{ etc.}$$

are meaningless when statements are substituted for "p" and "q." The following four rules, called collectively *Contradictories* (Contrad.) are a useful combination of statement logic and syllogistic logic:

$\overline{S))P}$	$\overline{S)(P}$	$\overline{S()P}$	$\overline{S((P}$
S((P	S()P	S)(P	S))P

EXERCISES

A. Put the following arguments in standard form, symbolize them, and check for validity by cancellation using either statement logic or syllogistic logic. If valid, give a proof using either statement logic or syllogistic logic.

   1. Everything that thinks exists;
I think;
Therefore I exist.

   2. One who knows and can do all things is God.
Christ knows and can do all things.
Therefore Christ is God.

   3. If there is a God, the impious will stand trial;
But there is a God;
Therefore the impious will stand trial before Him.

4. Unless Christ be God, there is no God;
    But there certainly is a God;
    Therefore Christ is God.
5. No one can serve God and Mammon;
    True Christians serve God;
    Therefore true Christians do not serve Mammon.
6. No one can serve God and Mammon;
    Some priests serve Mammon;
    Therefore some priests do not serve God.
7. Every simple thing is imperishable, because simple things do not decompose and what does not decompose is imperishable.
    The soul is simple, because a unit is without parts and indivisible;
    Therefore the soul is imperishable.
8. If God alters, He is altered by Himself or by another;
    God is not altered by another, for nothing is stronger than God, so as to alter Him; He is not altered by Himself, for, being perfect, He cannot change for the better, and what is perfect does not deteriorate for the worse;
    Therefore God is unalterable.
9. A virtuous person has no qualm of conscience;
    A person having no qualm of conscience is fearless;
    A fearless person is happy;
    Therefore a virtuous person is happy.
10. A person poor in spirit has knowledge of self and of God;
    A person having knowledge of self and of God manages his or her affairs as pleases God;
    A person managing his or her affairs as pleases God inherits the kingdom of heaven;
    A person inheriting the kingdom of heaven is blissful;
    Therefore a person, poor in spirit, is blissful.

B. Symbolize and prove the following arguments from Leibniz's *Syllogistic Abridgement of the Theodicy.*

1. Whoever does not choose the best is lacking in power or in knowledge or in goodness.
    God does not choose the best in creating this world.
    Therefore, God is lacking in power or in knowledge or in goodness.
2. Whoever makes things in which there is evil, which could have been made without any evil, and the making of which could have been omitted, does not choose the best.
    God has made a world in which there is evil, a world that could have been made without any evil, and the making of which could have been omitted altogether.
    Therefore, God has not chosen the best.
3. If there is more evil than good in intelligent creatures, then there is more evil than good in the work of God.
    There is more evil than good in intelligent creatures.
    Therefore, there is more evil than good in the work of God.
4. If it is always impossible not to sin, then it is always unjust to punish.

Now it is always impossible not to sin, or in other words every sin is necessary.

Therefore, it is always unjust to punish.

5. All that is predetermined is necessary.
   Every event is predetermined.
   Sin is an event.
   Therefore, every event is necessary and consequently sin is necessary.

6. That which is future, that which is foreseen, that which follows from its causes, is predetermined.
   Every event is such.
   Therefore, every event is predetermined.

7. Whoever can prevent the sin of another and does not do so, but rather contributes to it, although he is well informed of it, is accessory to that sin.
   God can prevent the sin of intelligent creatures, but he does not do so, and rather contributes to it by his concurrence and by the opportunities which he brings about, although he has a perfect knowledge of it.
   Therefore, God is an accessory to sin.

8. Whoever produces all that is real in a thing, is its cause.
   God produces all that is real in sin.
   Therefore, God is the cause of sin.

9. Whoever punishes those who have done as well as it was in their power to do, is unjust.
   God does so.
   Therefore, God is unjust.

10. Whoever gives only to some, and not to all, the means that produces in them effectively a good will and saving faith, has not sufficient goodness.
    God does this.
    Therefore, God has not sufficient goodness.

C. Symbolize the following arguments and prove their validity. (*Source*: Leibniz, *The Monadology*.)

   1. There must be simple substances since there are composites, and a composite is a collection of simple substances.

   2. Where there are no parts, divisibility is not possible. Simple substances have no parts. Therefore, it is not possible to divide them.

   3. Simple substances can neither begin by being formed out of parts nor end by being divided into parts. Since the only other way in which they can begin is by creation and the only other way in which they can end is by being annihilated, then, if they begin, they are created and, if they end, they are annihilated.

   4. Simple substances cannot be changed by being added to or by having their parts rearranged. External causes of change must either add something or rearrange parts. Therefore, the causes of change in simple substances must be internal.

   5. To change, something must either have parts or have many properties

and relations. Simple substances change, but have no parts. Therefore, they must have many properties and relations.

6. Since the soul is a simple substance and has many properties and relations, it is a mistake to say that no simple substance has many properties.

7. A soul in the wider sense is anything which has perceptions and desires. Simple substances have perceptions and desires and are therefore souls in the wider sense.

8. A soul in the narrower sense has clear perception and memory. Since simple substances have unclear perception and no memory, they are not souls in the stricter sense.

9. A soul in the narrower sense, which is unconscious, has desire and perception but not clear perception and does not have memory. Therefore, since a soul in the wider sense is what has unclear perception and desire but not memory, an unconscious soul in the narrow sense is the same as a soul in the wider sense.

10. No simple substance can be totally without perception. Since a soul is a simple substance, an unconscious soul is not totally without perception.

D. Take a valid argument from exercises A–C and give an argument for or against the truth of its premises.

6

Hume,
Probability,
and Causal Arguments

With Descartes we are already at the beginning of the scientific age: With David Hume (1711–1776) we move into an era where science was becoming increasingly important. Although Hume was not a philosopher of science, he contributed to our understanding of science in two ways: by his critique of the concept of causality and by his challenge to the methods of science. To deal with these two challenges by Hume, we will have to explore the more elementary part of the theory of probability.

Although, as we will see, Hume's positive idea of cause is open to many objections, his criticism of the accepted notions of causation in his time was a considerable advance in understanding. Because when we claim that event "a" causes event "b" we seem to be saying that if "a" occurs "b" *must* occur, many philosophers have confused the idea of causal necessity and the idea of strictly logical necessity. Hume analyzed logical necessity as purely a matter of relations between concepts, as when we say it must be true that all uncles are male because the concept of being an uncle includes the idea of being male. Hume then pointed out that causal relations are not a matter of relations between concepts: No amount of analyzing our concepts will tell us what causal relations hold: Only experience will do that. And Hume thought that experience could never give us any idea of necessity.

If we would satisfy ourselves, therefore, concerning the nature of that evidence, which assures us of matters of fact, we must enquire how we arrive at the knowledge of cause and effect.

I shall venture to affirm, as a general proposition, which admits of no exception, that the knowledge of this relation is not, in any instance, attained by reasonings *a priori*; but arises entirely from experience, when we find that any particular objects are constantly conjoined with each other. Let an object be presented to a man of ever so strong natural reason and abilities; if that object be entirely new to him, he will not be able, by the most accurate examination of its sensible qualities, to discover any of its causes or effects.[1]

If causal relations are not logical relations then what are they? To answer this question we must first master the elements of probability theory, which was first developed by Blaise Pascal (1623–1662) a century before Hume's time.

PROBABILITY

A probability is a *measure* that can be expressed by a number. By convention we usually express a probability as a fraction, or at least as some number between 0 and 1, whether that number can be expressed as a fraction or not. Some numbers less than 1 and more than 0 cannot be expressed by a fraction; for example, the square root of 2. Such numbers are called *irrational* numbers, and in advanced probability theory a probability can be expressed as an irrational number. But for our purposes we will always express probabilities as fractions.

What has probability? Actually the best answer to this is "events," but because of the great convenience of this way of doing things, we will talk instead of the probability of a *statement describing an event*. Thus, instead of talking about the probability that this coin I am about to flip will come up heads, we talk of the probability of the *statement*, "This coin I am about to flip will come up heads." Because we are talking about statements, we can use statement negation and statement connectives instead of introducing new machinery for ideas such as "this event does not happen" or "either event 'a' or event 'b' happens."

What is probability a measure *of*? This is a controversial topic. Some philosophers think that probability is a measure of how much we do or should *believe* a statement, with 1 representing complete confidence that the statement is true and 0 complete confidence that the statement is false. Some philosophers think that a probability represents a *frequency*: The statement that the probability of *S* is 3/4 means that *S* is true 3 out of 4 times in the long run. We will take the view that a probability expresses

[1] Hume, *An Enquiry Concerning Human Understanding* (Edinburgh, 1758), Section IV, Part I, Paragraphs 6 and 7.

the *degree of support* given to a statement by evidence. On this view, ordinary statement logic is a special case of probability theory, where the degree of support given to a statement by the evidence is 1 or 0. (We will explore this in detail later.)

The usual notation for expressing a statement like "the probability of S is 3/4" is "Pr(S) = 3/4" or "Prob(S) = 3/4." In this book we will use a simpler notation, which cuts down the need for parentheses and makes probability statements easier to read. We would write "The probability of S is 3/4" as

$$\overline{S} = 3/4 \quad (\text{not } Pr(S) = 3/4)$$

and "The probability of S or T is 5/8" as

$$\overline{S \vee T} = 5/8 \quad (\text{not } Pr(S \vee T) = 5/8)$$

We can now give a handful of simple rules for probability theory, using "p" and "q" as statement variables and our usual statement negation and connectives. The first rule is the *Convention Rule* (C.R.)

$$0 \leq \overline{p} \leq 1$$

This simply says that the convention for expressing probabilities we will use is to write them as a number greater than or equal to 0 ($0 \leq$) and less than or equal to 1 (≤ 1). The next rule is the *Negation Rule* (N.R.):

$$\overline{\hat{p}} = 1 - \overline{p}$$

This says that to get the probability of the negation of a statement we subtract the probability of that statement from 1. Thus, if the probability of drawing a heart card from a well-shuffled pack of cards is 1/4, the probability of *not* drawing a heart card is 3/4:

$$H \text{ \# A heart is drawn}$$

$$\overline{\hat{H}} = 1 - \overline{H} = 1 - 1/4 = 3/4$$

Notice that a probability itself is *not* a statement. "H" is a statement, but $\overline{H}$ is a *quantity*, which can enter into mathematical statements of equality, inequality, etc. For example:

$$\overline{H} = 3/4 \quad 0 < \overline{H} \quad \overline{H} < 1$$

We could use statement negation on this type of statement:

$$\overline{\overline{H} = 1/3} \quad \overline{\overline{H} < 0} \quad \overline{1 < \overline{H}}$$

but we will rarely do so. (To avoid confusion with our "arrow" angle connective, we will always write inequalities with the "open" side of the angle facing right: This avoids the visual confusion that might result from such an expression as "1 > $\overline{H}$," even though inequalities are always between quantities and arrow implication operators between statements.)

The *Addition Rule* (A.R.) gives us the probability of a disjunction when the probability of the disjuncts is known:

$$\overline{p \vee q} = \overline{p} + \overline{q} - \overline{p \wedge q}$$

In the cases where $\overline{p \wedge q} = 0$, this rule collapses into the *Simple Addition Rule* (S.A.R.):

$$\overline{p \vee q} = \overline{p} + \overline{q}$$

In many cases the condition is satisfied. If the chance of getting a heart on a draw from a well-shuffled deck of cards is 1/4 and the chance of getting a diamond is 1/4, then, because a card cannot be *both* a heart and a diamond, the probability is:

D **#** the card drawn is a diamond

$$\overline{H \vee D} = \overline{H} + \overline{D} = 1/4 + 1/4 = 1/2$$

But if I ask about the probability of getting a diamond or a jack, those are problems. The chance of getting a jack on a draw from a well-shuffled deck of cards is 4/52; the chance of getting a diamond is 13/52. But I cannot say:

J **#** The card drawn is a jack

$$\overline{D \vee J} = \overline{D} + \overline{J} = 4/52 + 13/52 = 17/52$$

because I have counted the Jack of Diamonds twice, once as diamond, once as a jack. Thus I must know that the probability of "J $\wedge$ D" is 1/52 and say:

$$\overline{J \vee D} = \overline{J} + \overline{D} - \overline{J \wedge D} = 4/52 + 13/52 - 1/52 = 16/52$$

Our next rule is a general rule for the probability of "p $\wedge$ q" where the probabilities of "p" and "q" are known. It is the *Multiplication Rule* (M.R.).

$$\overline{p \wedge q} = \overline{p} \times \overline{p > q}$$

This says that the probability of "p q" is the probability that "p" is true multiplied by the probability that *if* "p" is true "q" is true. Where $\overline{p > q} = \overline{q}$, this becomes the *Simple Multiplication Rule* (S.M.R.).

$$\overline{p \wedge q} = \overline{p} \times \overline{q}$$

Thus, consider the probability of getting a diamond twice by drawing from a well-shuffled deck, replacing the card, shuffling again, and drawing again. Since what was drawn the first time has no effect on what will be drawn the second time, then:

D^1 # Diamond on the first draw

D^2 # Diamond on the second draw

$\overline{D^1} = 1/4$

$\overline{D^2} = \overline{D^1 > D^2} = 1/4$

and

$\overline{D^1\ D^2} = \overline{D^1} \times \overline{D^2} = 1/4 \times 1/4 = 1/16$

However, not all probabilities are independent in this way. If I draw a diamond from the deck and do *not* replace it, then the probability that I will get a diamond on the next draw becomes 12/51, so for this situation:

$$\overline{D^1\ D^2} = \overline{D^1} \times \overline{D^1 > D^2} = 1/4 \times 12/51 = 12/204 = 3/51$$

(Because 1/16 is close to 3/51, the chances have not gone down drastically, but they have gone down.)

CONDITIONAL PROBABILITY

The general formula for the probability of a conditional is the *Conditional Probability Rule* (C.P.R.):

$$\overline{p > q} = \frac{\overline{q \wedge p}}{\overline{p}}$$

This says that the probability that if "p" is true then "q" is true is identical with the probability that both "q" and "p" are true divided by the probability that "p" is true. (The more usual, rather confusing, notation for $\overline{p > q}$ is "Pr(q/p)," read as "The probability of q if p is true" or "The probability of q *given* p.") Of course this definition is in a sense circular; because the rule for p ∧ q contains the probability of a conditional and the rule for p > q includes the probability of a conjunction, these two rules do not provide *independent* ways of determining these quantities. What the rules do, however, is show how the probabilities of conjunctions and conditionals are interrelated: how if one is known we can get the other.

To illustrate the Conditional Probability Rule consider a case where you may draw a court card but are not sure. What is the chance that the face on your card has a mustache? In almost every American deck of cards the King of Hearts does not have a mustache and neither does the Jack of Clubs. In most American decks all the other kings and jacks have mustaches, and suppose you know this is true of the deck you are using. Given:

$$\text{C \# The card drawn is a court card}$$

$$\text{M \# The face on the card has a mustache}$$

What is $\overline{C > M}$? We can use the formula:

$$C > M = \frac{\overline{M \wedge C}}{\overline{C}}$$

There are six mustached court cards so $\overline{M \wedge C} = 6/52$. There are 12 court cards in the deck so $\overline{C} = 12/52$. So:

$$\overline{C > M} = \frac{\overline{M \wedge C}}{\overline{C}} = \frac{6/52}{12/52} = 6/12$$

(Normally we divide fractions by inverting one of them and multiplying the numerators and denominators. But where the denominators are the same we can simply cross out the denominators and take the upper numerator as the numerator of the answer and the lower one as the denominator of the answer.)

Of course $\overline{C > M}$ is not the same as $\overline{M}$, which is 6/52. So if you *knew* you had a court card you could reason "My chances of having a mustached face on my card are 6/12(= 1/2) not 6/52, since I know the card is a court card, and half the court cards have mustaches.

In other words you could reason:

$$\overline{C > M} = 1/2$$

$$\overline{C} = 1$$

$$\overline{M} = 1/2$$

This is a special case of the general rule *Probabilistic Modus Ponens* (P.M.P.):

$$\overline{p > q} = m/n$$

$$\overline{p} = j/k$$

$$[m/n \times j/k] \le \overline{q}$$

(Provided the probabilities of the premises are independent) In the special case where one of the quantities, $\overline{p}$, or j/k is 1, the inequality in the conclusion becomes an equality. So ordinary *Modus Ponens* is also a special case:

$$\overline{p > q} = 1$$

$$\overline{p} = 1$$

$$\overline{q} = 1$$

Consider the case where I am drawing only from a shuffled pile of court cards. I have a 3/6 probability of having a red card. $\overline{R > M}$ is 3/6, since 3 out of 6 red court cards are mustached:

$$\overline{R > M} = 3/6$$

$$\overline{R} = 1/2$$

$$\overline{M} \ge 3/12$$

$\overline{M}$ is of course actually greater than 3/12: If I don't have one of the mustached red cards I may have one of the mustached black cards.

Let us now return to the question of what we mean by an event "a" *causing* an event "b." In many ways the notion of cause seems to resemble the notion of implication. If I know that a hole in a tire causes it to go flat, and know that there is a large hole in my spare tire, I expect my spare tire to be flat. This seems similar to "If A then B, A therefore B." However, in most ordinary uses of "a causes b," even if "a" has occurred we cannot be certain that "b" has occurred, for some unexpected factor may have intervened: for example, the hole may be temporarily plugged by some bit of debris that was inside the tire. Still, this doesn't happen often: If my spare tire has a large hole in it, I can be pretty sure it is flat. So the typical case of a causal claim is one where if the cause has occurred we are reasonably sure that the effect has occurred or will occur shortly.

To express this in the machinery available to us, we can do as we did in the case of probabilities and talk of the statement describing an event instead of the event itself. Thus, if:

O # There is a hole in my spare tire

F # My spare tire is flat

to say then "a hole in the spare tire will cause it to be flat is to say:

$$\overline{O > H} = 1 - 1/n$$

where 1/n is quite small and $\overline{O > H}$ is greater than $\overline{H}$ alone. We can then give a P.M.P. argument:

$$\overline{O > F} = 1 - 1/n$$
$$\overline{O} = 1$$
$$\overline{F} = 1 - 1/n$$

However, although the statement $\overline{O > F} = 1 - 1/n$ seems to be *implied* by the statement that a hole in the tire causes it to be flat, the probability statement does not seem to be equivalent to the causal claim. So we will introduce a new connective "}" such that

p } q # that p is true causes q to be true

In general:

$$\frac{p \} q}{p > q = 1 - 1/n}$$ Implication of
Causal Claim (I.C.C.)

where 1/n is small and $\overline{q} < \overline{p > q}$. Note that the two statements are not equivalent.

The I.C.C. rule entitles us to write the rules:

p } q	Causal	p } q	Causal
	Modus		Modus
p	Ponens	q̂	Tollens
$\overline{q} = 1 - 1/n$	(C.M.P.)	$\overline{\hat{p}} = 1 - 1/n$	(C.M.T.)

The new connective will also have causal analogues of H.S. and the equivalences Exp., I.A. and I.O.

p } q	[p ∧ q] } q	[p ∧ q] } r	p } [q ∧ r]
q } r			
p } r	p} [q } r]	p } r	p } q
		q } r	p } r

If p } q then $\overline{p > q}$ is quite high and the nonoccurrence of q would call for explanation. For example, consider the dialogue:

A: I had a hole in my spare tire when I checked it out today.
B: It must have been flat, then.
A: No it wasn't.
B: That's really surprising. What prevented it from going flat?

Because tires normally go flat when they have holes in them, a nonflat tire with a hole is surprising and in need of explanation.

HUME'S THEORY OF CAUSATION

Now Hume would grant that when we say that event "a" causes event "b" and event "a" has occurred, we expect "b" to occur and are surprised if it doesn't. But Hume argues that all there is to a causal statement is a past history of "a" being followed by "b," which has built up a psychological association between "a" and "b" so that when we see "a" we expect "b." Hume would deny that observing "a" gives us any *reason* for expecting "b." Expecting "b" when we have observed "a" is a matter of habit, not of reason.

> Suppose a person, though endowed with the strongest faculties of reason and reflection, to be brought on a sudden into this world; he would, indeed, immediately observe a continual succession of objects, and one event following another; but he would not be able to discover anything farther. He would not, at first, by any reasoning, be able to reach the idea of cause and effect; since the particular powers, by which all natural operations are performed, never appear to the senses; nor is it reasonable to conclude, merely because one event, in one instance, precedes another, that therefore the one is the cause, the other the effect. Their conjunction may be arbitrary and casual. There may be no reason to infer the existence of one from the appearance of the other. And in a word, such a person, without more experience, could never employ his conjecture or reasoning concerning any matter of fact, or be assured of anything beyond what was immediately present to his memory and senses.
>
> Suppose, again, that he has acquired more experience, and has lived so long in the world as to have observed familiar objects or events to be constantly conjoined together; what is the consequence of this experience? He immediately infers the existence of one object from the appearance of the other. Yet he has not, by all his experience, acquired any idea or knowledge of the secret power by which the one object produces the other; nor is it, by any process of reasoning, he is engaged to draw this inference. But still he finds himself determined to draw it: And though he should be convinced that his understanding has no part in the operation, he would nevertheless continue in the same course of thinking. There is some other principle which determines him to form such a conclusion.
>
> This principle is Custom or Habit. For wherever the repetition of any particular act or operation produces a propensity to renew the same act or operation, without being impelled by any reasoning or process of the understanding, we always say, that this propensity is the effect of *Custom.* By em-

ploying that word, we pretend not to have given the ultimate reason of such a propensity. We only point out a principle of human nature, which is universally acknowledged, and which is well known by its effects. Perhaps we can push our enquiries no farther, or pretend to give the cause of this cause; but must rest contented with it as the ultimate principle, which we can assign, of all our conclusions from experience. It is sufficient satisfaction, that we can go so far, without repining at the narrowness of our faculties because they will carry us no farther. And it is certain we here advance a very intelligible proposition at least, if not a true one, when we assert that, after the constant conjunction of two objects—heat and flame, for instance, weight and solidity—we are determined by custom alone to expect the one from the appearance of the other. This hypothesis seems even the only one which explains the difficulty, why we draw, from a thousand instances, an inference which we are not able to draw from one instance, that is, in no respect, different from them. Reason is incapable of any such variation. The conclusions which it draws from considering one circle are the same which it would form upon surveying all the circles in the universe.[2]

Many philosophers think that Hume has committed an error of reasoning here. True enough a description of an effect does not follow deductively from a description of its cause; we cannot deductively derive B from A and A } B. But simply because we do not have deductive reasons to accept B does not mean we have *no* reasons. These philosophers claim that Hume illegitimately assumed that the only kind of reasons we can have are deductive reasons, so if we have no deductive reasons to accept B we have no reasons. Another way of putting this is that Hume seems to suppose that if evidence does not give complete support to a conclusion it gives *no* support: that if the probability of the conclusion is not 1 we have no argument for the conclusion.

This may in fact account for a considerable part of Hume's objections, and it may be correct that Hume ignored the possibility of evidence giving partial support to a conclusion; ignored or denied in fact the whole notion of probability that we have been using. However, Hume would also issue the following challenge: How can we explain and justify the idea that evidence can give partial support to a conclusion; how can we justify probabilistic reasoning? Deductive logic is valid "no matter what": We do not need to know the state of the world to know that if A > B is true and A is true then B is true. But how can we justify probabilistic reasoning? By experience? If so, how can experience justify a conclusion that has not been experienced, which "goes beyond" experience?

HUME'S PROBLEM OF INDUCTION

This is what is sometimes called "Hume's Problem of Induction." By "induction" we mean just the kind of reasoning we have been discussing;

[2]*Enquiry*, Section V, Part I, Paragraphs 5, 6, 7.

reasoning that does not seem to be deductively valid and that gives only partial support to its conclusions.

The force of this objection can be brought out by considering one attempted answer to the problem. Empiricists like John Stuart Mill argued that we can justify induction by bringing in a general principle called the *Uniformity of Nature*. In observed cases (or in the past) all or most instances of "a" have been followed by "b." So in cases yet to be observed, "b" can be counted on to follow "a," since "nature is uniform"; that is, unobserved cases will resemble observed cases.

But a Humean would ask how we *know* that nature is uniform. If the answer is "by experience" the Humean will claim that this begs the question. Experienced cases are observed cases; the question remains how we can go from these observed (or past) cases to as yet unobserved (or future) cases.

To this it can be replied that probability theory is part of mathematics, and mathematics, like deductive logic, applies to all possible cases. When I am able to draw the conclusion that q is highly probable because $p > q$ is high and p is true, then of course q *may* be false: This is just to say that its probability is not 1. But q is not *likely* to be false; that is what is meant by saying that it has a high probability.

The Humean might reply that we *could* be totally mistaken, that probability theory might be a consistent conceptual structure that failed to apply to the world. But it can be shown that the only cases in which probability theory fails to apply to the world are if the world is *counterinductive*. The world could be counterinductive in two ways: First, we might live in a world of pure chance in which inductive arguments were always useless because $p \geq q$ always equalled $\bar{q}$. Second, we might live in a world in which something like Descartes' evil demon was manipulating events so as to frustrate our predictions. But there is no evidence at all that the universe is counterinductive and much evidence that it is not. If the universe were counterinductive in either of these ways, inductive reasoning would be useless, but it is not useless. Inductive reasoning has always worked and continues to work. (The universe could *become* counterinductive, but we have no reason to think that it will.)

When we carefully examine Humean skepticism about induction, we see that it is using a familiar skeptical ploy: making impossible or unreasonable demands and then complaining when they are not met. What would *satisfy* the Humean skeptic about induction? If inductive arguments were deductively valid? But they are, except that their conclusions are statements of probability. If the conclusions had probabilities of 1? But then inductive arguments would not be inductive, but deductive.

We can see that all of the true claims which the Humean skeptic makes are exactly what we would expect, given our account of induction. We are not certain of our conclusions? True, but that is just to say that inductive arguments do not give a probability of 1 to their conclusions. Induction could be useless? True, but only if the universe were counterinductive and we have no reason to suppose it is or will be, and much reason against those ideas.

In fact, we can see that Descartes' methodological doubt, which we discussed in the last chapter, was another kind of unreasonable skepticism. Descartes' definition of certainty as knowing beyond the possibility of doubt, and his methodological principle of rejecting all beliefs that are not certain in this sense, is bound to reject all beliefs that we hold on inductive evidence. But that is to assume, like Hume, that the only good evidence is deductive evidence. And that begs the question.

In fact, it is obvious that skeptics fail to meet their own standards. They certainly do not give us deductively valid arguments to show that induction is unjustified. If they claim that inductive conclusions *could* be mistaken, that is harmless, because that is in the nature of inductive argument. But if they try to show that inductive arguments are *probably* unjustified, then they are accepting probability arguments, and by the standards of probability arguments their case is negligible. So much for the skeptics.

Hume actually lays aside his skepticism and argues probabilistically in two interesting cases. One is the general problem of historical evidence and the other is the special problem of evidence for miraculous events. In the case of historical evidence, Hume argues:

> In every judgment which we can form concerning probability, as well as concerning knowledge, we ought always to correct the first judgment, derived from the nature of the object, by another judgment, derived from the nature of the understanding. It is certain a man of solid sense and long experience ought to have, and usually has, a greater assurance in his opinions than one that is foolish and ignorant, and that our sentiments have different degrees of authority, even with ourselves, in proportion to the degrees of our reason and experience. In the man of the best sense and longest experience, this authority is never entire, since even such-a-one must be conscious of many errors in the past, and must still dread the like for the future. Here then arises a new species of probability to correct and regulate the first, and fix its just standard and proportion. As demonstration is subject to the control of probability, so is probability liable to a new correction by a reflex act of the mind, wherein the nature of our understanding and our reasoning from the first probability become our objects.
>
> Having thus found in very probability, beside the original uncertainty inherent in the subject, a new uncertainty derived from the weakness of that faculty which judges, and having adjusted these two together, we are obliged by our reason to add a new doubt derived from the possibility of error in the estimation we make of the truth and fidelity of our faculties. This is a doubt which immediately occurs to us and of which, if we would closely pursue our reason, we cannot avoid giving a decision. But this decision, though it should be favorable to our preceding judgment, being founded only on probability, must weaken still further our first evidence, and must itself be weakened by

a fourth doubt of the same kind, and so on *in infinitum*, till at last there remain nothing of the original probability, however great we may suppose it to have been and however small the diminution by every new uncertainty. No finite object can subsist under a decrease repeated *in infinitum*, and even the vastest quantity which can enter into human imagination must in this manner be reduced to nothing. Let our first belief be ever so strong, it must infallibly perish by passing through so many new examinations, of which each diminishes somewhat of its force and vigor. When I reflect on the natural fallibility of my judgment, I have less confidence in my opinions than when I only consider the objects concerning which I reason; and when I proceed still further, to turn the scrutiny against every successive estimation I make of my faculties, all the rules of logic require a continual diminution, and at last a total extinction of belief and evidence.[3]

But something has gone wrong here. We can see what it is by considering a parallel case. Suppose you add up a column of figures and are not completely certain you have added them correctly. You add them again and get the same result, but again you are not *completely* certain that you have added them correctly. By Hume's reasoning every time you add the column and get the same answer you should get *less* certain. For ease in calculation, assume that each time you add the column you are 90 percent certain that you are right: If the column was added correctly

$$\overline{C} = 9/10$$

If I add twice, in Hume's view the probability is $9/10 \times 9/10 \times 81/100$, and by the time I have added the column seven times, *getting the same answer each time*, by Hume's reasoning my probability should be $4782969/10000000$, less than 1/2!

What has gone wrong is that Hume assumes that the probabilities are *independent* and that we can use the Simple Multiplication Rule. In fact, of course, the probabilities are *not* independent and we must use the regular Multiplication Rule. The probability that I was right the second time *if* I was right the first time is higher than the probability I was right the first time, and if this is so it can be shown that the probabilities "settle down" (technically "tend toward a limit") at quite a high probability. An easy calculation with a pocket calculator is to assume that the probability that you are right the second time given that you were right the first is $99/100$, the probability that you were right the third given that you were right the first and second is $999/1000$, and so on. It can be seen that the probability soon settles down around $89/100$ and hardly changes at all no matter how many multiplications you do. (There are many more mathematically sophisticated ways of showing that an increasing series like this tends to a

[3]Hume, *A Treatise of Human Nature* (London, 1740), Book I, Part IV, Paragraphs 5 and 6.

limit, but the "hands-on" experiment with a simple calculator is rather impressive to the average person.)

Naturally, in historical situations we do not have a simple case of independent or dependent probabilities. What we have is a complex mass of testimony, records, side-references, and cross-references that probably have to be assessed as a whole. Did Brutus and Cassius in fact stab Julius Caesar? If they did, this explains why so many historians and others say they did, mention in passing that they did, assume they did, etc. If they did not, what alternate hypothesis explains that mass of evidence?

Many philosophers think that the general pattern of reasoning from evidence to the probability of a hypothesis is given by the *Bayes Theorem* (B.T.):

$$\overline{p > q} = \frac{\overline{q} \times \overline{q > p}}{\overline{p}}$$

This is a simple consequence of the Multiplication Rule and the Conditional Probability Rule. Replacing "p" and "q" by "E" for evidence and "H" for hypothesis we get:

$$\overline{E > H} = \frac{\overline{H} \times \overline{H > E}}{\overline{E}}$$

Consider for example a case in which a number of independent witnesses have testified to a rather surprising and implausible event, say the sighting of a flying saucer. You are considering two hypotheses:

$$H^1 = \text{The witnesses are lying}$$

$$H^2 = \text{The witnesses are telling the truth}$$

The evidence you have to consider is the conviction, unanimity, and apparent reliability of the witnesses:

$$E \text{ \# Facts about the witnesses and about the circumstances}$$

Let us do a simple Bayes Theorem calculation. To begin with, assume that the witnesses are just as likely to be lying as telling the truth:

$$\overline{H^1} = 1/2$$

$$\overline{H^2} = 1/2$$

Even if the witnesses are telling the truth, they could still be mistaken, so let:

$$\overline{H^2 > E} = 9/10$$

Even if the witnesses are lying there *could* have been reasons for their unanimity, apparent conviction, and apparent reliability:

$$\overline{H^1 > E} = 1/100$$

In Bayes Theorem cases with two hypotheses we have a formula for E:

$$\overline{E} = [\overline{H^1} \times \overline{H^1 > E}] + [\overline{H^2} \times \overline{H^2 > E}]$$

We can now calculate the probabilities as follows:

$$\overline{E > H^1} = \frac{\overline{H^1} \times \overline{H^1 > E}}{\overline{E}}$$

$$\overline{E > H^2} = \frac{\overline{H^2} \times \overline{H^2 > E}}{\overline{E}}$$

$$\overline{H^1} \times \overline{H^1 > E} = 1/2 \times 1/100 = 1/200$$

$$\overline{H^2} \times \overline{H^2 > E} = 1/2 \times 9/10 = 9/20 = 90/200$$

$$\overline{E} = (\overline{H^1} \times \overline{H^1 > E}) + (\overline{H^2} \times \overline{H^2 > E}) = (1/2 \times 1/100) + (1/2 \times 9/10)$$

$$= 1/200 + 90/200 = 91/200$$

$$\overline{E > H^1} = \frac{1/2 \times 1/100}{91/200} = \frac{1/200}{91/200} = 1/91$$

$$\overline{E > H^2} = \frac{1/2 \times 9/10}{91/200} = \frac{90/200}{91/200} = 90/91$$

This is in some ways a surprising result. Because the testimony given was fairly likely if the witnesses were telling the truth and quite unlikely if they were lying and the other values were constant, the hypothesis that the witnesses were telling the truth receives a high value on the evidence. Given that the evidence is true we can use a P.M.P. argument:

$$\overline{E > H^2} = 90/91$$

$$\underline{E = 1}$$

$$90/91 \le H^2$$

Perhaps we have been too kind to the witnesses; let

$$\overline{H^1} = 9/10 \quad \text{and} \quad \overline{H^2} = 1/10$$

Then

$$\overline{E} = [\overline{H^1} \times \overline{H^1 > E}] + [\overline{H^2} \times \overline{H^2 > E}]$$

$$= [9/10 \times 1/100] + [1/10 \times 9/10]$$

$$= 9/1000 + 90/1000 = 99/1000$$

$$\overline{E > H^1} \times \frac{9/10 \times 1/100}{99/1000} \quad \frac{9/1000}{99/1000} = 9/99$$

$$\overline{E > H^2} = \frac{1/10 \times 9/10}{99/1000} \quad \frac{90/1000}{99/1000} = 90/99$$

So skewing the assumptions about the witnesses' truthfulness doesn't make all that much difference to the result, unless of course we say:

$$\overline{H^1} = 99/100$$

$$\overline{H^2} = 1/100$$

which gives us:

$$\overline{E} = (\overline{H^1} \times \overline{H^1 > E}) + (\overline{H^2} \times \overline{H^2 > E})$$

$$= [99/100 \times 1/100] + [1/100 \times 9/10]$$

$$= 99/10000 + 90/10000 = 189/10000$$

$$\overline{E > H^1} = \frac{99/100 \times 1/100}{189/10000} = \frac{99/10000}{189/10000} = 99/189$$

$$\overline{E > H^2} = \frac{1/100 \times 9/10}{189/10000} = \frac{90/10000}{189/10000} = 90/189$$

We at last have a lower probability for H^2 on E than for H^1 on E, but only by drastically unbalancing our assessment of the truthfulness of the witnesses.

In all of this, an important factor has been the *low* probability of $H^2 > E$ and the relatively high probability of $H^1 > E$. But that seems to be in the nature of the case: If the witnesses are lying it is hard to explain their unanimity, conviction, and apparent reliability (perhaps some are airline pilots in the sky, others law enforcement officers on the ground, etc.). On the other hand, if they are lying it seems hard to explain why independent witnesses of apparent reliability should convincingly tell the same story. Even if we change the probability of $H^1 > E$, we would have to raise it considerably to affect the figures that we have presented for illustration.

MIRACLES AND TESTIMONY

Hume's discussion of the reliability of testimony of miracles raises just these issues. His discussion consists of two parts, of which the first part seems to beg the question at issue:

> A miracle is a violation of the laws of nature: and as a firm and unalterable experience has established these laws, the proof against a miracle is as entire as any argument from experience can possibly be imagined. . . . Nothing is esteemed a miracle if it ever happens in the common course of nature . . . it is a miracle if a dead man comes to life because that has never been observed in any age or country. There must, therefore, be a uniform experience against every miraculous event, otherwise the event would not merit that appellation. And as a uniform experience amounts to a proof there is here a direct and full *proof* from the nature of the fact against the existence of any miracle.[4]

But this simply and obviously begs the question. If the question is "Do miracles occur?" we cannot assume at the outset that there is "a firm and *unalterable* experience" that laws of nature have never been violated. If you ask a traditional Christian if it has ever "been observed in any age or country" that a dead man has come to life, he or she would say Christ himself came back to life and also raised to life Lazarus, the widow's son, and the daughter of Jairus. (Christians might also mention several instances in the Old Testament and in the Acts of the Apostles.) They would certainly not grant that there was "uniform experience" against such events. Nor would Christians say that because there was not uniform experience against them that they were not miracles. Hume's implied definition of miracles amounts to *defining* miracles as "events which have never occurred," so obviously no defender of miracles would grant such a definition. A more neutral definition might be "an event which never occurs in the *ordinary* course of nature." (Hume himself seems to use this meaning in part of his argument.) The question then becomes: "Do events sometimes occur that do not occur in the *ordinary* course of nature?"

Hume's first argument is an exercise in assuming what needs to be proved, that is to say, in begging the question. And that seems to be the

[4]*Enquiry*, Section X, Part I, Paragraph 12.

plain sense of Hume's words. But some defenders of Hume interpret him in a somewhat different way. Imagine yourself, they say, as hearing a report of an event which there had been uniform experience against *up to that time*. Would you not feel that it was much more probable that the report was a lie or a mistake than that the event had occurred?

But if we think about this, it is an argument against *any* new and unique event. Up to a certain time there was "uniform experience" that human beings had never set foot on the moon. Does that mean that on hearing the reports of Neil Armstrong's moonwalk it would have been reasonable to reject them as lies or mistakes? Obviously an event should not be regarded as having *zero* probability if it has never occurred before: Otherwise we shut the door to new experience.

Suppose we say that an event that has never occurred before, or that we do not *know* has ever occurred before, has a *very low* probability? In that case we could do a Bayes Theorem calculation: What is the probability that a miracle has actually occurred, given some seemingly reliable testimony that it has? Let

$$H \text{ \# A miracle has occurred}$$

$$E \text{ \# Seemingly reliable testimony of a miracle}$$

We want to calculate:

$$\overline{E > H} = \frac{\overline{H} \times \overline{H > E}}{\overline{E}}$$

and contrast it with:

$$\overline{E > \hat{H}} = \frac{\hat{H} \times \overline{\hat{H} > E}}{\overline{E}}$$

In this case the theory of probability tells us that:

$$\overline{E} = (\overline{H} \times \overline{H > E}) + (\hat{H} \times \overline{\hat{H} > E})$$

Let us grant for the sake of argument that $\overline{H}$ is low; for simplicity in calculation let it be 1/100. That will mean that $\hat{H}$ is 99/100. We must now assign figures for $\overline{H > E}$ and $\hat{H} > E$. If a miracle has occurred, we would expect testimony that it has occurred, so let $\overline{H > E}$ be 1. What is the chance that we will get seemingly reliable testimony that a miracle has occurred if a miracle has *not* in fact occurred? This is the crucial figure: Let us first assume that it is quite low, say 1/100. On that assumption:

$$\overline{E > H} = \frac{\overline{H} \times \overline{H > E}}{(\overline{H} \times \overline{H > E}) + (\hat{H} \times \overline{\hat{H} > E})} = \frac{1/100 \times 1}{(1/100 + 1) + (99/100 \times 1/100)}$$

$$= \frac{1/100}{1/100 + 99/10000} = \frac{100/10000}{100/10000 + 99/10000}$$

$$= \frac{100/10000}{199/10000} = 100/199$$

$$\overline{E > \hat{H}} = \frac{99/100 + 1/100}{199/10000} = \frac{99/10000}{199/10000} = 99/199$$

making H slightly more probable than $\hat{H}$ on the evidence. But if it is fairly probable that if H is true then E is true, say $H > E = 1/10$, then the figures change:

$$\overline{E > H} = \frac{1/100 \times 1}{(1/100 \times 1) = (1/10 \times 99/100)} = \frac{1/100}{(1/100) + (99/1000)}$$

$$= \frac{10/1000}{10/1000 + 99/1000} = \frac{10/1000}{109/1000} = 10/109$$

$$\overline{E > \hat{H}} = \frac{99/100 \times 1/10}{109/1000} = 99/109$$

making H much more probable on E than $\hat{H}$ is. So a very important question is whether it is quite unlikely or fairly likely that we would get (false or mistaken) testimony of a miracle if no miracle had occurred.

Hume seems partly to recognize this when he says:

> No testimony is sufficient to establish a miracle, unless the testimony be of such a kind that its falsehood would be more miraculous than the fact it endeavors to establish. . . . When anyone tells me that he saw a dead man returned to life I immediately consider with myself whether it be more probable that this person should either deceive or be deceived . . . if the falsehood of his testimony would be more miraculous than the event which he relates; then and not till then can he pretend to command my belief or opinion.[5]

Hume seems quite sure that it will never be the case that it is more improbable that the testimony to a miracle will be false than that a miracle has occurred. We will examine his arguments for this shortly. It is not clear

---

[5]*Enquiry*, Section 10, Part I, Paragraph 13.

that Hume realizes that what he is discussing is a conditional probability, $\overline{H} > E$; he sometimes talks as if the probability in question were a simple probability, perhaps $\overline{E}$. But if we interpret Hume as saying $\overline{E} > H$ will not be high unless $\overline{H} > E$ is smaller than $\overline{H}$, then what he says is correct.

However, it is important to realize that we must compare the probability that a *particular* miracle, say the resurrection of Christ, has occurred with the probability that a *particular* set of testimony, say that of the four Evangelists, would be given if *that* miracle had not occurred. What Hume does is to discuss the fact that we have good reason to doubt many reports of miracles. But equally we have good reason to doubt many reports of, for example, atrocities in war. The fact that sometimes atrocity stories are invented or exaggerated for propaganda purposes does not mean that *no* atrocity reports are well supported and reliable. Similarly, from "Some reports of miracles are false" we cannot conclude "No reports of miracles are true."

However, Hume does propose some criteria for judging testimony. He says:

> There is not to be found in all history any miracle attested by a sufficient number of men, of such unquestioned good-sense, education and learning as to secure us against all delusion in themselves: of such undoubted integrity as to place them beyond all suspicion of any design to deceive others; of such credit and reputation in the eyes of mankind as to have a great deal to lose in case of their being detected in any falsehood; and at the same time attesting facts performed in such a public manner and in so celebrated a part of the world as to render the detection unavoidable: All of which circumstances are required to give us a full assurance in the testimony of men.[6]

Now these criteria are so stringent that it is dubious whether most reports of historical events could meet them. But if we take them as criteria for a probability of *zero* for $\hat{H} > E$, then the closer these criteria come to being met the lower the probability of $\hat{H} > E$ will be. And it is not at all clear that a sufficient number of these criteria are not met to a sufficient extent in some reports of miracles to give $\hat{H} > E$ a very low probability.

For example, in his discussion of Christ's resurrection, St. Paul mentions appearances to a number of members of the Christian community, including an appearance to 400 disciples of whom he says "many are still alive." Paul himself was a highly educated man with a good deal to lose by shifting from being a persecutor of the Christians to one of their leaders. Defenders of Christianity point out that those giving testimony to Christ's resurrection endangered their lives, not just their reputations, and that many did in fact die as witnesses to the truth of their testimony. Unless such terms as "education," "learning," "integrity," "public," and "celebrated part of the world" are to be interpreted in senses that are completely

[6]*Enquiry*, Section X, Part II, Paragraph 2.

question-begging, it is at least arguable that Hume's criteria can be met in the case of some miracles.

To sum up: If we assume at the outset that there is "uniform experience" that the laws of nature are never suspended, we beg the question. If we calculate the probability that a specific miracle has actually occurred given specific testimony, Hume is correct in his general point that the improbability of the testimony being given if the miracle did *not* occur must be greater than the improbability of the miracle. (Though Hume may be confused on details, it is $\overline{H > E}$ we compare with $\overline{H}$, not $\overline{E}$.)

Hume supplies criteria for giving a low probability to $H > E$, criteria that may be overly stringent. However, if these criteria are interpreted in a non-question-begging way it is at least arguable that they are met in the case of certain accounts of miracles. Whether they are or not is a matter for detailed historical investigation.

EXERCISES

A: For one of the following hypotheses,

(i) Assign a probability to the hypothesis (H).

(ii) Briefly state what evidence is relevant to the hypothesis (E).

(iii) Estimate how probable the evidence would be if the hypothesis were true $(H > E)$ and it were false $(\hat{H} > E)$.

(iv) Use probability theory to calculate $\hat{H}$, $\overline{E}$, and by using the Bayes Theorem $E > H$.

For your *estimate* use the scale:

.0 Certainly false
.1 Very improbable
.2
.3
.4
.5 About equally likely to be true or false
.6
.7
.8
.9 Highly probable
1.0 Certainly true

H1 God exists

H2 God sometimes works miracles

H3 Miracles sometimes occur

H4 Christ worked miracles

H5 Christ was God

H6 False accounts of miracles are frequently given

H7 False accounts of miracles are easily believed by many people

H8 David Hume believed miracles occur

H9 Pope John Paul II believes miracles occur

H10 The author of the book believes miracles occur

H11 Conspirators exist

H12 Conspirators sometimes bring about conspiracies

H13 Conspiracies exist

H14 The President was involved in a conspiracy

H15 The President was a conspirator

H16 False accounts of conspiracies are frequently given

H17 False accounts of conspiracies are easily believed by many people

H18 Our planet has been visited by alien space vehicles

H19 Alien space vehicles exist

H20 Air Force investigators believe that our planet has been visited by alien space vehicles

B.   For one of the hypotheses above, H1–H20,
   (i)   Give an argument for attaching a particular probability to that hypothesis.
   (ii) State the most plausible alternative hypothesis.
   (iii) Give an argument that the probability of the alternative hypothesis is (a) lower than, or (b) higher than the probability of the original hypothesis.
   (iv) State which other hypotheses in Exercise A are (a) inconsistent with, (b) imply, (c) are implied by the hypothesis you are discussing.
C.   For one hypothesis in Exercise A and some body of evidence relevant to that hypothesis,
   (i)   Give reasons for assigning a given probability to that evidence if that hypothesis were true.
   (ii) State the most plausible alternative hypothesis and give reasons for assigning a given probability to the evidence on the alternative hypothesis.
   (iii) Discuss whether the hypotheses are mutually exclusive.
   (iv) Discuss whether the two hypotheses are exhaustive (cover all possibilities).
D.   In the following statements about probability drawn from Hume's works,
   (1)   Compare what Hume is saying with the discussion of probability in this chapter.
   (ii) Argue in support of any point made by Hume that you agree with.
   (iii) Give arguments criticizing any point made by Hume that you disagree with.
   (iv) Discuss any apparent inconsistencies in Hume's view; for example, do all the quotations seem to improve a consistent view of probability?

1. Chance is nothing real in itself, and, properly speaking, is merely the negation of a cause. Its influence on the mind is contrary to that of causation; and it is essential to it, to leave the imagination perfectly indifferent, either to consider the existence or non-existence of that object, which is regarded as contingent. A cause traces the way to our thought, and in a manner forces us to survey such certain objects, in such certain relations. Chance can only destroy this determination of the thought, and leave the mind in its native situation of indifference; in which, upon the absence of a cause, it is instantly reinstated.

2. Since an entire indifference is essential to chance, no one chance can possibly be superior to another, otherwise than as it is composed of a superior number of equal chances. For if we affirm that one chance can, after any other manner, be superior to another, we must at the same time affirm, that there is something, which gives it the superiority, and determines the event rather to that side than the other: That is, in other words, we must allow of a cause, and destroy the supposition of chance; which we had before established. A perfect and total indifference can never in itself be either superior or inferior to another.

3. Where nothing limits the chances, every notion, that the most extravagant fancy can form, is upon a footing of equality; nor can there be any circumstance to give one the advantage above another. Thus unless we allow that there are some causes to make the dice fall, and preserve their form in their fall, and lie upon some one of their sides, we can form no calculation concerning the laws of hazard. But supposing these causes to operate, and supposing likewise all the rest to be indifferent and to be determined by chance, it is easy to arrive at a notion of a superior combination of chances. A die, that has four sides marked with a certain number of spots, and only two with another, affords us an obvious and easy instance of this superiority. The mind is here limited by the causes to such a precise number and quality of the events; and at the same time is undetermined in its choice of any particular event.

4. It is indeed evident, that we can never by the comparison of mere ideas make any discovery, which can be of consequence in this affair, and that it is impossible to prove with certainty, that any event must fall on that side where there is a superior number of chances. To suppose in this case any certainty, were to overthrow what we have established concerning the opposition of chances, and their perfect equality and indifference.

   It should be said, that though in an opposition of chances it is impossible to determine with *certainty*, on which side the event will fall, yet we can pronounce with certainty, that it is more likely and probable, it will be on that side where there is a superior number of chances, than where there is an inferior.

5. The likelihood and probability of chances is a superior number of equal chances; and consequently when we say it is likely the event will fall on the side, which is superior, rather than on the inferior, we do no more than affirm, that where there is a superior number of chances there is actually a superior, and where there is an inferior there is an inferior; which are identical propositions, and of no consequence.

6. We shall suppose a person to take a die, formed after such a manner as that four of its sides are marked with one figure, or one number of spots, and two

with another; and to put this die into the box with an intention of throwing it: This is plain, he must conclude the one figure to be more probable than the other, and give the preference to that which is inscribed on the greatest number of sides. He in a manner believes, that this will lie uppermost; though still with hesitation and doubt, in proportion to the number of chances, which are contrary: And according as these contrary chances diminish, and the superiority increases on the other side, his belief acquires new degrees of stability and assurance.

7.   This die formed as above, contains three circumstances worthy of our attention. *First*, certain causes, such as gravity, solidity, a cubical figure, etc., which determine it to fall, to preserve its form in its fall, and to turn up one of its sides. *Secondly*, a certain number of sides, which are supposed indifferent. *Thirdly*, a certain figure, inscribed on each side. These three particulars form the whole nature of the die, so far as relates to our present purpose; and consequently are the only circumstances regarded by the mind in its forming a judgment concerning the result of such a throw.

8.   There is no point of ancient history, of which we can have any assurance, but by passing through many millions of causes and effects, and through a chain of arguments of almost an immeasurable length. Before the knowledge of the fact could come to the first historian, it must be conveyed through many mouths; and after it is committed to writing, each new copy is a new object, of which the connection with the foregoing is known only by experience and observation. Perhaps, therefore, it may be concluded from the preceding reasoning, that the evidence of all ancient history must now be lost; or at least, will be lost in time, as the chain of causes increases, and runs on to a greater length. But as it seems contrary to common sense to think, that if the republic of letters, and the art of printing continue on the same footing as at present, our posterity, even after a thousand ages, can ever doubt if there has been such a man as Julius Caesar; this may be considered as an objection to the present system.

9.   And indeed it must be confessed, that in this manner of considering the subject, (which however is not a true one) there is no history or tradition, but what must in the end lose all its force and evidence. Every new probability diminishes the original conviction; and however great that conviction may be supposed, it is impossible it can subsist under such reiterated diminutions. This is true in general; though we shall find afterwards, that there is one very memorable exception, which is of vast consequence in the present subject of the understanding.

10.   If all the long chain of causes and effects, which connects any past event with any volume of history, were composed of parts different from each other, and which it were necessary for the mind distinctly to conceive, it is impossible we should preserve to the end any belief or evidence. But as most of these proofs are perfectly alike, the mind runs easily along them, jumps from one part to another with facility, and forms but a confused and general notion of each link. By this means a long chain of argument, has as little effect in diminishing the original vivacity, as a much shorter would have, if composed of parts, which were different from each other, and of which each required a distinct consideration.

— 7 —

Analogy,
Induction,
and Theistic Arguments

One of Hume's most influential works has been his *Dialogues on Natural Religion*. In this book Hume pits representatives of three different points of view against each other in a complex dialogue where two of the participants are often arguing against the third. This makes an interesting change from the dialogues of Plato where in most cases only two points of view are being considered at any one time. Hume's three protagonists are *Demea*, a supporter of deductive metaphysical arguments for the existence of God; *Cleanthes*, who supports an inductive "design" argument; and *Philo*, a philosophical skeptic who often seems to hide a basically skeptical attitude toward religion behind a facade of piety, claiming that it is impious to attempt to prove God's existence.

Most interpreters of Hume agree that Philo's piety *is* only a facade and that he is not genuinely a representative of the point of view discussed in Chapter 3, which rejects argument in religious matters for genuinely religious reasons. There is some disagreement, however, as to Hume's real attitude toward Cleanthes and his views. The most popular interpretation has been that Hume is completely on the side of Philo and uses the other two protagonists simply as foils for Philo's arguments. However, some interpreters have seen Hume as partly on Cleanthes' side, so that sometimes Philo represents Hume's view and sometimes Cleanthes does.

Be that as it may, Hume's *Dialogues* provides us a good opportunity to take another look at some of the arguments for God's existence discussed in Chapter 3. Hume considers Cleanthes' version of the Design Argument first, then Demea's version of one of the Cosmological Arguments. We will reverse the order and consider Demea first. Demea states his argument as follows:

> The argument, replied Demea, which I would insist on is the common one. Whatever exists must have a cause or reason of its existence, it being absolutely impossible for anything to produce itself or be the cause of its own existence. In mounting up, therefore, from effects to causes, we must either go on in tracing an infinite succession, without any ultimate cause at all, or must at last have recourse to some ultimate cause that is *necessarily* existent. Now, that the first supposition is absurd may be thus proved. In the infinite chain or succession of causes and effects, each single effect is determined to exist by the power and efficacy of that cause which immediately preceded; but the whole eternal chain or succession, taken together, is not determined or caused by anything; and yet it is evident that it requires a cause or reason, as much as any particular object which begins to exist in time. The question is still reasonable why this particular succession of causes existed from eternity, and not any other succession or no succession at all. If there be no necessarily existent being, any supposition which can be formed is equally possible; nor is there any more absurdity in nothing's having existed from eternity than there is in that succession of causes which constitutes the universe. What was it, then, which determined something to exist rather than nothing, and bestowed being on a particular possibility, exclusive of the rest? *External causes*, there are supposed to be none. *Chance* is a word without a meaning. Was it *nothing?* But that can never produce anything. We must, therefore, have resource to a necessarily existent Being who carries the *reason* of his existence in himself; and who cannot be supposed not to exist, without an express contradiction. There is, consequently, such a Being—that is, there is a Deity.[1]

Note several interesting things about this argument. First and most obviously, Demea seems to think that the kind of necessity which characterizes God is *logical* necessity: that God "cannot be supposed not to exist without an express (i.e., an explicit) *contradiction*." Now as we said earlier, the medieval idea of the kind of necessity that characterizes God had two elements, (1) always existing and (2) existing whether or not anything else exists. Demea's argument is thus very unlike the medieval arguments in that he substitutes logical necessity for the "causal independence" of the medievals.

Hume is able to argue convincingly that no statement of existence is characterized by *logical* necessity. Hume's test is the test of *conceivability:* We cannot conceive two plus two not making four, but we *can* conceive the nonexistence of anything that can be conceived to exist. Hume thus refutes the argument of his puppet Demea, but Hume seems to be arguing against

---

[1]David Hume, *Dialogues on Natural Religion* (London, 1979), Part IX, Paragraph 3.

a man of straw: He has given Demea the untenable position that God's nonexistence is *inconceivable*, then overturned this position by showing that we can conceive God's nonexistence. But Aquinas, for example, would have agreed entirely: He rejects the idea that God's existence is "self-evident," which is another way of saying that God's nonexistence is inconceivable.

Philo's second criticism of Demea is to ask why the material universe cannot be necessary being, and thus not in need of being caused by God. As so often, Hume seems inconsistent: If the idea of a necessary being is absurd, why entertain the idea with regard to the universe? But Hume is arguing dialectically against various positions that might be held by his opponents. "First, I deny that necessary existence is meaningful, *but* even if it were, why can't the universe be the necessary being. . . ."

To his credit, Hume considers an objection to the idea of the universe being necessary. Every part of the universe seems to be contingent: How can we get a necessary whole by adding contingent parts? But here he returns to the idea of necessity as the *in*conceivability of nonexistence, and therefore of contingency as the *conceivability* of nonexistence. If the universe is necessary, Hume says, it must be because some unknown factor makes it really inconceivable that it not exist, just as some mathematical operation such as "squaring the circle" may be really impossible for reasons we do not at first see. But such an "unknown factor," being unknown, may be as plausibly attributed to the universe as to God.

On the medieval view of necessary existence as eternal, causally independent existence, the argument becomes "Every part of the universe is causally dependent and exists for a limited time. How then can a whole made up of such parts be eternal and causally independent?" One possible answer is that the universe consists of an infinite regress of caused beings, each of which exists for a finite time. But the infinite sequence is eternal and since each part of it has a cause, the *whole* does not need a cause.

This is in fact Hume's next move: In response to Demea's denial of infinite regress he says, "In such a chain too, or succession of objects each part is caused by that which preceded it and causes that which succeeds it. Where then is the difficulty? But the *whole*, you say wants (i.e., needs) a cause. . . . (if) I show you the particular causes of twenty particles of matter, I should think it very unreasonable should you afterwards ask me what was the cause of the whole twenty. This is sufficiently explained in showing the cause of the parts."

But of course Hume has worked a bit of sleight of hand here. In explaining the existence of 20 particles of matter, at least one explanation must refer to something outside the 20. Even if number 19 caused number 20, number 18 caused number 19 and so on, what caused number 1? One of the others? But that would make causation go in a circle, which seems absurd. Yet if we deny circular causality, at least one cause of any finite collection of things must lie outside that collection. Do we really change the situation by making it an *infinite* collection? On this point philosophers are still arguing.

But to return to Demea's argument; a feature of it which is seldom noticed is that despite Hume's intention to make Demea a representative of purely *a priori* arguments, there is a curiously inductive undercurrent to Demea's arguments. "The question is still reasonable why this particular succession of causes existed from eternity and not any other succession or no succession at all. If there be no necessarily existent being, any supposition which can be formed is *equally possible* [my emphasis], nor is there any more absurdity in nothing's having existed from eternity than there is in that succession of causes which constitutes the universe. What was it then, which determined something to exist rather than nothing, and bestowed being on a particular possibility, exclusive of the rest? *External causes*, there are supposed to be none. *Chance* is a word without a meaning. Was it *nothing*? But that can never produce anything. We must therefore have recourse to a necessarily existent Being who carries the *reason* of his existence in himself."

Now it looks as if this argument might be reconstructed as follows:

If no necessarily existing being, every possible sequence, including no sequence at all, is equally likely.

If a necessarily existing being, then the actual sequence is more probable than any other.

Therefore there must be a necessary being.

INDUCTIVE ARGUMENTS

This is plainly not a deductive argument. Can it be reconstructed as an inductive argument? And if so, how? Consider a case that may be parallel. While waiting in an airport for a delayed flight, a smooth-talking stranger talks you into a game of tossing coins: You win if heads comes up, he wins if tails comes up. He throws five tails in a row, winning five dollars from you. You then reason as follows:

If he is not cheating, any sequence of heads and tails is equally likely.

If he is cheating, the actual sequence is more probable than any other.

Therefore he is probably cheating.

We can reconstruct this as a Bayesian argument as follows:

C # The stranger is cheating

O # Observed sequence, five tails

If he is not cheating and the coin is fair, the probability of five tails in a row is 1/32, so:

$$\overline{\hat{C} > 0} = 1/32$$

If he is cheating, the observed sequence is just what you would expect:

$$\overline{C > 0} = 1$$

How likely is it in general that he is cheating? We could arbitrarily set this at 1/2, so:

$$\overline{C} = 1/2$$
$$\overline{\hat{C}} = 1/2$$

We could then do a Bayesian calculation:

$$\overline{0 > C} = \frac{\overline{C} \times \overline{C > 0}}{\overline{0}}$$

$$\overline{0 > \hat{C}} = \frac{\overline{\hat{C}} \times \overline{\hat{C} > 0}}{\overline{0}}$$

We know that

$$\overline{0} = (\overline{C} \times \overline{C > 0}) + (\overline{\hat{C}} \times \overline{\hat{C} > 0})$$

so

$$\overline{0 > C} = \frac{1/2 \times 1}{(1/2 \times 1) + (1/2 \times 1/32)} = \frac{1/2}{33/64} = \frac{32}{33}$$

$$\overline{0 > \hat{C}} = \frac{1/2 \times 1/32}{(1/2 \times 1) + (1/2 \times 1/32)} = \frac{1/64}{33/64} = \frac{1}{33}$$

So we have very good reason indeed to accept the hypothesis that the stranger is cheating since the probability is 32/33 = .969. But this high probability was gotten partly by assuming that it was equally likely that the stranger was cheating and that he was not. Perhaps this is unfair. Is there in fact any reasonable way of deciding what $\overline{C}$ is?

Suppose that there is not, and that we cannot do a complete Bayesian calculation? A contemporary philosopher, Robert Nozick,[2] has suggested a schema for probabilistic arguments in such cases:

$$\text{If} \quad \overline{H > E} \geq .95$$

$$\widehat{H} > E \leq .05$$

$$E$$

$$\overline{\widehat{H} > E} < \overline{H}$$

$$\text{Infer} \quad H$$

Since $1 > .95$ and $1/32 = .03123$, which is less than $.05$, and we have observed the five tails, Nozick's first three conditions are satisfied. Now all we need to decide is whether $\overline{C}$ is greater than $\widehat{C} > 0$. Since $\widehat{C} > 0$ is quite low, we do not need to be abnormally suspicious to conclude that we should accept the hypothesis that the stranger is cheating.

DEMEA'S ARGUMENT

Now let us reconstruct Demea's argument as a Nozick-style argument, for we have no realistic figures for the prior probabilities involved.

Let N # A necessary being has created the Universe.

O # Observed sequence of events in the Universe.

Then we might think of Demea as arguing:

$$\overline{N > 0} \geq .95$$

$$\widehat{N} > 0 \leq .05$$

$$0$$

$$\overline{\widehat{N} > 0} < \overline{N}$$

$$\text{Therefore accept N}$$

Now of these premises 0 is obviously true: It is just that the observed sequence of events is what it is. $\widehat{N} > 0 \leq .05$ seems highly plausible granted Demea's point that if there is no necessary being, all of a vast, perhaps infinite, range of possibilities are *equally* likely. The hypothesis of a necessary

[2]Robert Nozick, *Philosophical Explanations*, Cambridge, MA: Harvard University Press, 1981, p. 254–55.

being is arguably at least a serious possibility, so $\overline{\hat{N} > 0} < \overline{N}$ would seem to be plausible, since $\hat{N} > 0$ will be extremely low. Thus a great deal of the controversy will center on whether it is true that

$$\overline{N > 0} \geq .95$$

Why should the observed order of the universe be highly likely, given that there is a necessary being? Naturally, if there is a necessary being it will be certain that there is something rather than nothing, but why should the actual observed order be more probable than any alternative?

I think Demea has no answer for this, but perhaps Cleanthes does. In fact, Hume has put his criticisms of Demea into the mouth of Cleanthes rather than Philo, and has made the defender of the Design Argument the critic of the Cosmological Arguments. This "divide and conquer" strategy may be the key to Hume's apparent success. Arguably, what we need to do is to *combine* the Design and Cosmological arguments; something rather than nothing is certain given a necessary being (in the medieval sense, an eternal and causally independent being). An orderly and understandable universe is highly probable given a necessary being, which is also an intelligent designer. So the argument can be reformulated with the evidence to be explained being restated as "an observed sequence of events which is orderly and understandable."

Let U # The observed sequence of events exists, and is orderly and understandable.

Then if G # God, a necessary being who is the creator and intelligent designer of the universe, exists

Then the argument is

$$\overline{G > U} \geq .95$$
$$\overline{\hat{G} > U} \leq .05$$
$$U$$
$$\overline{\hat{G} > U} < \overline{G}$$

Therefore accept G

So a theist will argue that all of the premises should be accepted and therefore so should the conclusion.

What could Hume reply? He can hardly deny the basic principles of probability theory involved; these *are* logically true. In fact, the condition that

$$\overline{\hat{H} > E} < \overline{H}$$

is precisely the one he has invoked in his discussion of miracles. For this reason we can call it *Hume's Constraint*. It looks as if Hume can hardly deny that

$$\overline{\hat{G} > U} \leq .05$$

unless he gives us some reason to suppose that this is not as low as it appears, and Hume does not seem to do this. He also seems to give no arguments to show that a God who is both creator and designer would not be a very good explanation of (that is, give a high probability to) such features of the universe as existence, order, and understandability.

Thus, Hume's only strategy would seem to be to lower the probability $\overline{G}$ or raise the probability $\hat{G} > U$, so that Hume's Constraint is violated, and the argument does not go through. In fact, given his discussion of miracles, this is precisely what we would expect him to do.

Hume can hardly deny that a necessary Creator or Designer gives a probability of one to the existence of something rather than nothing. What he can try to show is the probability of order and understandability is higher than we have said on a nontheistic hypothesis (and lower on a theistic hypothesis perhaps, though this is not essential to his aim).

Philo's criticism of Cleanthes' version of the Design Argument can be understood in just this way. Philo says, in effect, "Perhaps a God of the traditional kind would explain the apparent order and understandability of the universe. But there are other hypotheses which would explain it *equally as well*, and which are as probable *a priori* as traditional theism. Thus, $\hat{G} > 0$ is *not* less than $\overline{G}$ and we cannot conclude to G, even if $\overline{G > U} \geq$ .95 and U is true."

ANALOGY ARGUMENTS

However, before we attack this argument directly we must take a brief look at the idea of "argument from analogy," since Hume regards arguments about the orderliness and understandability of the universe as analogy arguments, and has Cleanthes state his argument as an analogy argument. Cleanthes states the Design Argument as follows:

Not to lose any time in circumlocutions, said Cleanthes, addressing himself to Demea, much less in replying to the pious declamations of Philo, I shall briefly explain how I conceive this matter. Look round the world: Contemplate the whole and every part of it: You will find it to be nothing but one great machine, subdivided into an infinite number of lesser machines, which again admit of subdivisions to a degree beyond what human senses and faculties can trace and explain. All these various machines, and even their most minute parts, are adjusted to each other with an accuracy which ravishes into admiration all men who have ever contemplated them. The curious adapting of means to ends, throughout all nature, resembles exactly, though it much exceeds, the productions of human contrivance—of human design, thought, wisdom, and intelligence. Since therefore, the effects resemble each other, we are led to infer, by all the rules of analogy, that the causes also resemble, and that the Author of Nature is somewhat similar to the mind of man, though possessed of much larger faculties, proportioned to the grandeur of the work which he has executed. By this argument *a posteriori*, and by this argument alone, do we prove at once the existence of a Deity and his similarity to human mind and intelligence.[3]

Now according to many logic texts, the form of an analogy argument is as follows:

Case A has characteristics m,n,o . . . and also characteristic x.

Case B has characteristics m,n,o . . .

Case B probably has characteristic x.

Stated in this way, Cleanthes' argument is:

A machine has parts accurately adjusted to each other, a curious adaptation of means to ends, and is a product of design.

The universe has parts accurately adjusted to each other, a curious adaptation of means to ends.

The universe is probably a product of design.

Call this the *Simple Argument from Analogy*. The first thing that strikes us about it is that it is much weaker than it might be. Cleanthes could easily have given another argument, which we will call the *Sophisticated Argument from Analogy*:

Machines have an adaptation of means to ends, behave in a predictable way, and so are understandable and orderly and this is because they are products of intelligent design.

[3] *Dialogues on Natural Religion*, Part II, Paragraph 5.

The universe has an adaptation of means to ends, behaves in a predictable way, and so is orderly and understandable.

Therefore, the universe probably has these features because it is the product of intelligent design.

In general, how do we move from the premises of an argument from analogy to the conclusion? We could regard it as a *deductive* argument:

> Everything which has m,n,o . . . has x.
>
> Case B has m,n,o . . .
>
> Therefore, Case B has x.

This would be a simple Barburu syllogism and be valid, but the major premise seems much too strong. Another way to regard analogy arguments is as Bayesian arguments. We want to know how likely x is, given m,n,o, and if we let

$$X \text{ # Observed case has x}$$

$$M \text{ # Observed case has m,n,o} \ldots$$

Assume that

$$\overline{X} = .5$$

$$\overline{X > M} = .95$$

$$\overline{\hat{X} > M} = .05$$

then

$$\overline{M} = (\overline{X} \times \overline{X > M}) + (\overline{\hat{X}} \times \overline{\hat{X} > M})$$

$$\text{and} \quad \overline{M > X} = \frac{\overline{X} \times \overline{X > M}}{\overline{M}} = \frac{.5 \times .95}{.475 + .025} = \frac{.475}{.5} = .95$$

But of course our value for $\overline{X}$ was arbitrary and we may have no way of giving $\overline{X}$ a reasonable value. The values of .95 for $\overline{X > M}$ and .05 for $\hat{X} > M$ reflect the idea that m,n,o . . . are highly correlated with x: Where we observe x we should expect to find m,n,o . . . and where we do not find x, we should not expect m,n,o . . . . If this is the case, we can ignore the prior probability of X and give a Nozick-type argument:

$$\overline{X > M} \geq .95$$

$$\overline{\hat{X} > M} \leq .05$$

$$M$$

$$\overline{\hat{X} > M < \overline{X}}$$

Accept X

This amounts to saying that, since the presence of x leads us to expect m,n,o and the absence of x leads us to expect m,n,o . . . to be absent, then given that $\overline{X}$ is greater than $\hat{X}> M$, we should infer X from the presence of m,n,o . . . . This seems a reasonable way to look at analogy arguments. Consider the example:

W # My car won't start, my lights won't go on, and my radio won't play.

B # My battery is dead.

$$\overline{B > W} \geq .95$$

$$\overline{\hat{B}> W} \leq .05$$

$$W$$

$$\overline{\hat{B}> W < \overline{B}}$$

Therefore, accept B

The argument seems very plausible, even though I may start by thinking of some case *in the past* where W was true and was explained by B. Arguably, the role of the past case is to suggest to my mind the general principles:

$$\overline{B > W} \geq .95$$

$$\overline{\hat{B} > W} \leq .05$$

If these principles are not true, the past case shows nothing about the present case. If they are true, they apply equally to the past case and the present case. In the past case I might have checked and found B was true, increasing my confidence that B explains W. If I had checked and found not B instead of B, it would have *decreased* my confidence in B > W and *increased* my confidence in $\hat{B} > W$.

As a general point about analogy arguments, Hume suggests that they hold good only where we can get this kind of "double check" on $\overline{H > E} \geq$ .95 and $\hat{H} > E \geq$ .05 by seeing that when E was true then H was true in a number of previous cases. But this seems both too weak and too strong. Even if H has been observed to be true in a number of cases where E was true, this does not show that H explains E or makes it probable. And we can know on general principles that H makes E probable without ever having observed H and E together. I am quite sure that if I cut someone's head into four equal pieces, the person would die, even though I have never *observed* these two things together. I am sure that if I dropped a cat from a second story window, the cat would *probably* be hurt, even though I have never done this or seen it done.

Philo's general strategy in trying to refute Cleanthes' rather weak Simple Argument from Analogy is to cite a number of hypotheses where if the hypothesis were true the observed evidence would be probable. His strategy might be regarded in this way: "Here are a number of analogy arguments which are *just as good as* the machine analogy. Since they all lead to the conclusion "accept H" and we cannot accept all of the H's (since they are incompatible), *therefore* we should accept none of the conclusions, including the conclusion of the machine analogy."

This seems reasonable, but *are* all the arguments *just as good* as the machine analogy? And if they are, is this true if we replace the Simple Argument with the Sophisticated Argument? Consider one of Hume's "Parallel Arguments":

A living organism has parts accurately adjusted to each other, a curious adaptation of means to ends, and is not the product of design.

The universe has parts accurately adjusted to each other, a curious adaptation of means to ends.

Therefore, probably the universe is not the product of design.

But even in this simple form we can see the argument begs the question. Living organisms are part of the universe: If the universe is the product of design, then so are living organisms. How can we pretend to be investigating whether the universe as a whole is the product of design while assuming as true that *parts* of the universe are not products of design? If living organisms are *known* not to be the product of design, this implies the universe isn't either, since if it is, they are. So this argument begs the question at issue.

If we try to generalize the case of living organisms to get a general principle, what will this general principle be? Probably something on the order of "The probability of adaptation of means to ends given no design is high" or at least "The probability of adaptation of means to ends given no design is higher than the probability of design." But the proponent of the design argument will hardly grant either generalization, especially since the case cited begs the question.

How can we avoid begging the question here? The proponent of the Design Argument will claim that any "naturally occurring" example of adaptation of means to ends is a *part* of the adaptation of means to ends in the universe as a whole, and to say that it is *not* the product of design is to beg the question. On the other hand, humans do originate orderly adaptations of means to ends, which are not part of "naturally occurring" adaptation of means to ends. The challenge to the opponent of the Design Argument is to give an example of an "order originating" mechanism that is *neither* part of the "natural order" *nor* the product of *human* design.

The opponent of the Design Argument will reject this formulation of the problem. The "natural" adaptation of means to ends should be taken as what has to be explained by *either* theory: It cannot be taken as favoring one hypothesis at the outset. The proponent of the Design Argument favors the analogy of "natural" order with (human) design-originated order. All that the opponent of the argument has to do is to give *another* hypothesis A, which is inconsistent with the hypothesis D of design, and such that the relation of this hypothesis to "natural" adaptation of means to ends, N is such that

$$\overline{A > N} \geq .95$$

$$\overline{A > N} \geq \overline{\hat{D} > N}$$

Let us suppose that chance, C, design, D, and our alternate hypothesis A are the three competing explanations for N, the "natural" adaptation of means to ends, and are incompatible. Then

$$\overline{D} + \overline{C} + \overline{A} = 1$$

(since $\overline{D \vee C \vee A} = 1$ and they are mutually exclusive). Grant for the sake of argument that

$$\overline{D > N} = .95$$

$$\overline{C > N} = .015$$

We could *consistently* assume that

$$\overline{A > N} = .96$$

since if

$$\overline{D} = .3$$
$$\overline{A} = .3$$
$$\overline{C} = .4$$

then

$$\overline{N > D} = \frac{\overline{D} \times \overline{D > N}}{\overline{N}} = \frac{.285}{.579} = .4922$$

$$\overline{C > N} = \frac{\overline{C} \times \overline{C > N}}{\overline{N}} = \frac{.006}{.579} = .010$$

$$\overline{A > N} = \frac{\overline{A} \times \overline{A > N}}{\overline{N}} = \frac{.288}{.579} = .4974$$

since

$$\overline{N} = (\overline{D} \times \overline{D > N}) + (\overline{C} \times \overline{C > N}) + (\overline{A} \times \overline{A > N})$$
$$= (.3 \times .95) + (.4 \times .015) + (.3 \times .96)$$
$$= .579$$

This result depends on arbitrary probabilities for the hypotheses. We cannot apply the simple version of Nozick's schema, which assumes a simple "dichotomous" or "two-way" situation.

A reasonable generalization of Nozick's schema to "three-way" (or more) cases is to accept the hypothesis that makes the observed facts *most* probable, provided that the probability of that hypothesis is not smaller than that of the competing hypothesis, which gives the next highest probability to the evidence. In our example, A satisfies these conditions, but the difference in probabilities as calculated by Bayes' Theorem is so small as to give us pause about accepting A. Thus, we will be most confident of the generalized Nozick schema when the H to be accepted makes the observed evidence *much* more likely than any competing hypotheses or $\overline{H}$ is much more probable than any competing hypothesis.

But Hume is not trying to *establish* any competing hypothesis; he is merely trying to show that the hypothesis of design does not make the observed evidence *more* probable than any competing hypothesis while at the same time being at least as probable as any competing hypothesis: In other words, that D does not fit the revised Nozick schema.

Can he do this? Probably not with the examples he in fact uses. Hume has Philo throw out a number of suggestions and though he sometimes asserts that they are as plausible as the Design hypothesis, there is no real effort to show this. After all, millions of people have taken the Design hypothesis seriously, while hardly anyone has seriously believed in any of Hume's alternate suggestions. Furthemore, Hume makes no real effort to show that these alternate hypotheses make the observed state of affairs as likely or more likely than the Design hypothesis. So if this is what Hume was attempting to do, it would seem that he has failed. (Some of Hume's suggestions are used as exercises at the end of this chapter, so you can examine them in more detail there.)

THE EVOLUTIONARY SCENARIO

However, many contemporary thinkers believe they can succeed where Hume failed: provide an alternative hypothesis that gives as good or better an explanation of the observed facts as the Design hypothesis and is at least as likely. This alternative hypothesis might be called the *Evolutionary Scenario.*

The high points of the Evolutionary Scenario are as follows: The physical universe has always existed in some form, and it exists whether or not anything else exists (that is, it is a "necessary being" in the medieval sense). The matter-energy of the universe has certain inherent laws of development, according to which the universe develops in a certain way. However, these laws do not determine every detail of the universe: There is considerable room for random variation. Such features of the universe as the development of stars, planets, etc., are due to the internal laws of matter and energy, but such things as the origin of life on a particular planet at a particular time are due to random variation within the framework of these laws. Thus, life is a "cosmic accident" but such accidents are bound to occur sooner or later in the long history of the universe.

Once life has come into being it develops by "natural selection" of the kind first suggested by Darwin and elaborated by later biological science. Hence, such features of the universe as plant and animal species and the development of intelligent animals such as ourselves are explained by Darwinian natural selection. Such features of human society as morality, religion, and so on are explained by the fact that they serve evolutionary needs.

The Evolutionary Scenario is a powerful competitor to the Theistic View that an eternal and causally independent God created and designed the universe and implanted morality and religion in human beings. Large numbers of people accept the Evolutionary Scenario as the best explanation of the observed facts about the universe. On the other hand, many theists have faced the challenge of the Evolutionary Scenario, and they believe that they can show that the Theistic View does a much better job of explaining our experience of the universe.

One issue that is highly relevant to the question as to whether the Theistic View or the Evolutionary Scenario is the best explanation of our experience is the existence of moral evil and physical suffering in the universe. Many nontheists have rejected religion because they do not see how the existence of a God in the traditional sense, all-powerful and all good, is consistent with the existence of evil and suffering. In the "accidental universe" of the Evolutionary Scenario, suffering is simply a spur to evolutionary development, injustice a result of the way the universe develops. Because there is no supreme power of goodness, evil and suffering are not surprising.

The nontheist's argument can be put as follows:

E # The Evolutionary Scenario is true.

T # The Theistic View is true.

S # Suffering and evil exist.

$$\overline{E > S} \geq .95$$

$$\overline{T > S} \leq .05$$

S

$$\overline{T > S} < \overline{E}$$

Accept E

This assumes that T and E are the only real competitors, that $T > \hat{E}$ and $E > \hat{T}$.

Much of the last part of Hume's *Dialogues* may be taken as an attempt to give arguments supporting the premises of this schema. Hume paints an extremely gloomy picture of human life and then asks, "Is this what we would expect if there was an all-good, all powerful God? Surely not."

> But allowing you what never will be believed, at least, what you never possibly can prove, that animal or, at least, human happiness in this life exceeds its misery, you have yet done nothing: for this is not, by any means, what we expect from infinite power, infinite wisdom, and infinite goodness. Why is there any misery at all in the world? Not by chance, surely. From some cause then. Is it from the intention of the Deity? But he is perfectly benevolent. Is it contrary to his intention? But he is almighty. Nothing can shake the solidity of this reasoning, so short, so clear, so decisive, except we assert that these subjects exceed all human capacity, and that our common measures of truth and falsehood are not applicable to them—a topic which I have all along insisted on, but which you have, from the beginning, rejected with scorn and indignation.[1]

[1] *Dialogues on Natural Religion*, Part X, Paragraph 31.

Of Philo's two opponents, Demea suggests that present miseries must be seen in the light of eternal happiness. Cleanthes rejects this as an unprovable hypothesis and tries to argue that life is not as black as Philo has painted it. This is a good example of Hume's "divide and conquer" tactics: Most religious believers would both want to challenge Hume's gloomy picture of life *and* argue that a future life must be considered as part of the whole picture of human suffering. If suffering now is the only way we can be brought to recognize and repent our evildoing, then suffering will be both the effect of and the cure for moral evil.

Moral evil is seen as the result of human freedom: Human beings have the ability to say no to God's plans for them, which means that when they do say yes their assent is genuinely a gift to God. Thus, free will gives us the dignity of being not wholly "takers" in our relationship with God, but to some extent "givers" also.

Religious believers thus challenge the premise of Hume's argument that if the Theistic View is true then evil and suffering are very improbable. They can also turn Hume's argument against him: The Evolutionary Scenario explains the *facts* of suffering and injustice but not our indignation against injustice and suffering. If these things are "natural," why do we feel so outraged by them? Thus, the theist argues that if

I # The facts of suffering and injustice *plus* our indignation of them

$\overline{T > I} \geq .95$

$\overline{E > I} \leq .05$

I

$\overline{E > I} < \overline{T}$

Therefore accept T.

These philosophical issues can only be raised here, not settled; again, the point is that logical techniques can only clarify the issues and show us what is at stake in the premises.

A final philosophical problem to which Hume applies the idea of analogy is the problem of inductive reasoning itself. Are all of our inferences from past experience to predictions of the future basically analogy arguments of the form:

In past cases, state of affairs A resulted in state of affairs B.

The present case resembles the past cases in a number of ways.

Therefore probably in the present case, state of affairs A will result in state of affairs B.

To give a specific example:

In past cases when I stayed up too late, drank too much, and mixed my drinks, I had a hangover the next day.

I am now staying up too late, drinking too much, and mixing my drinks.

Probably tomorrow morning I will have a hangover.

Hume's own view of analogy raises a problem about this kind of reasoning. Since in his view we can only use analogy arguments if we have "double-checked" that very kind of *A* against that very kind of *B*, haven't I done that in this case? No, says Hume, because all observed cases were *present* or *past* hangovers: What I am trying to infer to is a *future* hangover. Of course, these past hangovers were *once* future, but they are *now* past. As one exponent of Hume put the point, the problem is to infer future-futures from past-futures, and we have never and *can* never observe future-futures: Any future we observe becomes a past-future.

There is no real solution to this problem on Hume's view; that is why philosophers speak of "Hume's Problem of Induction." However, the problem arises from an unrealistic demand placed on analogy arguments, a demand that cannot *in principle* be met.

If we regard analogy arguments as Nozick-style arguments, the argument becomes:

> D # Drinking late, too much, and mixing drinks.
>
> H # Hangover the next day.
>
> $\overline{\mathrm{H} > \mathrm{D}} \geq .95$
>
> $\overline{\hat{\mathrm{H}} > \mathrm{D}} \leq .05$
>
> D
>
> $\overline{\hat{\mathrm{H}} > \mathrm{D}} < \overline{\mathrm{H}}$
>
> Therefore accept H

In this example, $\overline{\mathrm{H} > \mathrm{D}} \geq .95$, $\overline{\hat{\mathrm{H}} > \mathrm{D}} \leq .05$ are accepted on the basis of experience.

Can we treat inductive arguments in general as Nozick-style arguments? And if we do, how can we avoid Hume's problem about the impossibility of arguing to future-future events on the basis of past-future events?

Let us consider a famous Humean example, set it up as a Nozick-style argument, and see how Hume might object to it. Can we be confident that the sun will rise tomorrow on the basis of our experience that it has always risen in the past? If we let

$$T \; \# \; \text{Sun will rise tomorrow}$$

$$P \; \# \; \text{Sun has always risen in past}$$

then we can argue

$$\overline{T > P} \geq .95$$

$$\overline{\hat{T} > P} \leq .05$$

$$P$$

$$\overline{\hat{T} > P} < \overline{T}$$

Why is $\overline{\hat{T} > P}$ low? Because if the sun's rising tomorrow was an improbable event then all of its risings in the past would be improbable too, and the conjunction of all the past risings would be very improbable. Say that the chance of the sun's rising tomorrow was even .99, but that the situation was otherwise in every respect like the situation in which the sun had risen in the past. Then each of those risings would also have a probability of .99, but the conjunction of millions of events with a probability of .99 would be a very tiny probability. Another way of saying this is to say that if there were a real possibility of the sun not rising, this possibility would have been realized at some time in the past. Certain hands of cards, such as a royal flush, are extremely improbable, but over the millions of hands of cards that have been played, they have happened ever so often.

On the other hand, if the probability that the sun will rise tomorrow is one or very close to one, then the conjunction of similar events in the past will also have a high probability, so $\overline{T > P} \geq .95$. Since we have argued that $\hat{T} > P$ must be tiny and we have been given no reason to think $\overline{T}$ is equally tiny, it looks as if $\hat{T} > P < \overline{T}$. Since P has been observed, all of the conditions for a Nozick-type argument are fulfilled and we should accept T.

The argument can be put informally as follows: "You claim that there is some serious doubt that the sun will rise tomorrow, but you do not claim that the conditions are any different from the conditions under which it has always risen in the past. But if that is so then its rising millions of times in the past is an immensely improbable event. On the other hand, if the sun is almost certain to rise tomorrow, then its rising millions of times in the past in similar circumstances is also very likely. You have given me no reason to suppose that it is *very* improbable that the sun will rise tomorrow, so it is surely more probable than the sun's having risen all those times in the past if it will not rise tomorrow under the same conditions under which it has always risen. So I conclude that the sun will rise tomorrow: Any other supposition makes my past experience too improbable."

A Humean reply might be: "Your argument proves too much; it is an argument against any new and unexpected event occurring. If a chicken could reason it might reason that 'on every previous morning the farmer has fed me and never harmed me, so on this morning he will do the same.' But that very morning the farmer might chop the chicken's head off and have it cooked for dinner."

Of course, the reply to this is that when something new occurs after a long sequence of similar events, we think that the conditions have changed in some way. If the chicken had not led too sheltered a life it might have seen that farmers periodically kill animals for food. The sun might fail to rise, since we know that there are astronomical events that could stop a planet from rotating. If the supposition is that some such event will have occurred by tomorrow, we must see how likely that is. But Hume's doubt is not based on astronomical speculation: It is based on a *logical* fear that past evidence gives us no real grounds for prediction. Against this fear, a Nozick-style argument is effective, for it shows that the great weight of probability is on the side of future events resembling past events provided conditions have not changed.

The Humean can still maintain that the sun *may* not rise tomorrow. Of course, it *may* not: Even extremely high probability is not absolute certainty. But where the probability is overwhelmingly on one side, we can treat it as certainty for all practical purposes. We cannot have the same certainty about the future as we have about simple mathematical truths, but we do not need to.

There may be hidden flaws in this "inverse" justification of induction, but granted the basic idea that we should accept the hypothesis that makes the observed evidence most likely unless it can be shown to be less probable than the best competing hypothesis, this justification and the other probabilistic arguments in this chapter seem effective.

As against Humean skepticism we can argue that if a hypothesis renders the observed evidence highly probable it can only be overturned by a hypothesis that is more probable and that makes the observed evidence more probable. No such hypothesis has even been suggested in the case of "the problem of induction." Whether the Evolutionary Scenario or the Theistic view does the best job of explaining our total experience is of course a matter of lively and continuing controversy. But if we are to be inductively reasonable, it is not enough to show that a competing hypothesis can be put forward; we must decide which competing hypothesis does the best job of explaining the evidence.

This is essentially the method of science; even if an accepted theory is not completely successful, it is not abandoned until and unless we can find a theory that does a better job at explaining the same facts. To refuse to accept a new theory that explains the facts better is unreasonable, but it is also unreasonable to abandon the best available theory until we find a competing theory that is better.

EXERCISES

A. For one of the following hypotheses give an estimate of:
  (a) The probability of the hypothesis (H)
  (b) The probability of available evidence given the hypothesis ($\overline{H > E}$)
  (c) The probability of available evidence if the hypothesis is false ($\hat{H} > E$)
  (d) Specify the nature of the available evidence.
    Calculate the following:
  (e) The probability that the hypothesis is false $\hat{H}$)
  (f) The probability of the evidence ($\overline{E} = (\overline{H} \times \overline{H > E}) + (\hat{H} \times \overset{\wedge}{H > E})$)
  (g) The probability of the hypothesis if the evidence is observed

$$\left(\overline{E > H} = \frac{\overline{H} \times \overline{H > E}}{\overline{E}} \right)$$

  For your *estimate* use the scale:
  .0 Certainly false
  .1 Very improbable
  .2
  .3
  .4
  .5 About equally likely to be true or false
  .6
  .7
  .8
  .9 Highly probable
  1.0 Certainly true

H1. The world was designed by an aging god who has since died.

H2. The world was designed by a committee of gods.

H3. The world is an organism that grows and develops by the laws of its own nature.

H4. Miracles have occurred that support non-Christian religions.

H5. Inconsistent miracles have occurred in support of competing religious claims.

B. For each of the above hypotheses, argue that Nozick's Schema does or does not apply. The conditions under which Nozick's Schema applies are:
  (1) $\overline{H > E}$ is high
  (2) $\hat{H} > E$ is low
  (3) E is observed

(4) $\overline{H}$ is higher than $\overline{\hat{H} > E}$

If you think Nozick's Schema does apply, do you agree that we should accept H? Why or why not? If Nozick's Schema does not apply, which condition is not satisfied?

C. For one of the above hypotheses, give an argument for attaching a given prior probability to that hypothesis.

D. For one of the above hypotheses and some specified set of evidence, give an argument for assigning a given probability to $H > E$ and to $\hat{H} > E$.

8

Kant and Necessity

The tradition of abstract rational thinking represented by Descartes and the tradition of appeal to concrete empirical facts represented by Hume seemed to be developing separately, with increasingly little contact. The rationalist approach characterized much thinking on the continent of Europe, and the empirical approach was dominant in England. The next great philosophical movement was started by Immanuel Kant (1724–1804) in Germany, and it can be thought of as an attempt to unite both the empirical approach and the rationalist approach.

A weakness of pure empiricism is that it has no adequate way of dealing with necessity and possibility. Hume's theory of causation is a good example of this. There is no place for any necessity in his theory except the logical necessity that comes from the meaning of words (for example, "Uncles are male."). So Hume cannot do justice to our feeling that there is some sort of necessity involved in causal relations and in the laws of nature. Nor can he make a workable distinction between pure logical possibility (the absence of self-contradiction) and "causal possibility" (for example, it is logically but not causally possible for a material object to go faster than the speed of light).

On the other hand, rationalist theories too often confuse other kinds of necessity with logical necessity. For Leibniz causal necessity was ultimately the same as logical necessity; since God must always act for the best, this world must logically be the best of all possible worlds and its laws and causal regularities *could not* have been other than they are.

Kant's way out of the dilemma of either ignoring other kinds of necessity or running them together with logical necessity was to say that there is a kind of necessity distinct from narrowly logical necessity, but that this was grounded on empirical facts about the way we perceive and organize the universe.

ANALYTIC AND SYNTHETIC

Kant distinguished between *analytic* statements, which are true or false because of the meaning of their terms (for example, "Uncles are male") and *synthetic* statements, whose truth or falsity does not depend on the meaning of their terms (for example, "Uncles are fond of their nephews and nieces"). He then made a second distincton between *a priori* statements, which we can know to be true without empirical investigation, and *a posteriori* statements, whose truth or falsity cannot be known without empirical investigation. Analytic statements are a priori, so "Uncles are male" is an example of an a priori statement as well as of an analytic statement. *Some* synthetic statements are a posteriori, so "Uncles are fond of their nephews and nieces" is an example of an a posteriori statement as well as an example of a synthetic statement: Its truth or falsity is *not determined* by the meaning of its terms, and we must undertake an empirical investigation to find out if it is true. Because a statement could not be both analytic and a posteriori, the category "analytic a posteriori" is empty.

But Kant raised the possibility of *synthetic a priori* statements, which could be known to be true without empirical investigation but whose truth or falsity did *not* just depend on the meaning of their terms. For Kant a mathematical statement such as "$7 + 5 = 12$" was an example of such a synthetic a priori truth. Kant asked whether we knew that there were synthetic a priori statements and if so how they were possible.

For an empiricist like Hume the answer to the first question is no, so the second question doesn't arise. For Hume the only a priori statements are analytic; synthetic a priori statements are *impossible*, so we do not need to ask *how* they are possible. In general, the empiricist schools of philosophy after Hume share his view; the only a priori truths are analytic, and all synthetic statements are a posteriori.

Before we tackle directly the question of whether there *are* synthetic a priori truths it will be useful to see how Kant thought such truths are possible. Once we have a better idea of what Kant thought the nature of such statements was, we can return to the question of whether there are any such statements.

To begin with, let us consider some basic facts about experience. All the material objects we experience seem to occupy *space*: They have size, shape, and are at various distances from us and from each other. And all of our experience, including our experience of our own thoughts, seems to take place in *time*: One event or thought happens before or after or at the same time as another event or thought. Things and thoughts *change*: They have characteristics at one time that they do not have at another.

But what *are* space and time? They are not material objects; we cannot see or touch or taste them. But they don't seem to depend on our thoughts either: They are not just *a* way of thinking about experience, which some people employ and others don't; we can't escape seeing objects as in space and events as in time. Some theories of space take the expression *"in* space" seriously and think of space as a sort of "container," which seems to amount to thinking of it as a sort of substance. Isaac Newton, the greatest scientist at the time of Hume and Kant, favored this view. But Aristotle earlier and Liebniz at the time of Newton favored a *relational* view of space; in this view, space is not a substance but a set of relations between objects.

Kant's solution to this problem was that space and time were *ways of experiencing*. Whether "things in themselves" are spatial and temporal we have no way of knowing. But *phenomena*, things as they appear to us, must be spatial and temporal because we cannot help *experiencing* them as spatial and temporal.

Kant offered a similar solution to the problem of causality and necessity. Causal relations are necessary relations because whether or not things in themselves have causal relations with each other we *must* experience reality in terms of causal relations. A useful, though somewhat oversimple, analogy is this: If everything we saw looked blue this could be because the things actually *were* blue *or* because we were wearing blue spectacles (that is, eyeglasses), which made those things look blue. Kant's view is analogous to the possibility that things look blue because of blue spectacles: We see reality as spatial and temporal because our mind is, so to speak, wearing "spatiotemporal spectacles."

In the "blue spectacle" case we could check out the hypothesis by removing the spectacles and seeing if things still looked blue, or we could ask someone without spectacles if everything looked blue to him or her. But in Kant's view the spatiotemporal (and causal) spectacles cannot be removed, and everyone is wearing them.

Presently we will criticize this view of Kant's, but for the moment let us first try to understand it better. Notice that it gives a certain kind of objectivity to space, time, and causality. We can count on every human being seeing reality as spaciotemporal and causal, just as we can count on every human being needing water to live. At the same time there is an element of subjectivity: Space, time, and causality do not represent the way the world really *is*, but only the way it must appear to *us*. Still, since the world must appear to us in this way we can count on it, plan on it, rely on it; the world as we must experience it is intelligible.

MODAL LOGIC

For Kant, causality is only one of a set of fundamental "categories," of which we will say more later. But in order to understand and assess Kant's view better we will now introduce some new logical techniques, namely the logic of necessity and possibility, which is called *modal logic*. We can get modal logic out of the statement logic we introduced in Chapter 2 by introducing one or two new operators on statements. The first operator is a *necessity* operator; to say that a statement, *p*, is necessary we write

$$\Box \, p$$

and this can be combined with the negation operator:

"Necessarily not p" is $\Box \, \hat{p}$

"Not necessarily p" is $\hat{\Box} \, p$

"Not necessarily not-p" is $\hat{\Box} \, \hat{p}$

We can *define* our next operator "possibly p" which we write as

$$\Diamond \, p$$

in terms of the necessity operator and negation:

$\Diamond \, p$ is defined as $\hat{\Box} \, \hat{p}$

There are two basic rules governing these operators:

$\Box \, p$	*Necesse*		p	*Esse ad*
—	*ad esse*		—	*posse*
p	(N.E.)		$\Diamond \, p$	(E.P.)

The first rule says that if something is necessarily true, it is true; the second says that if it is true then it is possibly true. The definition of possibility in terms of necessity also gives us a set of rules collectively called *Modal Operator Exchange* (M.O.E.).

$\Box \, p$	$\hat{\Box} \, p$	$\Box \, \hat{p}$	$\hat{\Box} \, \hat{p}$
═══	═══	═══	═══
$\hat{\Diamond} \, \hat{p}$	$\Diamond \, \hat{p}$	$\hat{\Diamond} \, p$	$\Diamond \, p$

These six rules (N.E., E.P., and the four varieties of M.O.E.) are the basic rules of the first stage or "system" of modal logic, which we will call S.1.

To return to Kant, we can say that for him a statement is necessarily true just in case it is true *in every case we are capable of experiencing*. A statement is possibly true if it is true in *some* case we are capable of experiencing. Thus, "Material objects are in space" is a necessary truth because in every case we are capable of experiencing, material objects are in space. "There is a material object larger than any I have experienced so far" is possible, since I am capable of experiencing a material object larger than any I have experienced so far.

Given Kant's meaning of necessity and possibility, all six of our rules make good sense. If it is true in every case I can experience that material objects are in space, it would seem that I must regard "material objects are in space" as true. If I experience a red object I must be capable of doing so, so "a red object exists" must be possible. On the other hand, if "material objects are in space" is true in every case I am capable of experiencing, then it must be false that in some case I am capable of experiencing I experience an object not in space (that is, "$\Box$ p" implies "$\Diamond$ p̂").

Now when we combine our new operators with the connectives "$\lor$," "$\land$," "$>$," and "$< >$" we need a new set of rules. To indicate the difference between "necessarily A, and in addition B" and "necessarily both A and B" we will write the necessity or possibility operators in front of parentheses, which indicate the "scope" of the operator; thus,

$$\text{"necessarily p, and also q" is } \Box p \land q$$

while

$$\text{"necessarily both p and q" is } \Box (p \land q)$$

Given this notation, we can write the rules collectively, called *Modal Operator Distribution* (M.O.D).

$$\frac{\Box (p \land q)}{\Box p \land \Box q} \qquad \frac{\Diamond (p \lor q)}{\Diamond p \lor \Diamond q} \qquad \frac{\Box p \lor \Box q}{\Box (p \lor q)} \qquad \frac{\Diamond (p \land q)}{\Diamond p \land \Diamond q}$$

These rules are the essential rules of our second stage or system of modal logic, S.2.

Even in S.1 we could have introduced a new connective, *Strict Implication*, which is defined by the rule

$$\frac{p \gg q}{\Box (p > q)} \qquad \begin{array}{l}\text{Definition of Strict Implication}\\ \text{(D.S.I.)}\end{array}$$

Now because of the rule N.E., such rules as M.P. and M.T. will hold for Strict Implication

$$p \gg q \qquad\qquad\qquad p \gg q$$

$$\frac{p}{q} \qquad \text{and} \qquad \frac{\hat{q}}{\hat{p}}$$

and will be true because we could argue as follows:

1	$p \gg q$	P
2	p	P
3	$\square\,(p > q)$	1 D.S.I.
4	$p > q$	3 N.E.
5	p	2,4 M.P.

and

1	$p \gg q$	p
2	p	P
3	$\square\,(p > q)$	1 D.S.I.
4	$p > q$	3 N.E.
5	$\hat{p}$	2,4 M.T.

Because we know we can always do this, we will simply apply M.P. and M.T. to Strict Implication without further ado. For similar reasons, *Strict Transportation* (S. Transp) is a rule

$$\frac{p \gg q}{\hat{q} \gg \hat{p}}$$

But there are also some rules that apply to Strict Implication but that do *not* hold for our regular single arrow "if . . . then." These rules are the essential rules of the next stage system of modal logic, S.3, and they are collectively called *Consequences of Strict Implication* (C.S.I.)

$$\frac{p \gg q}{\square\,p \gg \square\,q} \qquad\qquad \frac{p \gg q}{\Diamond\,p \gg \Diamond\,q}$$

The system S.3 contains all the rules of S.1 and S.2, also, so with a few additions it is a workable and plausible system of modal logic. One useful addition is a *Definition of Strict Equivalence* (D.S.E.).

$$\frac{p <> q}{\Box\,(p <> q)}$$

Another is *Strict Hypothetical Syllogism* (S.H.S)

$$\frac{\begin{array}{c} p >> q \\ q >> r \end{array}}{p >> r}$$

The rules that define the next two systems, S.4 and S.5, are highly controversial. The basic rules of S.4 are the *Weak Reduction Principles* (W.R.P.),

$$\frac{\Box\,p}{\Box\Box\,p} \qquad \frac{\Diamond\,\Diamond\,p}{\Diamond\,p}$$

and the basic rules of the S.5 system are the *Strong Reduction Principles* (S.R.P.),

$$\frac{\Diamond\,\Box\,p}{\Box\,p} \qquad \frac{\Diamond\,p}{\Box\,\Diamond\,p}$$

The Weak Reduction Principles act to eliminate "iterated" (repeated) modal operators of the same kind. By the W.R.P. "□ □ □ □ p" is the same as "□ p" and "◇ ◇ p" is the same as "◇ p." The W.R.P. says you don't add information by *repeating* "necessarily" or "possibly." In this way it is like Double Negation, for by D.N.

$$\overset{\wedge\wedge\wedge}{p} \qquad \text{would be the same as p}$$

$$\overset{\wedge\wedge\wedge\wedge}{\hat{p}} \qquad \text{would be the same as } \hat{p}$$

and in general, any even number of "nots" boils down to a positive statement, while any odd number boils down to a single negative.

In Kant's view, what would an expression like "□ □ p" mean? Since in Kant's theory "□ p" means "In every case we are capable of experiencing, p is true", "□ □ p" would mean "In every case we are capable of experiencing, it is true that in every case we are capable of experiencing, p is true." Does the repetition add anything? It looks as if it might. Experiencing that p is true might be one thing; experiencing that we experience p is true might be something different. Experiencing that I have a sore finger might be a "direct" experience, whereas experiencing that I experience having a sore finger might involve a certain amount of introspection; asking myself "What am I experiencing now" and answering "I am having the experience of feeling pain in my finger."

But if there is a difference between "experiencing p" and "experiencing that I experience p," both Weak Reduction Principles are highly suspect and perhaps Kant should reject them. Compare this with the case of analytic a priori truths. These are "necessary" in the sense that, given the meaning of their terms, the statement must be true: for example, given that "uncle" has the meaning it does, uncles must be males. But is it analytic that the word "uncle" has the meaning it does? Surely not: It is a contingent fact that the word "uncle" has the meaning it does; we might have used the word "uncle" to mean what we now mean by "uncle or aunt" and in that case "uncles are male" would not have been analytic. So if one sense of "it is necessary that p" is "it is analytically true (true by the meaning of terms) that p" then for this meaning the rule

$$\frac{\Box \, p}{\Box \Box \, p}$$

is just false: It is not analytically true that uncles are male; instead, it is synthetically true that it is analytically true that uncles are males.

The Strong Reduction Principle is even more suspect. If "necessarily true" is interpreted as "analytically true" then the rule

$$\frac{\Diamond \, \Box \, p}{\Box \, p}$$

would say that if it was not analytically false that it is analytically true that p is true, then it *is* analytically true that p is true. But if it is not a matter of the meaning of words, but a matter of contingent fact that words mean what they do, then it is not true that if it is not analytically true that p is analytically true then p is analytically true.

Similarly, in Kant's view if there is a difference between having an experience and experiencing having the experience, then it is highly dubious that if it is not true that we are never capable of not experiencing that we are never capable of experiencing p then we are never capable of experiencing not p.

THE MODAL ONTOLOGICAL ARGUMENT

So tentatively we should conclude that the Kantian view of necessity rules out an S.4 or S.5 system of modal logic. This idea is strengthened by Kant's discussion of the Ontological Argument for the existence of God. For our purpose the argument can be stated as follows:

> **If God exists then it is necessarily true that God exists.**
>
> **Possibly God exists.**
> _____
> **Therefore God exists.**

In symbols:

$$G \gg \Box G \qquad G \,\#\, \text{God exists}$$
$$\Diamond G$$
$$\overline{}$$
$$G$$

The conclusion can be proved as follows:

1	$G \gg \Box G$	P
2	$\Diamond G$	P
3	$\Diamond G \gg \Diamond \Box G$	1, C.S.I. (S.3)
4	$\Diamond \Box G$	2,3 M.P.
5	$\Box G$	4 S.R.P. (S.5)
6	G	5 N.E. (S.1)

Now it is quite surprising that so strong a conclusion can be proved from such apparently harmless premises. Further, some of the logical principles involved seem quite acceptable: *Modus Ponens, Necesse ad Esse,* even Consequences of Strict Implication. So the real weight falls on the two premises and the Strong Reduction Principle. Defenders of the argument argue on various grounds that S.5 is an acceptable system of modal logic, perhaps even the best system, then they argue that the existence of God is at least *possible* and that surely if God exists at all God exists necessarily.

One possible reply to this argument is to claim an ambiguity. That God's existence is possible may mean no more than that there is no contradiction in supposing God exists. But for this narrowly logical sense of possibility the corresponding sense of necessity is "it is analytically true that." And if this is what we mean it is not at all plausible that if God exists, God's existence is necessary; this would be to say "If God exists it is analytically true that God exists," and as Hume had already argued, anything that can be thought of as existing can be thought of as not existing without contradiction. The idea of an existence statement being necessary in the sense of being analytically true seems to be a confusion.

Kant seems to endorse this line of argument. He says,

> If, in an identical proposition, I reject the predicate while retaining the subject, contradiction results; and I therefore say that the former belongs necessarily to the latter. But if we reject subject and predicate alike, there is no contradiction; for nothing is then left that can be contradicted. To posit a triangle, and yet to reject its three angles, is self-contradictory; but there is no contradiction in rejecting the triangle together with its three angles. The same holds true of the concept of an absolutely necessary being. If its existence is rejected, we reject the thing itself with all its predicates; and no question of contradiction can then arise. There is nothing outside it that would then be contradicted, since the necessity of the thing is not supposed to be derived from anything external; nor is there anything internal that would be contradicted, since in rejecting the thing itself we have at the same time rejected all its internal properties. "God is omnipotent" is a necessary judgment. The omnipotence cannot be rejected if we posit a Deity, that is, an infinite being; for the two concepts are identical. But if we say, "There is no God", neither the omnipotence nor any other of its predicates is given; they are one and all rejected together with the subject, and there is therefore not the least contradiction in such a judgment.[1]

In reply to this one might say that by "G > □ G" we do not mean that, if God exists, God's existence is analytic, but that if God exists, God's existence is necessary in some other sense, for example, the medieval sense of "always existing and causally independent." Here Kant has some points of his own to make and is not merely retracing Hume's steps.

For Kant the only sense of necessity aside from "analytically true" is Kant's own sense of necessity as "true in every case we are capable of experiencing." Now in this sense of necessity the premise "G > □ G" is more plausible. For *if* there were a being which always existed and existed whether or not anything else existed surely it would be true that it existed in every state *we* were able to experience. But now the *second* premise becomes questionable; how do we know that in *some* state we *are* capable of experiencing God *does* exist? It is no longer a matter simply of the absence

---

[1] Kant, *Critique of Pure Reason* (Riga, 1781), I. First Part Second Division, Chapter III, Section 4 (A595, B623).

of contradiction: There has to be a state of experience in which we are sure God exists.

Within many religious views we cannot have a direct experience of God, at least in this life. In Kant's terminology this point can be made by saying that if God exists then God is a "thing in itself," not a phenomenon. As a thing in itself God is beyond the realm of possible experience and thus is something of which we can say nothing. As Kant states:

> It is evident, from what has been said, that the concept of an absolutely necessary being is a concept of pure reason, that is, a mere idea the objective reality of which is very far from being proved by the fact that reason requires it. For the idea instructs us only in regard to a certain unattainable completeness, and so serves rather to limit the understanding than to extend it to new objects. But we are here faced by what is indeed strange and perplexing, namely, that while the inference from a given existence in general to some absolutely necessary being seems to be both imperative and legitimate, all those conditions under which alone the understanding can form a concept of such a necessity are so many obstacles in the way of our doing so. . . . A concept is always possible if it is not self-contradictory. This is the logical criterion of possibility. . . . But it may none the less be an empty concept, unless the objective reality of the synthesis through which the concept is generated has been specifically proved; and such proof, as we have shown above, rests on principles of possible experience, and not on the principle of analysis (the law of contradiction). This is a warning against arguing directly from the logical possibility of concepts to the real possibility of things.[2]

Now if we *did* in some way have an experience which gave us good grounds for thinking God existed, we could argue by *Esse ad Posse*, "This experience shows that God exists so it is possible God exists." But even aside from Kant's denial that we could have such an experience, we would have no need of the Ontological Argument: We would know God existed because of the experience! Thus, the argument would be useless if it was sound, for one of the premises would be equivalent to the conclusion.

Actually, as we will see, Kant did think that one kind of experience, moral experience, gives us grounds for thinking God exists. But for Kant, to say that we had *experienced* God, as some mystics have claimed, would be to reduce God to a phenomenon, subject to the limitations of our minds. But anything so subject could not be God.

Could we perhaps argue to God from experiences we *do* have, as in the Cosmological Arguments? Kant answers no:

> I have stated that in this cosmological argument there lies hidden a whole nest of dialectical assumptions, which the transcendental critique can easily detect and destroy. These deceptive principles I shall merely enumerate, leaving to the reader, who by this time will be sufficiently expert in these matters, the task of investigating them further, and of refuting them.

---

[2] *Critique*, I. First Part, 2nd Division, Chapter III, Section 4 (A592, B620).

We find, for instance, the transcendental principle whereby from the contingent we infer a cause. This principle is applicable only in the sensible world; outside that world it has no meaning whatsoever. For the mere intellectual concept of the contingent cannot give rise to any synthetic proposition, such as that of causality. The principle of causality has no meaning and no criterion for its application save only in the sensible world. But in the cosmological proof it is precisely in order to enable us to advance beyond the sensible world that it is employed.[3]

In other words, no causal argument can give us reason to think God exists, for causal arguments are applicable only in the realm of phenomena.

Thus, as we might expect, Kant rejects the Ontological Argument. Because the principles of S.5, the Strong Reduction Principles, are highly implausible for Kant's sense of necessity and we need the S.R.P. for the validity of the Ontological Argument, it is not surprising that Kant rejects the Ontological Argument. Because he believed that the Cosmological Argument depends upon the Ontological Argument, he also rejected the Cosmological Argument. Thus, if Kant is right, both arguments fail.

But is Kant right? *Should* we define necessity as truth in all cases that we are capable of experiencing? Take a very simple counterexample. Suppose all human beings were color-blind and saw everything in shades of black, gray, and white (like a black-and-white movie). Now every object we were capable of experiencing we would see as black, white, or gray, but that would not mean that everything *was* black, white, or gray. Roses would remain red, corn would be yellow, leaves remain green, whether or not we could experience them as such. At best I could argue:

Everything I am capable of experiencing seems black, white, or gray.

Therefore everything seems black, white, or gray *to me*.

This is basically an enthymetic argument; to be valid it needs a further premise to the effect that if I can only experience a thing in a certain way, then *to me* that is the way it is. Even that is ambiguous; I might know, as many color-blind people do, that other people could see colors I do not. Thus, I might argue that despite the way this rose inevitably seemed to me it in fact had different characteristics from the ones I was capable of experiencing.

An instance where we often correct our experience by reason is in the case of optical illusions. In the two lines below:

[3] *Critique* I, First Part, 2nd Division, Chapter III, Section 5 (A607, B637).

the top line may *look* longer to me no matter how I try, but I can know that they are of equal length.

Similarly, in science many cases abound in which we cannot experience something at all, or can only experience it indirectly. Subatomic particles are not "objects of possible experience" although certain experiences such as seeing tracks made by particles in a cloud chamber come close to being indirect experiences of subatomic particles. If we cannot argue to God because God is not an object of possible experience, how can science argue to unobservably small particles such as neutrinos or events such as the Big Bang, which could in principle never be observed by bodily senses such as ours?

In fact, there seems to be an important ambiguity in Kant's philosophy between the truism "We can only *experience* those things which we are capable of experiencing" and the far from truistic claim "We can only *know* those things which we are capable of experiencing." If this second claim were true it would elminate much, perhaps most, of our scientific knowledge.

KANT'S ANTINOMIES

An interesting application and illustration of Kant's view is found in what Kant calls the "Antinomies of Pure Reason." In Kant's theory we can only use categories like causality as applied to possible experiences; we cannot reflect on the nature of causality itself, for that would be to treat a *form* of experience as if *it* were capable of being experienced. Kant thinks that whenever we try to think about the nature of causality (which is one of what he calls the "transcendental ideas") we are bound to find ourselves with equally good arguments for incompatible statements; this is what he calls an *antinomy*. The third of these "conflicts of the transcendental ideas" is as follows:

Thesis

Causality in accordance with laws of nature is not the only causality from which the appearances of the world can one and all be derived. To explain these appearances it is necessary to assume that there is also another causality, that of freedom.

Proof

Let us assume that there is no other causality than that in accordance with laws of nature. This being so, everything which *takes place* presupposes a preceding state upon which it inevitably follows according to a rule. But the preceding state must itself be something which has taken place (having come to be in a time in which it previously was not); for if it had always existed, its consequence also would have always existed, and would not have only just arisen. The causality of the cause through which something takes place is itself, therefore, something that has *taken place*, which again presupposes, in accordance with the law of nature, a preceding state and its causality, and this in similar manner a still earlier state, and so on. If, therefore, everything takes place solely in accordance with laws of nature, there will always be only a relative and never a first beginning, and consequently no completeness of the series on the side of the causes that arise the one from the other. But the law of nature is just this, that nothing takes place without a cause *sufficiently* determined *a priori.* The proposition that no causality is possible save in accordance with laws of nature, when taken in unlimited universality, is therefore self-contradictory; and this cannot, therefore, be regarded as the sole kind of causality.

We must, then assume a causality through which something takes place, the cause of which is not itself determined, in accordance with necessary laws, by another cause antecedent to it, that is to say, an *absolute spontaneity* of the cause, whereby a series of appearances, which proceeds in accordance with laws of nature, begins *of itself.* This is transcendental freedom, without which, even in the [ordinary] course of nature, the series of appearances on the side of the causes can never be complete.

Antithesis

There is no freedom; everything in the world takes place solely in accordance with laws of nature.

Proof

Assume that there is freedom in the transcendental sense, as a special kind of causality in accordance with which the events in the world can have come about, namely, a power of absolutely beginning a state, and therefore also of absolutely beginning a series of consequences of that state; it then follows that not only will a series have its absolute beginning in this spontaneity, but that the very determination of this spontaneity to originate the series, that is to say, the causality itself, will have an absolute beginning; there will be no antecedent through which this act, in taking place, is determined in accordance with fixed laws. But every beginning of action presupposes a state of the not yet acting cause; and a *dynamical* beginning of the action, if it is also a first beginning, presupposes a state which has no *causal* connection with the preceding state of the cause, that is to say, in nowise follows from it. Transcendental freedom thus stands opposed to the law of causality; and the kind of connection which it assumes as holding between the successive states of the active causes renders all unity of experience impossible. It is not to be met with in any experience, and is therefore an empty thought-entity.

In nature alone, therefore, [not in freedom], must we seek for the connection and order of cosmical events. Freedom (independence) from the laws of nature is no doubt a liberation from compulsion, but also from the guidance of all rules. For it is not permissible to say that the *laws* of freedom enter into the causality exhibited in the course of nature, and so take the place of natural laws. If freedom were determined in accordance with laws, it would not be freedom; it would simply be nature under another name. Nature and transcendental freedom differ as do conformity to law and lawlessness. Nature does indeed impose upon the understanding the exacting task of always seeking the origin of events ever higher in the series of causes, their causality being always conditioned. But in compensation it holds out the promise of thoroughgoing unity of experience in accordance with laws. The illusion of freedom, on the other hand, offers a point of rest to the enquiring understanding in the chain of causes, conducting it to an unconditioned causality which begins to act of itself. This causality is, however, blind, and abrogates those rules through which alone a completely coherent experience is possible.[1]

We might paraphrase Kant's argument for the thesis as follows: If *every* event has a sufficient cause then the chain of causality extends to infinity. But then each sufficient cause would depend on an infinite number of previous sufficient causes. Thus, every sufficient cause has a sort of essential incompleteness, which prevents it from really explaining the event it is a cause of. But the whole point of a sufficient cause is to explain the event it is a cause of, so sufficient causes cannot "do their job," so to speak, and the whole idea of a sufficient cause is inconsistent.

Kant's argument for the antithesis can be paraphrased as follows: If there is a purely spontaneous event, not determined by a sufficient cause, it would be unintelligible because we would have no grounds for predicting it or putting it in an orderly picture of nature. Thus, spontaneous events would also undermine the whole idea of causal explanation and make an intelligible picture of nature impossible, so the idea of a spontaneous event is also inconsistent.

The "antinomy" arises because the two views of causality ("every event has a sufficient cause" and "some events do not have sufficient causes") seem to be mutually exclusive and to exhaust the possibilities: No third position seems possible. But then every possible theoretical view of causation seems to lead to inconsistency and make the universe unintelligible.

The moral Kant draws from this is that we cannot reason theoretically about causality; we must simply use the concept to apply to phenomena, not try to theorize about it as if *it* were an object of possible experience. Causality and the other "transcendental" ideas are necessary to make sense of experience, but we cannot in the same way make sense of them. To give an analogy, light enables us to see objects but we cannot see light itself in the same sense we see objects.

However, before we grant Kant this sweeping conclusion let us see if there is a way out of his antinomy. Hegel, Kant's great successor, argued that wherever we have a thesis and antithesis that both seem well supported but are inconsistent, we should find a *synthesis* that does justice to the truth in both thesis and antithesis but rejects some false or incomplete element in both.

DIALECTICAL ARGUMENTS

Many interesting arguments in philosophy are in this *dialectical* form or can be put into that form. A *dialectical argument* has three parts: a *Thesis* (T), an *Antithesis* (A), and a *Synthesis* (S). The thesis and antithesis are *con-*

---

[1] *Critique*, I, First Part, 2nd Division, Chapter 11, Section 2 (A445, B473).

traries: They cannot both be true, but they can both be false. The synthesis contains the true elements in *both* the thesis and the antithesis. It follows from these requirements that the thesis and antithesis must be either *compound* or *general*. Two simple forms of dialectical argument are:

D1

T. A and B

A. not A and not B

S. A and not B (*or* not A and B)

D2

T. Every S is P

A. No S is P

S. Some S is P and Some S is not P

In the first form of dialectical argument the thesis and antithesis each contain one true and one false statement. The synthesis accepts the true statements and rejects the false ones. Even though "A" and "not A," "B" and "not B" are contradictory, the compound statements "A and B" and "not A and not B" are contrary, for though they cannot both be true they *can* both be false, and if the synthesis "A and not B" is true both *are* false.

A familiar dialectical argument is the debate between Strict Determinists, Compatibilists, and Free-Willers. From the Free-Will point of view the dialect is:

Thesis (Strict Determinism)

Moral Responsibility is incompatible with every event having a sufficient cause. (Since every event has a sufficient cause) we are not morally responsible.

Antithesis (Compatibilism)

Moral responsibility is compatible with every event having a sufficient cause. (Every event has a sufficient cause, but) we are morally responsible.

Synthesis (Free Will)

Moral responsibility is incompatible with every event having a sufficient cause. We are morally responsible (so not every event has a sufficient cause).

But from the Strict Determinist's point of view, the Free Will view and the Compatibilist view are the thesis and antithesis, respectively, and the Strict Determinist point of view is the synthesis. Similarly, from the Compatibilist's point of view, the Strict Determinist point of view and the

Free Will view are the thesis and antithesis, respectively, and the Compatibilist point of view is the synthesis. Thus, if

I # "Every event has a sufficient cause" is incompatible with moral
responsibility

and

R # We are morally responsible

the three dialectical arguments are

Free Willer	Strict Determinist	Compatibilist
T: I and not R	T: I and R	T: I and not R
A: Not I and R	A: Not I and R	A: I and R
S: I and R	S: I and not R	S: Not I and R

One point of putting the arguments in this way is that it makes clear what points are in dispute between the three parties and on what points they are allies.

Similarly, in Hume's *Dialogues on Natural Religion*, if we let

C # The Cosmological Arguments are sound

D # The Design Argument is sound

then the three positions represented in the dialogue are:

Demea	Cleanthes	Philo
T: Not C and D	T: C and not D	T: Not C and D
A: Not C and not D	A: Not C and not D	A: C and not D
S: C and not D	S: Not C and D	S: Not C and not D

Now is there any way of putting Kant's antinomy about causation into this form? I think there is.

The hidden assumption, it seems to me, is an assumption about the nature of intelligible expansion, which might be put roughly as "Any adequate explanation must be a *complete* explanation." If we let

C # Every adequate explanation is a complete explanation

S # Every event has a sufficient cause

Then the thesis is

$$\hat{S} \wedge C$$

the antithesis is

$$S \wedge C$$

which are, of course, contrary and not contradictory (they can't both be true but can both be false). There are two possible syntheses:

$$S \wedge \hat{C} \text{ or } \hat{S} \wedge \hat{C}$$

The first synthesis says that every event has a sufficient cause but that a "complete" explanation is not necessary for adequacy; the second says that some event lacks a sufficient cause and that a complete explanation is not necessary. To better understand the thesis and antithesis and the two syntheses, let us examine the arguments for each.

For the thesis, let

I # There are an infinite chain of sufficient causes

O # Some explanation is complete

A # Some explanation is adequate

C # Every adequate explanation is complete

Then the argument will be

1	$S \wedge C$	S cancels S >
2	$S > I$	> I cancels I >
3	$I > \hat{O}$	> $\hat{O}$ cancels $\hat{O}$ >
4	$\hat{O} > (C > \hat{A})$	C cancels C > leaving $\hat{A}$

which cancels to the conclusion Â and can be proved as follows:

$$
\begin{array}{lll}
1 & S \wedge C & P \\
2 & S > I & P \\
3 & I > \hat{O} & P \\
4 & \hat{O} > (C > \hat{A}) & P \\
5 & S & 1 \text{ Conj.} \\
6 & C & 1 \text{ Conj.} \\
7 & I & 2,5 \text{ M.P.} \\
8 & \hat{O} & 3,6 \text{ M.P.} \\
9 & C > \hat{A} & 4,8 \text{ M.P.} \\
10 & \hat{A} & 6,9 \text{ M.P.}
\end{array}
$$

Of the four premises, the first is the antithesis: What we are trying to do is assume the antithesis and show that if the antithesis is true then no explanation is adequate, so this is our reason for accepting the thesis. The proof shows that given the antithesis and other plausible premises we can show that it is false that some explanation is adequate, which of course is equivalent to "No explanation is adequate." The second premise

$$S > I$$

seems to be true for the reasons given by Kant; if every event must have a sufficient cause we are forced to an infinite regress of causes for reasons like those discussed in Chapter 3. The third premise

$$I > \hat{O}$$

seems to be true given the understanding of a "complete" explanation, which Kant has: We will say more about this presently. Given that idea of a complete explanation, the fourth premise

$$\hat{O} > (C > \hat{A})$$

seems to be true also, and unless we deny C or S or both, we must accept the conclusion.

Kant's argument for the antithesis can be symbolized as follows. Let F # Every event is determined in accordance with fixed laws and S, O, C, and A be as above.

The argument is:

1 $\hat{S} \wedge C$	$\hat{S}$ cancels $\hat{S} >$
2 $\hat{S} > \hat{F}$	$\hat{F}$ cancels $\hat{F} >$
3 $\hat{F} > \hat{O}$	$> \hat{O}$ cancels $\hat{O} >$
4 $\hat{O} > (C > \hat{A})$	C cancels C $>$ leaving $\hat{A}$

which cancels to the conclusion $\hat{A}$.

The proof is as follows:

1	$\hat{S} \wedge C$	
2	$\hat{S} > \hat{F}$	
3	$\hat{F} > \hat{O}$	
4	$\hat{O} > (\hat{C} > \hat{A})$	
5	S	1 Conj.
6	C	1 Conj.
7	$\hat{F}$	2,5 M.P.
8	$\hat{O}$	3,7 M.P.
9	$C > \hat{A}$	4,8 M.P.
10	$\hat{A}$	6,9 M.P.

Premise 1 is the thesis, which we are assuming in order to derive the conclusion that no explanation is adequate. Premise 2 simply says that if some events have no sufficient causes then not every event is determined by fixed laws, which seems true by definition. Given Kant's sense of complete explanation, we can grant that, if not every event is determined by fixed laws, no explanation is complete, for even chains of explanations that contain sufficient causes will eventually run into an event that does not have a sufficient cause. We have already discussed premise 4, which is the same as Premise 4 in the previous argument. Thus, if we assume the antithesis it seems we must conclude again that no explanation is adequate. If the thesis and antithesis exhausted the possibilities we would be forced to the conclusion that no explanation could possibly be adequate: This would be true if the thesis were true and also true if the antithesis were true.

But the thesis and antithesis do *not* exhaust the possibilities; we can accept either of the two "syntheses," each of which contain $\hat{C}$ as a conjunct. Since C is essential to the two proofs we have just given, we could not get $\hat{A}$ as a conclusion from either proof (only the weaker $(C > \hat{A})$.

It is now time to explore what Kant *meant* by a complete explanation. It would seem that his idea of a complete explanation was something like this:

> A complete explanation is an explanation that leaves no causal question un-answered.

An explanation by a sufficient cause cannot be complete, for an explanation by sufficient cause leaves unanswered the question as to the sufficient cause of the sufficient cause. An explanation by a spontaneous event cannot be complete, for if an event is spontaneous we cannot give a sufficient cause for it. Thus, by his very definition of "complete explanation," Kant has ruled out any possibility of adequate explanation.

A defender of the first synthesis, $S \wedge \hat{C}$, could reply to Kant as follows: "Every event does have a sufficient cause, and I grant your point that any explanation by a sufficient cause leaves unanswered the question as to the sufficient cause of that sufficient cause, and by your definition of 'complete explanation' is incomplete. But I disagree that an explanation which is not complete in your sense is inadequate. Just because an explanation doesn't answer *every* causal question does *not* mean it is inadequate. Our knowledge is always finite; you are unreasonably demanding infinite knowledge from finite minds, the skeptical trick of demanding the impossible and com-plaining when you don't (because you can't) get it."

A defender of the second synthesis, $\hat{S} \wedge \hat{C}$, could argue as follows: "Of course an event with no sufficient cause is not *determined* by any fixed law: That is just what is meant by having no sufficient cause. But that does not mean that explanations by spontaneous events are inadequate. For a spontaneous event you cannot answer the question 'What is its sufficient cause,' but this is not a legitimate question for spontaneous events; in the nature of the case they *can't* have sufficient causes. To ask 'What is the sufficient cause of this spontaneous event' is like asking 'Where are the corners of this circle?' Circles don't *have* corners; spontaneous events don't *have* sufficient causes, so it is meaningless to ask for the sufficient cause of a spontaneous event. This does not mean that spontaneous events are unintelligible: They can obey statistical laws (as quantum events do) or have reasons (as free human actions do). And every spontaneous event has necessary conditions; even a theist who believes that God's creation of the universe was a spontaneous (free) act thinks that God's eternal existence was a necessary condition for creation."

KANT'S CATEGORIES

Whether such replies are adequate and whether they refute Kant's position is a matter that requires much more detailed philosophical discussion of Kant's philosophy. As one step in the better understanding of this philosophy we will conclude this chapter with a brief discussion of Kant's Categories.

For Kant, causality was only one of 12 "pure concepts of the understanding" that are given in the following Table of Categories:

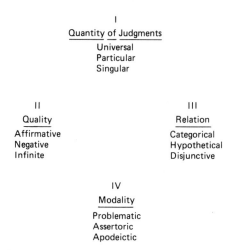

Table of Categories

I
Of Quantity
Unity
Plurality
Totality

II
Of Quality
Reality
Negation
Limitation

III
Of Relation
Of Inherence and Subsistence
(substantia et accidens)
Of Causality and Dependence
(cause and effect)
Of Community (reciprocity between
agent and patient)

IV
Of Modality
Possibility--Impossibility
Existence--Non-existence
Necessity--Contingency

Where did Kant get these particular categories and subcategories? From the accepted logic of his time. A little earlier Kant has given a "Table of Judgments" as follows:

I
Quantity of Judgments
Universal
Particular
Singular

II
Quality
Affirmative
Negative
Infinite

III
Relation
Categorical
Hypothetical
Disjunctive

IV
Modality
Problematic
Assertoric
Apodeictic

The "quality" and "quantity" of judgments are plainly those of the traditional Aristotelian logic, which we discussed in Chapter 4, but to fill out his schema of three subcategories in each category, Kant has added "infinite" to *positive* and *negative*. Universal, particular, and singular judgments plainly have the form

Every S is P

Some S is P

N is P

All of these are affirmative: The corresponding negatives are

No S is P

Some S is not P

N is not P

But what is an "infinite" judgment? Kant's explanation is not particularly helpful, and as we will see this is a problem for his list of Categories.

The subcategories of judgment "problematic," "assertoric," and "apodeictic" correspond to our "◇p," "p," and "□p." This suggests that the categories are basically applied to the same subject matter and that we could give a combined table as follows:

	POSITIVE	NEGATIVE	INFINITE
Assertoric:			
Universal	S))P	S)(P	?
Particular	S()P	S((P	?
Singular	*N*))P	*N*)(P	?
Problematic:			
Universal	◇[S))P]	◇[S)(P]	?
Particular	◇[S()P]	◇[S((P]	?
Singular	◇[*N*))P]	◇[*N*)(P]	?
Apodeictic:			
Universal	□[S))P]	□[S)(P]	?
Particular	□[S()P]	□[S((P]	?
Singular	□[*N*))P]	□[*N*)(P]	?

Now how does the third category, that of relation, come in? Perhaps we can interpret it as follows:

Categorical: p

Hypothetical: p > q

Disjunctive: p ∨ q

Applying this to the schema we have, we can substitute any of the standard-form Syllogistic Logic statements for A and B and get such statements as:

Categorical: S))P

Hypothetical: S))P > S()P

Disjunctive: S()P ∨ S((P

(The latter two would be logical truths on the Aristotelian interpretation of the Square of Opposition, see Appendix III.) Probably what Kant had in mind here was the "mixed" logic which we saw in Leibniz (an author Kant frequently mentions) where we move back and forth easily between Categorical Syllogisms, Hypothetical Syllogisms, and Disjunctive Syllogisms, and where the antecedent and consequent of a conditional or the disjuncts of a disjunction can be "Every . . . ," "No . . . ," "Some . . . ," or "Some . . . not . . ." statements *or* statements about individuals. Thus, Kant might claim that every premise of every argument would have one of the following forms or some combination of them:

   I. Apodeictic
      A. Categorical
         1. Universal
            a. Positive S))P
            b. Negative S)(P
            c. Infinite ?
         2. Particular
            a. Positive S()P
            b. Negative S((P
            c. Infinite ?
         3. Singular
            a. Positive *N*))P
            b. Negative *N*)(P
            c. Infinite ?
      B. Hypothetical
         1. Universal
            a. Positive S))P > S()P
            b. Negative S)(P > S((P
            c. Infinite ?
         2. Particular
            a. Positive S()P > P()S
            b. Negative S((P > $\hat{P}$((Ŝ
            c. Infinite ?
         3. Singular
            a. Positive *N*))P > *N*()P
            b. Negative *N*)(P > *N*((P
            c. Infinite ?
      C. Disjunctive
         1. Universal
            a. Positive S))M ∨ M))P

        b. Negative S)(M ∨ M)(P
        c. Infinite ?
    2. Particular
        a. Positive S()M ∨ M()P
        b. Negative S((M ∨ S((P
        c. Infinite ?
    3. Singular
        a. Positive *N*))M ∨ *N*))P
        b. Negative *N*)(M ∨ *N*)(P
        c. Infinite ?

  II. Problematic
    A. Categorical
      1. Universal
        a. Positive ◇ [S))P]
        b. Negative ◇ [S)(P]
        c. Infinite ?
                    etc.

 III. Apodeictic
    A. Categorical
      1. Universal
        a. Positive □ [S))P]
        b. Negative □ [S)(P]
        c. Infinite ?
                    etc.

Except for the puzzle of what we should fill in for the question marks opposite "Infinite," all this makes perfectly good sense.

How does all this tie up with the Categories themselves? The Category of Quantity is relatively straightforward. To the *judgment* that every S is P corresponds to the fact that the totality of S's have property P, the judgment that no S is P corresponds to the fact that the totality of S's lack P (for example, "No duck is four-legged; look at the totality of ducks; all lack four legs").

The Category of Quality is partially clear; positive statements about things imply their reality; negative statements simply deny some reality. "Limitation" is explained no more clearly than the subcategory of "infinite" judgments.

In the fourth category, Modality, possibilities correspond to statements of possibility; existing things are the basis of assertions, and necessities correspond to statements of necessity. We begin to see that for Kant, the "architecture" of the universe and the types of things in it could be organized by using the logical categories of judgment as a guide.

But how do the categories of Relation correspond to judgments of relation? Remember that our "base" was the standard-form statements of Aristotelian logic. Thus, a "categorical" statement will always have a subject-predicate form, always affirm or deny a property of a subject. So "substances" and properties that "inhere" in those subjects correspond to simple categorical statements. In a causal relation we have a case where *if* "a" occurs *then* "b" occurs, so we can see why the logical subcategory of the hypothetical has become the category of Causality.

But what about Community? The explanatory parentheses say "reciprocity between agent [what acts] and patient [what is acted on]." Kant's thought here seems to be that any agent/patient situation can be described in *either* of two ways; for example, "Johnny hit the ball" *or* "The ball was hit by Johnny." But this is one of the weakest transitions from logic to the world: Surely not all "either-or" relationships are reciprocal in this sense.

Can we make any sense at all of the logical subcategory of Infinity and the corresponding subcategory of Limitation? Kant's example of an "infinite" judgment is "the soul is nonmortal," of which he says:

> . . . *infinite judgments* must, in transcendental logic, be distinguished from those that are *affirmative*, although in general logic they are rightly classed with them, and do not constitute a separate member of the division. General logic abstracts from all content of the predicate (even though it be negative); it enquires only whether the predicate be ascribed to the subject or opposed to it. But transcendental logic also considers what may be the worth or content of a logical affirmation that is thus made by means of a merely negative predicate, and what is thereby achieved in the way of addition to our total knowledge. If I should say of the soul, "It is not mortal," by this negative judgment I should at least have warded off error. Now by the proposition, "The soul is non-mortal," I have, so far as the logical form is concerned, really made an affirmation. I locate the soul in the unlimited sphere of non-mortal beings. Since the mortal constitutes one part of the whole extension of possible beings, and the non-mortal the other, nothing more is said by my proposition than that the soul is one of the infinite number of things which remain over when I take away all that is mortal. The infinite sphere of all that is possible is thereby only so far limited that the mortal is excluded from it, and that the soul is located in the remaining part of its extension. But, even allowing for such exclusion, this extension still remains infinite, and several more parts of it may be taken away without the concept of the soul being thereby in the least increased, or determined in an affirmative manner. These judgments, though infinite in respect of their logical extension, are thus, in respect of the content of their knowledge, limitative only, and cannot therefore be passed over in a transcendental table of all moments of thought in judgments, since the function of the understanding thereby expressed may perhaps be of importance in the field of its pure *a priori* knowledge.[5]

But this just seems wrong whether we interpret "the soul is nonmortal" as "S))M" or "S))M"; in either case it is simply equivalent to a *negative* judgment "S)(M" or "S)(M." The supposed category of "infinite" statements is not positive at all; it collapses into a negative statement. Kant seems partly to realize this when he says of the subcategory of Limitation that "*limitation is simply reality combined with negation.*" It does not help much to be told that

[5] *Critique* I First Part, First Division, Chapter 11, Section 1 (A72, B97).

Thus *allness* or *totality* is just plurality considered as unity; *limitation* is simply reality combined with negation; *community* is the causality of substances reciprocally determining one another; lastly, *necessity* is just the existence which is given through possibility itself. It must not be supposed, however, that the third category is therefore merely a derivative, and not a primary, concept of the pure understanding. For the combination of the first and second concepts, in order that the third may be produced, requires a special act of the understanding, which is not identical with that which is exercised in the case of the first and the second.[6]

I conclude, then, that Kant's attempt to derive categories from the kind of logic available to him is an interesting failure. There is a fair amount of correspondence between the logical categories and subcategories and the "ontological" categories and subcategories, but the correspondence breaks down at points. "Infinity" is a false subcategory, and there seems no real correspondence between Disjunction and Community, especially if Community is to be "the causality of substances mutually determining each other."

Kant's procedure also is open to an interesting objection: The kind of "metalogical" statements he makes *about* the Categories do not fall into any of the logical categories, just as the Categories themselves are not the kind of thing that come under the Categories (that is, they are not substances, causes, etc.). In one sense Kant should welcome this result; it reinforces his view that we cannot talk or think *about* such categories as Causality, only *apply* these categories to phenomena. But how is the talking and thinking that Kant does in analyzing and describing the Categories to be legitimized? The dilemma for Kant is this: If his own theorizing about the Categories is to be legitimate, why cannot other theoretical employments of them be legitimized? And if every kind of theorizing about "pure concepts" is suspect, why is Kant's theorizing legitimate? Whether Kant can give a convincing answer to this dilemma is one of the most crucial questions about his philosophy.

EXERCISES

A. Translate the following statements into the symbolism of propositional modal logic, and check the truth of the starred assertions that appear before each group. (*Source*: Aristotle, *On Interpretation*.)

*A The following pairs must be considered as five contradictory pairs.

  1. It may be   It cannot be
  2. It is possible   It is not possible

[6] *Critique* I, First Part, First Division Chapter 11, Section 3 (B111).

3. It is impossible   It is not impossible
4. It is necessary   It is not necessary
5. It is true   It is not true

*B   From the statements on the left, those on the right follow.

6. It may be   It is possible
                            It is not impossible
                            It is not necessary
7. It is possible   It may be
8. It may not be   It is not necessary that it should not be
                            It is not impossible that it should not be
9. It is not possible   It is necessary that it should be
                            It is impossible that it should not be
10. It cannot not be   It is necessary that it should be
                            It is impossible that it should not be

*C   The expressions in the following group are all equivalent.

11. It may be
12. It is possible
13. It is not impossible that it should be
14. It is not necessary that it should be

*D   The expressions in the following group are all equivalent.

15. It cannot be
16. It is not possible
17. It is impossible that it should be
18. It is necessary that it should not be

*E   The following group are all equivalent.

19. It may not be
20. It is possible that it should not be
21. It is not impossible that it should be
22. It is not necessary that it should not be

*F   The following group are all equivalent.

23. It cannot not be
24. It is not possible that it should not be
25. It is impossible that it should not be
26. It is necessary that it should be

*G   The statements on the left are contradictories of those on the right.

27. It is impossible   It may be
                                                It is possible
28. It is not impossible that it should be   It cannot be
                                                It is not possible

*H   The following pair are contraries.

29. It is necessary   It is impossible

*I   The following pair are subcontraries.

30. It may be   It may not be

B. These exercises are intended to give practice in the use of repeated modal operators and do not bear directly on the differences between the systems. Translate from English to symbols, using the dictionary:

G # God exists   E # Evil exists   F # Freedom exists

1. It is possible that it is necessary that God exists.
2. If it is possible that freedom exists, then it is necessary that it is possible that evil exists.
3. If God exists, then, if it is possible that evil exists, it is necessary that it is necessary that evil exists.
4. If it is possible that it is necessary that God exists, then it is necessary that it is possible that evil exists.
5. If it is necessary that God exists, then it is necessary that it be possible that freedom exists.
6. If it is necessary that freedom exists, then it is possible that it is necessary that God exists.
7. If it is necessary that evil exists, then it is not necessary that it is necessary that God exists.
8. If it is possible that it is necessary that evil exists or possible that it is necessary that freedom exists, then it is possible that it is not necessary that God exists.
9. If it is possible that, if God exists, then freedom exists, then it is possible that it is necessary that evil exists.
10. If it is necessary that, if God exists, then freedom exists, then it is necessary that it is possible that it is necessary that evil exists.

C. Symbolize and provide proofs for the following, using the techniques of this chapter.

1. A perfect being exists and exists necessarily or does not exist and does not exist necessarily. A perfect being is possible. Therefore it exists.
2. A perfect being exists necessarily or does not exist necessarily. A perfect being possibly may not exist. Therefore it does not exist.
3. A perfect being, if it exists at all, exists necessarily. A perfect being possibly may not exist; therefore it does not exist.
4. A perfect being exists necessarily if it exists at all, and such a being is possible. If it is true that, if a perfect being exists at all, it exists necessarily, then, if it is possible that it should exist, it exists. Therefore, a perfect being exists.
5. A perfect being either exists and exists necessarily or exists and possibly may not exist or does not exist and does not exist necessarily or does not exist and may exist. If such a being exists at all, it exists necessarily. Such a being is possible. Therefore, it exists.

D. 1. Construct an argument using statements from exercises A or B as premises.
    2. Argue for or against the premises of one of the arguments in exercise C.

9

Analyzing Philosophical Arguments

We are now ready to put together what we have learned so far and use it in the analysis of philosophical arguments taken in their original context rather than cut up and "packaged" as exercises. We will develop several standard patterns into which philosophical arguments can be put in order to display their structure and also to make sure that every part of the argument receives proper attention.

Let us begin with an argument that was given at the end of the last chapter. I came to the conclusion that Kant's scheme of categories was a failure (I said "an interesting failure" but will drop the adjective for the sake of simplicity). This is what we call a *thesis*, a claim that needs to be proved. Often in a thesis there are one or more terms that need to be clarified: This can best be done by a *definition*, formal or informal. We can expand the meaning of "failure" in this context as follows:

> A philosophical theory is a *failure* when it does not carry out the claims or intentions, explicit or implicit, of its author.

We can now present in outline the *argument* given in support of the thesis, giving the *explicit premises*, any *assumed premises*, and the *conclusion*. My argument could be reconstructed as follows:

If some of the categories are not independent of others and some of the logical categories do not really lead to the ontological categories, then Kant has not carried out his claims and intentions.

If Kant has not carried out his claims and intentions, his theory of categories is a failure.

Some categories are not independent of others.

Some of the logical categories do not really lead to the ontological categories.

Therefore, Kant's theory of categories is a failure.

We now have to put the argument in symbolic form and test it for validity, and if valid give a proof. Let

I # Every category is independent of every other

L # Every logical category leads to the corresponding ontological category

C # Kant has carried out his claims and intentions

F # Kant's theory of categories is a failure

Then the argument is

$$1 \; (\hat{I} \wedge \hat{L}) > \hat{C}$$
$$2 \; \hat{C} > F \qquad \text{Conclusion: F}$$
$$3 \; \hat{I}$$
$$4 \; \hat{L}$$

The argument cancels to its conclusion:

$$1 \; (\hat{I} \wedge \hat{L}) > \hat{C}$$
$$2 \; \hat{C} > F \qquad \hat{I} \text{ cancels } \hat{I} >$$
$$3 \; \hat{I} \qquad\quad\; \hat{L} \text{ cancels } \hat{L} >$$
$$4 \; \hat{L} \qquad\quad\; > \hat{C} \text{ cancels } \hat{C} >$$
$$\text{leaving F}$$

The proof is as follows

$$1 \ (\hat{I} \wedge \hat{L}) > \hat{C}$$

$$2 \ \hat{C} > F$$

$$3 \ \hat{I}$$

$$4 \ \hat{L}$$

5 $\hat{I} \wedge \hat{L}$ 3,4 Conj

6 $\hat{C}$ 1,5 M.P.

7 F   2,6 M.P.

Thus, the argument is valid. We next need to give *reasons* in support of any premises that need support:

Premise 1: Because Kant has claimed that each category is independent of the others and that each logical category leads to the corresponding onto-logical category, it is clear that if either or both of these claims is false then Kant has not carried out his claims and intentions.

Premise 2: This is true by the definition of "failure" we have given.

Premise 3: The logical category of the "Infinite" reduces to the category "Negation"; thus they are not independent, and the ontological category of Limitation is by Kant's own admission a combination of Reality and Negation.

Premise 4: The logical category of Disjunction is too weak to lead to the ontological category of Community; not all "either . . . or" relations are re-lations of "reciprocal causation."

FORM A

Eventually we will expand this schema to take account of objections and replies to the objections. But for the moment let us lay out the steps we have gone through:

1. Thesis
2. Definition of Key Term(s)
3. Explicit Premises
4. Assumed Premise(s) (if any)
5. Conclusion (same as thesis)
6. Symbolization
7. Cancellation check for validity
8. Proof
9. Support for premises
(10. Objections and replies)

These ten steps will apply to any deductive argument: We will call this schema *Form A* and use it to analyze a variety of deductive arguments. An argument can turn out to be a bad one at any of these steps:

1. It may not have a clear *thesis*.
2. Some key term may be so vague or ambiguous that it cannot be *defined*, or cannot be defined in a way useful for the argument.
3. When we try to find *explicit premises*, there may be none, or none that can be clearly stated.
4. The argument may need *assumed premises* that cannot be supplied for one reason or another.
5. There may be no *conclusion* from the argument, or a conclusion different from the thesis.
6. When we begin to *symbolize* the argument we may find difficulties not apparent in the ordinary language form.
7. The argument may not be *valid* by cancellation.
8. There may be problems in the *proof*.
9. There may be no good *supporting arguments* for the premises.
10. Some *objection* to the supporting arguments may be convincing and no *reply* to it can be found.

On the other hand, if an argument passes all these tests, it is likely to be a good one; our only reservation will be that we may eventually discover *further* objections that will undermine the supporting arguments for the premises. A Form-A argument can be used with syllogistic logic or mixed-statement and syllogistic logic, as well as with statement logic, though our example used statement logic. In some cases, elements may be left out; for example, there may be no assumed premises or no terms in need of definition.

Let us now turn to the application of Form A to some "live" arguments. First consider an argument that can be dealt with by Form A. In a famous paper the American philosopher Norman Malcolm argued as follows:

> If God . . . does not exist then He cannot *come* into existence. For if He did He would either have been *caused* to come into existence or have *happened* to come into existence, and in either case He would be a limited being, which by our conception of Him He is not. Since He cannot come into existence, if He does not exist His existence is impossible. If He does exist He cannot have come into existence (for the reasons given), nor can He cease to exist, for nothing could cause Him to cease to exist nor could it just happen that He ceased to exist. So if God exists His existence is necessary. Thus God's existence is either impossible or necessary. It can be the former only if the concept of such a being is self-contradictory or in some way logically absurd. Assuming that this is not so, it follows that He necessarily exists.[1]

[1]Norman Malcolm "Anselm's Ontological Argument," *Philosophical Review* Vol. LXIX 1960.

We can reconstruct the argument as follows:

1. Thesis: God exists

2. Definition of key terms:
   God: the all-powerful, all good being who always exists

3. Explicit premises:

(1). If God does not exist, it is not possible that God begins to exist.

(2). If it is not possible that God begins to exist, then either God exists or it is not possible that God exists.

(3). It is possible that God exists.

4. Assumed premises: none

5. Conclusion: God exists

6. Symbolization: Let

$$G \# \text{God exists}$$

$$P \# \text{It is possible that God exists}$$

$$B \# \text{It is possible that God begins to exist}$$

$$(1)\ \hat{G} > \hat{B}$$

$$(2)\ \hat{B} > (G \vee \hat{P})$$

$$(3)\ P$$

7. Cancellation check

$$(1)\ \hat{G} > \hat{B} \qquad > \hat{B} \text{ cancels } \hat{B}>$$

$$(2)\ \hat{B} > (G \vee \hat{P}) \qquad P \text{ cancels } \hat{P}$$

$$(3)\ P \qquad \hat{G} > \text{ becomes } G$$

$$\text{Two G's are left}$$

Argument cancels to conclusion

8. Proof

$$(1)\ \hat{G} > \hat{B}$$

$$(2)\ \hat{B} > (G \vee \hat{P})$$

$$(3)\ P$$

(4) $\hat{G} > (G \vee \hat{P})$ (1),(2) H.S.

(5) $\hat{\hat{G}} \vee G \vee \hat{P}$ (4) C.I.

(6) $G \vee G \vee \hat{P}$ (5) D.N.

(7) $G \vee G$ (3),(6) D.S.

(8) G (7) Rep.

9. Support for premises:

(1) As Malcolm argues, if God did not exist, God would either have to begin to exist by being caused or just happen to begin to exist: Either is incompatible with the concept of God.

(2) If God *can't* begin to exist, then either God necessarily *does* exist or else God *can't* exist: There seems to be no other alternative.

(3) As Malcolm says, the only grounds we could have for saying that God's existence is not possible would be that God's existence was self-contradictory. But there is no discernible self-contradiction in the concept of God.

10. Objections:

Objection 1: The symbolization fails to capture the argument; we need the notion that God's existence is necessary. If N # God exists necessarily then the argument is

(1) $\hat{G} > \hat{B}$

(2) $\hat{B} > (N \vee \hat{P})$

(3) P

and Malcolm's conclusion is "N." The argument does not cancel to this conclusion.

Reply to Objection 1: The valid version of the argument given is quite strong enough for most purposes. However, if we accept the suggested revision we need merely add an assumed premise:

(4) $N > G$

and prove G as follows:

(1) $\hat{G} > \hat{B}$

(2) $\hat{B} > (N \lor \hat{P})$

(3) P

*(4) N > G

(5) $\hat{G} > (N \lor \hat{P})$ (1),(2) H.S.

(6) $\hat{G} \lor N \lor \hat{P}$ (5) C.I.

(7) $\hat{G} \lor N$ (6),(3) D.S.

(8) $G \lor N$ (7) D.N.

(9) $\hat{N} \lor G$ (4) Cl

(10) $G \lor G$ (8),(9) C.C.

(11) G   (10) Rep

It is conceded that the argument as given doesn't prove "N", but there is no need to, and Malcolm can be interpreted as merely saying that "G" *follows* necessarily from the premises. If the stronger conclusion "N" is desired we might appeal to an additional assumed premise

$$G > N$$

and justify it by arguments that are an extension of Malcolm's line of argument about God *ceasing* to exist. A subproof would be:

Let C # God possibly ceases to exist

(1) $G > (\hat{C} > N)$ P

(2) $\hat{C}$ P

(3) $(G \land \hat{C}) > N$ (1) Exp.

(4) $(\hat{C} \land G) > N$ (3) Com.

(5) $\hat{C} > (G > N)$ (4) Exp.

(6) $G > N$ (2),(5) M.P.

The premises could be justified by Malcolm's argument "Nothing could cause Him to cease to exist nor could it just happen that He ceased to exist," based on the definition of God given at the beginning of our analysis.

Objection 2: The terms "necessary" and "possible" are being used ambiguously and nothing follows as to the actual existence of God. From the *logical* possibility of God and the fact that by definition *if* God exists then God is causally independent we cannot infer that God actually exists. Specifically in premise (3) and its justification, "possible" is taken in the merely logical sense, whereas in the consequence of premise (2) and in the subargument for "G > N" the terms "possible" and "necessary" are taken in the sense of "ontological" possibility and necessity.

Reply to Objection 2: This is one of the most serious criticisms of the Ontological Argument: Its defenders must either deny the ambiguity or show that God is possible in the sense of ontological possibility. Both courses have difficulties and the argument continues.

Another possible version of the argument has the same thesis and definition, but continues as follows:

3. Explicit premises:

(1). If it is possible that God exists, but God does not exist, then it is possible that God begins to exist.

(2). It is possible that God exists.

(3). It is not possible that God begins to exist.

4. Assumed premises: none

5. Conclusion: God exists

6. Symbolization: Let

G # God exists

P # It is possible that God exists

B # It is possible that God begins to exist

$$(1)\ (P \wedge \hat{G}) > B$$
$$(2)\ P$$
$$(3)\ \hat{B}$$

7. Cancellation check

$(1)\ (P \wedge \hat{G}) > B$	P cancels P >
$(2)\ P$	$\hat{B}$ cancels > B
$(3)\ \hat{B}$	$\hat{G} >$ becomes G

Argument cancels to conclusion.

8. Proof

(1) $(P \wedge \hat{G}) > B$

(2) P

(3) $\hat{B}$

(4) $P > (\hat{G} > B)$ (1) Exp.

(5) $\hat{G} > B$ (2),(4) M.P.

(6) $\hat{\hat{G}}$ (3),(5) M.T.

(7) G (6) D.N.

9. Support for premises

(1). Surely it is true in general that if something possibly exists and does not exist then it is possible that that thing should begin to exist. If this is true in general it must be true of God.

(2). There seems to be no contradiction in the concept of God: Surely it is *possible* that such a being exists.

(3). Since God is, by definition, eternal, surely it is contradictory to say that it is possible that God *begins* to exist.

10. Objections and Replies:

Objection 1: The argument proves too much. Consider some very feeble and far from divine being that has existed from eternity: Call this being the Eternal Mariner. Precisely the same argument would prove the existence of the Eternal Mariner: All we need to do is substitute "Eternal Mariner" for "God" throughout the argument.

Reply to Objection 1: The Eternal Mariner, so far as the idea is clear, seem to be *contingently* eternal; so it is *possible* that the Eternal Mariner *could* have had a beginning. Thus Premise (3) is false for the Eternal Mariner. God, however, by nature could not be anything but eternal, so Premise (3) is true for God.

Objection 2: The justification of Premise (1) is faulty, since some things that *might* have existed but don't are such that they *couldn't* have a beginning. So the general principle is not true and we cannot apply it to the case of God.

Reply to Objection 2: Anything that *could* not begin to exist would either be impossible, in which case the first conjunct of the antecedent of the general principle would not be satisfied, or it would be the same as God, which merely reinforces the argument. . . .

There is, of course, a great deal more to be said on both sides of the argument, but we will break off the example here. The point of this illustration is that some quite sophisticated arguments have a fairly simple logical structure and that we can identify the points at issue clearly and conveniently by putting the argument in deductive form.

FORM B

Let us now look at a similar schema, *Form B*, for *inductive* arguments. Our example for Form B will be an argument that miracles occur, given the testimony we have.

1. Thesis: Accept the hypothesis that miracles occur on the evidence of testimony available.

2. Definition: *Miracle*: A suspension of the laws of nature caused by God.

3. Summary of evidence: Stories of miracles have been told by witnesses who were in a position to observe the alleged miracles and who often suffered persecution or death for their testimony.

4. Probability of the Hypothesis:
No numerical value, perhaps low but higher than that of the evidence if the opposing hypothesis is true.
Probability of the evidence if the hypothesis is true:
No numerical value, but high.
Probability of the evidence if the hypothesis is false:
No numerical value, but lower than the probability of the hypothesis.

5. Conclusion: Accept the hypothesis that miracles occur on the evidence available.

6. Symbolization:

$$M \ \# \ \text{Miracles occur}$$

$$T \ \# \ \text{Miracle stories are told}$$

$$\overline{M > T} \quad \text{is high}$$

$$\overline{\hat{M} > T} \quad \text{is low}$$

$$T$$

$$\overline{\hat{M} > T} \quad \text{is lower than } \overline{M}$$

$$\text{Accept } M$$

7. Probability of the hypothesis given the evidence:
   Unknown, since no numerical value.

8. Evaluation of the hypothesis: Accept: Nozick's Schema is satisfied.

9. Support for probabilities assigned:

   $\overline{M}$: <u>We can</u> concede that $\overline{M}$ is low, as long as it is higher than
   <u> $\hat{M} > T$</u>

   $M > T$: Of course, if miracles occur people would be excited by
   <u>   </u> them and tell about them.

   $\hat{M} > T$: There seems no adequate reason for people to give
   <u>   </u> accounts of miracles if they have not occurred.

   $\hat{M} > T < \overline{M}$: We cannot rule out the possibility of miracles if
   there are good reasons to think God exists, and
   there are such reasons. People would not lay themselves open to ridicule and persecution by telling
   false miracle stories. So $\hat{M} > T$ is not higher than
   $\overline{M}$, and may be considerably lower.

10. Objections and Replies:

    Objection: Hume's objections that people are quite likely to tell
    miracle stories even if miracles don't occur (see Chapter 7):
    Thus, $\overline{M}$ is not higher than $\hat{M} > T$ and Nozick's Schema cannot
    be used as Hume's Constraint is violated.
    Reply: Hume exaggerates the extent to which motives such as
    credulity will cause people to tell false miracle stories; thus,
    Hume's Constraint is *not* violated.

As can be seen from this example, the elements of Form B are:

1. Thesis

2. Definitions of key terms

3. Summary of evidence

4. Probability of the hypothesis,
   Probability of the evidence if the hypothesis is true,
   Probability of the evidence if the hypothesis is false.

5. Conclusion

6. Symbolization

7. Probability of the hypothesis if the evidence is observed

8. Evaluation of the hypothesis (accept or reject)

9. Support for probabilities assigned

10. Objections and replies

If we have numerical figures for the probabilities that we can defend, we will be able to give precise answers to 3, 4, and 5, and *calculate* 7 using Bayes' Theorem. However, in philosophy we rarely have exact numerical probabilities and we will usually use Nozick's Schema. Form B is applicable to either kind of case.

As there are no obviously correct philosophical examples of Form-B arguments where we have exact probabilities, consider a scientific case: Suppose that a certain test for AIDS detects 90 percent of those who have the disease, but gives a "false positive" result in 20 percent of cases. Suppose that only 1 percent of the population has AIDS. A person named Jan is tested and the test is positive. How worried should Jan be? (These figures are roughly correct for current AIDS tests, incidentally, though the percentage for AIDS victims in the population is too high).

1. Thesis: Reject the hypothesis that Jan has AIDS on the evidence of a positive result on the California Blot test.

2. California Blot test: A blood test for AIDS that consists of detecting by chemical means certain antibodies that are formed when the AIDS virus is present.

3. Summary of evidence: Reliability of test; detects 90 percent of those with AIDS, gives 20 percent false positives. Frequency of AIDS in population is stipulated to be one percent

4. Probability that Jan has AIDS: .01
Probability of a positive test result if Jan has AIDS: .9
Probability of a positive test result if Jan doesn't have AIDS: .2

5. Conclusion: Reject the hypothesis that Jan has AIDS on the evidence of a positive reaction on the California Blot test.

6. Symbolization:

J # Jan has AIDS

P # Jan has tested positive on California Blot test

$\bar{J} = .01$

$\overline{J > P} = .9$

$\overline{\hat{J} > P} = .2$

$$\overline{P > J} = \frac{\bar{J} \times \overline{J > P}}{\bar{P}}$$

$\bar{P} = (\bar{J} \times \overline{J > P}) + (\bar{\hat{J}} \times \overline{\hat{J} > P})$

$\bar{\hat{J}} = 1 - \bar{J}$

$\bar{P} = (.01 \times .9) + (.99 \times .2) = .207$

7. Probability of the hypothesis if the evidence is true:

$$\overline{P > J} = \frac{.01 \times .9}{.207} = \frac{.009}{.207} = .0434782$$

8. Evaluation of Hypothesis:

Reject the hypothesis as there is only about one chance in 20 that Jan has AIDS

9. Support for probabilities given:

References to medical literature

10. Objections and Replies:

Objection: Even though the probability is low, AIDS is so deadly that Jan and others concerned should accept the hypothesis "to be on the safe side." Reply: Jan and others should instead accept the limited hypothesis "There is about one chance in twenty that Jan has AIDS", and take precautions and seek further medical advice on the basis of *that* hypothesis.

Obviously this example is highly schematic: Things such as "references to medical literature" need to be filled in for the argument to have any force. But it gives us a fairly realistic picture of a Form-B argument where we have exact probabilities.

As in the case of Form A, the argument can fail at any stage: The thesis may be unclear or a definition impossible; we may not be able to give even an estimate of the probabilities or arrive at a judgment on the hypothesis on the evidence, or the calculation of the value of the hypothesis may give a result contrary to the thesis. The arguments in support of the probabilities assigned may be unsuccessful or the objections strong or not answerable.

For an example of an argument that we can analyze using Form B we turn to an argument against determinism by the American philosopher James N. Jordan:

Suppose that our assessments of arguments are the results of sufficient causal conditions whose complete statement involves no reference to "rational insight into a nexus between premises and conclusion," no mention of judgment "in accordance with objective laws or principles." Would it not be merely fortuitous if our assessments were in accord with what "objective laws or principles" prescribe as conditions for sound argumentation? Let us admit that the sufficient conditions of rational judgment need not be felt as compulsive foreign intrusions. Would there not still be a problem about knowing when, if ever, our assessments are reliable, if their sufficient conditions are logically indifferent to criteria of truth and validity?

Suppose we are asked to accept the proposition that all our rational assessments have sufficient—not just necessary—causal conditions. In order to show that we ought to believe this, someone would need to produce evidence which is seen to conform to criteria of reasonable trustworthiness and which is recognized to confer, by virtue of some principle of deductive or probable inference, certainty or sufficient probability upon it. But if the proposition is true, this could never happen, for it implies that whether anyone believes it and what he considers trustworthy evidence and acceptable principles of inference are determined altogether by conditions that have no assured congruence with the proposition's own merits or with criteria of sound argumentation whose validity consists of more than that we accept them. Whether we believe the proposition and what considerations we undertake before making a decision depend simply on sufficient and necessary causal conditions that logically need not be, and quite probably are not, relevant to the issues involved in assessing propositions for truth and arguments for validity. If our rational assessments are conditioned solely by factors whose exhaustive statement would omit mention of the recognized accordance of our deliberations with criteria of trustworthy evidence and correct inference, then the recognition of the relevance of these criteria is either inefficacious or absent. Of course, one still might occasionally believe what is true, but this would always be the outcome of happy circumstances, never of reasoned investigation. And if this is true of our rational assessment of any argument, it is true of our attempts to determine the strengths and weaknesses of any argument for the proposition in question. If the latter is true, any argument for it is self-defeating, for it entails that no argument can be known to be sound. The result was tersely expressed by A.E. Taylor: "Each of us, if we are to push the 'determinist' theory to its logical conclusion, thinks what he does think, and that is all there is to be said on the matter; which of us thinks *truly* is a question which, even if it has an intelligible meaning, is, and eternally must remain, without an answer.[2]

We can set up the argument as follows:

1. Thesis: Causal determinism should be rejected.

2. Definitions:
Causal determinism: the view that every event has a sufficient cause.

3. Evidence:

We can produce evidence for some views that conform to criteria of reasonable trustworthiness.

4. Probability of the hypothesis:

No numerical value, but higher than the probability that we could produce evidence that meets criteria of reasonable trustworthiness for any view if causal determinism were not rejected.

Probability of the evidence if the hypothesis is true:
No numerical value, but high.
Probability of the evidence if the hypothesis is false:
No numerical value, but very low.

5. Conclusion: Causal determinism should be rejected.

[2]James N. Jordan, "Determinism's Dilemma," *Review of Metaphysics* Vol. 23 (1969). Used by permission.

6. Symbolization

R # Causal determinism should be rejected

P # We can produce evidence for some views that conform to criteria of reasonable trustworthiness

$$\overline{R > P} \geq .95$$

$$\overline{\hat{R} > P} \leq .05$$

$$P$$

$$\overline{\hat{R} > P} < \overline{R}$$

Accept R

7. Probability of the hypothesis:
Unknown, since no numerical value.

8. Evaluation of the hypothesis:
Accept; Nozick's Schema is satisfied.

9. Support for probability assigned:

$\overline{R > P} \geq .95$: If, as we normally assume, we are free to consider evidence and come to a decision on the basis of that evidence then there is a very good chance that we will be able to find evidence that meets criteria of reasonable trustworthiness for some views.

$\overline{R > P} \leq .05$: If determinism were true, as Jordan argues, "whether anyone believes it and what he considers trustworthy evidence. . . are determined altogether by conditions which have no assured congruence with the proposition's own merits or with criteria of sound argumentation. . . one might still occasionally believe what is true, but this would always be the result of happy circumstances. . . ."

P: Unless we assume that we can produce evidence that meets reasonable criteria for some views, we can have no reason to accept any view, whether it be determinism or some other view. By the very fact of giving arguments, the determinist shows he or she accepts P.

$\overline{\hat{R} > P} < \overline{R}$: Since we have argued that $\hat{R} > P$ is very small, and the rejection of determinism had not shown to be very improbable, this inequality seems to hold.

10. Objections and Replies:

Objection 1: $\overline{R}$ is not especially high; in fact, it is very low, for that every event has a sufficient cause is a presupposition of science and carries with it the authority of science.

Reply to Objection 1: In fact, modern science, which accepts quantum indeterminacy, has *rejected* the principle that every event has a sufficient cause: Whatever the relevance of quantum indeterminacy to free will in general it certainly undercuts the appeal to the authority of science to support causal determinism.

Objection 2: $\hat{\overline{R}} > P$ is not especially low, for we can argue on scientific grounds that natural selection will favor the development of minds that accept hypotheses or reasonable criteria. Our minds are such minds and thus it is quite likely that even if causal determinism is true we will accept hypotheses that have evidence that meets reasonable criteria.

Reply to Objection 2: The theory of evolution by natural selection, whatever its other virtues or faults, contains an essential reference to *random* variation. Thus, it is incompatible with causal determinism.

Objection 3: The probability of $\overline{R} > P$ is not especially high: The mere fact that causal determinism is false does not mean that it is very probable that we can find good evidence for some hypotheses.

Reply to Objection 3: This is probably a point in Jordan's argument that needs more work. However, one can argue that the very concept of good evidence implies the possibility of being swayed *only* by the evidence, not by any nonrational factors. The falsity of causal determinism makes this possible, but admittedly does not *ensure* it: Additional argument may be necessary. Here we leave the argument to further philosophical discussion, having sufficiently made our logical points.

The exercises for this chapter contain a number of brief philosophical arguments. Decide whether Form A or Form B is appropriate for each argument if this is not indicated. Then give the thesis of the argument, define any key terms in need of definition, and summarize the argument or evidence. (In a Form-A argument there may be assumed premises. In a Form-B argument we assign probabilities before giving the conclusion.) After symbolizing in a Form-A argument we do a cancellation check for validity and give a proof; in a Form-B argument we calculate a probability for a Bayesian argument or assess the conclusion by the Nozick schema. Step 9 in a Form-A argument is supporting the premises; in a Form-B argument it is defending the probability assignments. The final step in either argument pattern is to consider objections and replies.

EXERCISES

A. Take one of the valid deductive arguments from the Exercises that follow Chapters 2 through 5 and set it up as a Form-A argument, defining key terms, distinguishing explicit and assumed premises, supporting the premises and giving objections and replies. (If you have already done this exercise as an assignment you should have a number of the components of Form A and will only need to expand and organize them.)

B. Take one of the inductive arguments from the Exercises that follow Chapters 6 and 7 and set it up as a Form-B argument, defining key terms, giving objections and replies and so on. (If you have done this exercise as an assignment you will already have a number of the components of Form B and will only need to expand and arrange them.)

C. Take one of the modal logic arguments from the Exercise that follows Chapter 8 and set up as far as possible as a Form-A argument. (You may not be able to do a cancellation check as we have no cancellation techniques for modal logic as such.)

D. The following excerpts are from a fictional dialogue between a dying philosopher, Gertrude Weirob, and her friend, Sam Miller. Miller is attempting to prove the possibility of survival after death and Weirob is raising objections. For each excerpt give a Form-A or Form-B analysis, reconstructing the argument, finding the conclusion if it is not expressed, and defining key terms.[3]

    1. WEIROB: You reason on the principle, "Same body, same self."

         MILLER: No, I do not claim that. But I also do not extend a principle, found reliable on earth, to such a different situation as is represented by the Hereafter. That a correlation between bodies and souls has been found on earth does not make it inconceivable or impossible that they should separate. Principles found to work in one circumstance may not be assumed to work in vastly altered circumstances. January and snow go together here, and one would be a fool to expect otherwise. But the principle does not apply in southern California.

    2. WEIROB: So the principle "Same body, same soul" is a well-confirmed regularity, not something you know "a priori." But if such judgments were really about souls, they would all be groundless and without foundation. For we have no direct method of observing sameness of soul, and so—we can have no indirect method either.

    3. MILLER: Your reasoning has some force. But I suspect the problem lies in my defense of my position, and not the position itself. Look here—there *is* a way to test the hypothesis of a correlation after all. When I entered the room, I expected you to react just as you did—argumentatively and skeptically. Had the person with this body reacted completely differently perhaps I would have been forced to conclude it was not you. For example, had she complained about not being able to appear on the six o'clock news, and missing Harry Reasoner, and so forth, I might eventually have been persuaded it *was* Barbara Walters and not you. Similarity of psychological characteristics—a person's attitudes, beliefs, memories,

   [3](*Source:* John Perry: *A Dialogue on Personal Identity and Immortality*). Hackett Publishing Company 1978 Used by permission of the publisher.

prejudices, and the like—is observable. These are correlated with identity of body on the one side, and of course with sameness of soul on the other. So the correlation between body and soul can be established after all by this intermediate link.

4. WEIROB: And so just because you judge as to personal identity by reference to similarity of states of mind, it does not follow that the mind, or soul, is the same in each case. My point is this. For all you know, the immaterial soul which you think is lodged in my body might change from day to day, from hour to hour, from minute to minute, replaced each time by another soul psychologically similar. You cannot see it or touch it, so how would you know?

5. MILLER: I see. But wait. I believe my problem is that I simply forgot a main tenet of my theory. The correlation can be established in my own case. I know that *my* soul and my body are intimately and consistently found together. From this one case I can generalize, at least as concerns life in this world, that sameness of body is a reliable sign of sameness of soul. This leaves me free to regard it as intelligible, in the case of death, that the link between the particular soul and the particular body it has been joined with is broken.

6. WEIROB: This would be quite an extrapolation, wouldn't it, from one case directly observed, to a couple of billion in which only the body is observed? For I take it that we are in the habit of assuming, for every person now on earth, as well as those who have already come and gone, that the principle "one body, one soul" is in effect.

7. MILLER: This does not seem an insurmountable obstacle. Since there is nothing special about my case, I assume the arrangement I find in it applies universally until given some reason to believe otherwise. And I never have been.

8. WEIROB: But I grant you that a single *person* has been associated with your body since you were born. The question is whether one immaterial soul has been so associated—or more precisely, whether you are in a position to know it. You believe that a judgment that one and the same person has had your body all these many years is a judgment that one and the same immaterial soul has been lodged in it. I say that such judgments concerning the soul are totally mysterious, and that if our knowledge of sameness of persons consisted in knowledge of sameness of immaterial soul, it too would be totally mysterious. To point out, as you do, that it is not mysterious, but perhaps the most secure knowledge we have, the foundation of all reason and action, is simply to make the point that it cannot consist of knowledge of identity of an immaterial soul.

9. WEIROB: Well, consider these possibilities. One is that a single soul, one and the same, has been with this body I call mine since it was born. The other is that one soul was associated with it until five years ago and then another, psychologically similar, inheriting all the old memories and beliefs, took over. A third hypothesis is that every five years a new soul takes over. A fourth is that every five minutes a new soul takes over. The most radical is that there is a constant flow of souls through this body, each psychologically similar to the preceding, as there is a constant flow of water molecules down the Blue River. What evidence do I have that the first hypothesis, the "single soul hypothesis," is true, and not one of the others? Because I am the same person I was five minutes or five years ago? But the issue in question is simply whether from sameness of person, which isn't in doubt, we can infer sameness of soul. Sameness of body? But how do I establish a stable relationship between soul and body? Sameness of thoughts and sensations? But they are in constant flux.

10. WEIROB: By the nature of the case, if the soul cannot be observed, it cannot be observed to be the same. Indeed, no sense has ever been assigned to the phrase "same soul." Nor could any sense be attached to it! One would have to say what a single soul looked like or felt like, how an encounter with a single soul at different times differed from encounters with different souls. But this can hardly be done, since a soul according to your conception doesn't look or feel like *anything* at all. And so of course "souls" can afford no principle of identity. And so they cannot be used to bridge the gulf between my existence now and my existence in the hereafter.

10

Constructing
a Philosophical Argument

You have now seen some ways of analyzing the arguments of others. But suppose that you wish to come up with an original philosophical argument for some conclusion that you believe is true but wish to establish more firmly both for yourself and for others. Both Aristotle, in his books *Topics* and *Prior Analytics*, and the medieval philosophers discussed this problem, but it has largely been neglected in recent logical work.

Aristotle, working with the syllogistic logic that he had developed, saw the problem as finding a common term to link two terms he wanted to put into a standard-form statement. Thus, to prove "Virtue is desirable" we would need to find a middle term that would fit into a syllogism of the pattern:

> Every X is desirable
>
> Every virtue is X
> ───────────────
> Every virtue is desirable.

which, of course, would be a valid Barbara syllogism. But how do we find an appropriate "x"? Aristotle suggested that we make a list of things that follow *from* virtue, and things that desirability follows from. Thus, if virtue is noble, praiseworthy, and helpful and if things that are enjoyable, profitable, or helpful are all desirable, we could notice that "helpful" appears on both lists and set up our Barbara syllogism as:

Every helpful thing is desirable

Every virtue is helpful

_____

Every virtue is desirable.

Similar considerations would apply if we were trying to reach a negative conclusion; for example, "No vice is desirable." If vice is ignoble, blameworthy, and unhelpful, then with the same list for "desirable" we could give the Celarent syllogism:

No unhelpful thing is desirable

Every vice is unhelpful

_____

No vice is desirable.

THE *PONS ASINORUM*

The medievals worked out these suggestions of Aristotle into a diagram of the various ways in which the major and minor terms of a syllogism could be combined with a middle term to achieve various kinds of conclusions. Remembering that on the medieval view the *A* statement implied the corresponding *I* statement, we can give this diagram as follows:

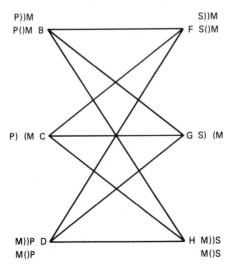

Most, though not all, of the horizontal and diagonal lines link premises that will yield a conclusion by the medieval rules. The ones that do are:

1	BG	P))M	3	CF	P)(M	6	DF	M))P
		S)(M			S))M			S))M
		———			———			———
		S)(P			S)(P			S))P

2	BH	P()M	4	CF	P)(M	7	DF	M))P
		M))S			S()M			S()M
		———			———			———
		S()P			S((P			S()P

5	CH	P)(M	8	DH	M))P
		M()S			S()M
		———			———
		S((P			S()P

Notice that this list contains almost all of the simplest and most basic syllogistic forms: Barbara, Celarent, Darii, Ferio, and the variations of Celarent and Darii where the order of positive/negative and universal/particular is reversed. It does *not* contain Baroco or Bocardo because these could not be obtained from the universal premises by Aristotelian methods.

But we can add these:

BG   P))M

S((M

———

S((P

CH   M((P

M))S

———

S((P

since in the medieval view we could obtain "S((M" from "S)(M" and "M((P" from P)(M. The medievals had memory rhymes to remember the valid combinations, but in our enlarged and simplified version of the diagram every combination occurs except the two horizontal lines across from each other, BF and CG. The BF combination is impossible because the middle term cannot be distributed; the CG because we would have two negative premises.

If all this seems complicated, it is humbling to remember that the medieval logicians called this diagram the *pons asinorum* or "donkey's bridge." The idea is that just as it is difficult to get a stubborn donkey to cross a bridge, it is hard to get a beginning student to master a complicated set of combinations like those in this diagram. But the medievals definitely regarded the "donkey's bridge" as something that only a "donkey" couldn't get over!

CONSTRUCTING ARGUMENTS

The *pons asinorum* is mainly of historical interest, but we sometimes face the problem of finding premises to justify a conclusion, and these Aristotelian and medieval techniques can give us a hint how to do so. For conclusions in the standard-form statements of syllogistic logic we can, in fact, use somewhat expanded and simplified versions of the *pons asinorum*.

However, we can also broaden the basic technique to other kinds of arguments. Consider how Crito might be pictured as thinking in his appeals to Socrates to escape from prison. "How can I convince this stubborn old man to escape? Well, if he doesn't what will be the consequences? His children will be left fatherless for one thing. Can I make that into an argument? Well, surely leaving the children fatherless will injure them, and injuring your children is unjust. So his not escaping will lead to injustice, and he doesn't want to do anything unjust. . . ." With a little more work we could arrive at one of the arguments attributed to Crito in Plato's dialogue.

Or consider the reasoning of the person who wishes to deny that the existence of God can be proved. Why not? Perhaps because he or she thinks the existence of God is a matter of faith and believes matters of faith cannot be proved. So the idea of a matter of faith is the link, the "middle term," between the idea of God and the idea of unprovability.

Let us give a more extended example of constructing a philosophical argument. Suppose that a philosophical feminist wants to show that women should be regarded and treated equally with men. She or he might start out with the conviction that it is *unfair* to treat women and men unequally because there is no difference between them that justifies unequal treatment. How could this conviction be turned into an argument that would convince others? The feminist might start with a statement of general principles:

If there are no differences between men and women that justify unequal treatment, it is unfair to treat them unequally.

If it is unfair to treat men and women unequally, then men and women should not be treated unequally.

These sound like principles no reasonable person could disagree with. But now how can we establish that there are no differences between men and women that justify unequal treatment? A good technique might be to consider alleged differences and show that none of them justify unequal treatment. A good general strategy might be to show that a given difference is not used as a basis for unequal treatment of men; therefore, it should not be used as a basis for unequal treatment of men and women.

For example, whether or not it is true that men on the average are physically stronger than women, weaker men are not generally given lower wages, fewer privileges, etc., than stronger men. Again, even if there were differences between the way men and women think, we do not in general allocate wages, privileges, etc., on the basis of *how* men think (though of course how *well* they think may be relevant to some raises, promotions, etc.).

Again, some people have suggested that women are more emotional than men, or that their wages are in general less essential to their households than are the wages of men. But we do not in general inquire into such factors in paying and promoting men. So we might begin to work out an argument pattern:

If X is not a basis for unequal treatment in the case of men, it should not be a basis for unequal treatment of men and women.

We might also give a premise that draws together various alleged justifications for unequal treatment:

If there are any differences between men and women that justify unequal treatment, they will be either physical, mental, emotional, or economic.

We then need a set of similar premises:

If physical differences between men are not a justification for unequal treatment, then physical differences between women are not.

Physical differences between men are not a justification for unequal treatment.

We go through similar steps for mental, emotional, and economic differences. At this stage we can draw together the argument and symbolize it as follows:

 J # There are differences between men and women that justify unequal treatment

 U # It is unfair to treat men and women unequally

S # Men and women should be treated unequally

P # Physical differences justify treating men and women unequally

Y # Physical differences justify treating men unequally

M # Mental differences justify treating men and women unequally

N # Mental differences justify treating men unequally

E # Emotional differences justify treating men and women unequally

O # Emotional differences justify treating men unequally

C # Economic differences justify treating men and women unequally

D # Economic differences justify treating men unequally

The argument can then be symbolized, and it can be seen that it cancels to the conclusion "$\hat{S}$" as follows:

1	$\hat{J} > U$	$> U$ cancels U
2	$U > \hat{S}$	$\hat{Y}$ cancels $> Y$
3	$J > (P \lor M \lor E \lor C)$	$P >$ cancels P
4	$P > Y$	$\hat{N}$ cancels $> N$
5	$\hat{Y}$	M cancels M $>$
6	$M > N$	$\hat{O}$ cancels $> O$
7	$\hat{N}$	E cancels E $>$
8	$E > O$	$\hat{D}$ cancels $> D$
9	$\hat{O}$	C $>$ cancels C
10	$C > D$	J $>$ becomes $\hat{J}$
11	$\hat{D}$	$\hat{J}$ cancels $\hat{J} >$ leaving $\hat{S}$

The conclusion can be proved as follows:

12	$\hat{P}$	4,5 M.T.
13	$\hat{M}$	6,7 M.T.
14	$\hat{P} \land \hat{M}$	12,13 Conj
15	$\overline{P \lor M}$	14 DeM
16	$\hat{E}$	8,9 M.T.
17	$\hat{C}$	10,11 M.T.

18	$\hat{E} \wedge \hat{C}$	11,12 Conj.
19	$\overline{E \vee C}$	13 DeM.
20	$\overline{P \vee M} \wedge \overline{E \vee C}$	15,19 Conj.
21	$\overline{P \vee M \vee E \vee C}$	20 DeM.
22	$\hat{J}$	3, 21 M.T.
23	U	1,22 M.P.
24	$\hat{S}$	2,23 M.P.

For a philosophical audience this argument could be set up as a Form-A argument, with terms defined and each premise defended. For a nontechnical presentation for a more general audience, however, it would be better to set up the argument more informally; for example:

> Any reasonable person should admit that if there are no differences between men and women that justify unequal treatment that it is unfair to treat men and women unequally. And if it is unfair to treat men and women unequally, we should not do it.
>
> What are some of the differences between men and women that have been alleged to justify unequal treatment? They fall under four general headings: physical, mental, emotional, and economic. We will take each one in turn and show that since this factor is not used as a basis for discrimination among *men* it is not reasonable to use it to discriminate between men and women.
>
> Consider the physical differences first. . . .
>
> We see, then, that none of the kinds of differences between men and women that have been alleged to justify unequal treatment do in fact justify unequal treatment. Thus, it seems that there are no differences between men and women that justify unequal treatment, and thus unequal treatment is unfair and ought not to exist.

It would take too much of this chapter to examine each kind of alleged difference in detail, but we can see the general strategy: For example, whether or not women's contributions to their households are less necessary than men's contribution to *their* households, the fact is that employers do not pay men more or less according to how necessary their contributions are to their households, and it is unfair to do so in the case of women.

This strategy avoids a great deal of factual debate about actual economic contributions of men and women to their respective households, and so on; the point is that if we don't consider this factor in the case of men we shouldn't consider it between women and men.

Form A concludes with objections and replies: In an informal presentation it might be a good idea to consider possible objections when each point is being argued, and answer each of them on the spot. Thus, for example, questions about differences between men and women based on the fact that women bear children might be considered along with the discussion of physical differences, and so on. The strongest objections should be anticipated and brought forward, for only in this way can we have any hope of convincing the readers of the argument that all the pros and cons have been considered, and that enough has been said to convince a reasonable person of the conclusion. Any attempt to weaken the objections by giving them in ways that do not do justice to the position will be counterproductive in the long run, since merely knocking down "men of straw" will not convince an intelligent reader.

STRATEGIES OF ARGUMENT

The technique we used of *dividing* possible differences and considering each one separately is related to some techniques proposed by Aristotle in the *Topics*. To prove a general truth he recommends subdividing it and arguing each subdivision separately, as we did in the argument above. If we arrive at a subdivision where we cannot prove the general thesis we can give our thesis in a modified form; for example, "Except for the special case of childbearing, there are no differences between men and women that give any plausible reasons for different treatment. . . ."

If we are trying to *dis*prove a general thesis then even one counterexample is enough to disprove the thesis, but the main thrust of the thesis can often be saved by modifying or qualifying the thesis. Thus, if a Republican was trying to claim that all major wars have started when a Democrat was in office, and the Civil War is brought up as a counterexample, the Republican could change the thesis to "all major *foreign* wars have started when a Democrat was in office". If the War of 1812 is used as counterexample, the thesis might be qualified again to: "Since the founding of the Democratic Party, every major foreign war has started when a Democrat was in office. . . ."

It may be that eventually a thesis will be so qualified as to lose all its force. However, in many cases a qualified thesis is merely more realistic and true to the facts; qualifying a thesis does not usually mean abandoning it.

Of course we rarely begin an argument completely from scratch: We have some idea of the relevant factors pro and con for most theses. It is often useful to list the pros and cons and then arrange them into arguments, objections, and replies. In an actual debate or discussion it may be quite useful to see what points are *not* in dispute and which points of agreement can be built on and which points of disagreement can be explored.

It is often both courteous and good psychology to emphasize agreements before going on to explore disagreements; for instance, "We are both agreed that unfair actions should not be done and that treating people unequally if there are no differences between them is unfair. With regard to physical differences, we agree that physical strength is not a major factor in most jobs, and that in fact women typically have more stamina than men. So now let us look at a major physical difference, that women bear children, and see if *it* justifies any unequal treatment and if so what kind. . . ."

Sometimes we may have to "agree to disagree" on some points and arrive at a limited agreement on a qualified thesis; for example, "We don't seem to be able to arrive at agreement on what is fair with regard to pregnancy leave, but we do seem to be agreed that while a woman is on the job she should receive equal pay for equal work. . . ." Such limited agreements may in fact be of more use than a situation where one side of an argument technically "wins" but leaves proponents of the other side unhappy and only superficially convinced.

This applies primarily to "live" arguments, but even in written arguments it is usually wise to limit oneself to the most moderate thesis one can honestly defend. The exception to this is the case where the thesis you wish to defend has been so ignored or underrated that only the strongest statement of it will secure attention and a moderate or qualified statement of the thesis would be disregarded. Even in such cases *over*stating your thesis is unwise; having to withdraw part of your thesis may discredit it. Thus, "There are *no* differences between men and women" is an overstatement. "Not a single difference between men and women justifies unequal treatment" is merely a strong unqualified statement of a thesis, and "Setting aside the matter of childbearing, no other difference between men and women can be shown to give reasonable grounds for unequal treatment" would be a qualified statement of the thesis.

It may often be good strategy to deny that you are defending an overstatement of a thesis and "set aside" parts of the thesis that for one reason or another cannot be debated then and there; for instance, "I am not saying that there are no differences between men and women, and I am not concerned now with the question of which differences are biological and which are due to social conditioning. What I do want to claim is that whatever differences exist do not justify the following kinds of unequal treatment. . . ."

Another strategy of effective argument is to give frequent illustrations and applications of general principles. An argument that is completely abstract will lose the attention of many readers or listeners. Great teachers often teach in parables, as Christ did, or, like Socrates, begin with the concrete situation in which their listeners find themselves. For example, before discussing righteousness and unrighteousness in general, Socrates listens to the details of Euthyphro's dispute with his father.

Thus, a good way to begin a discussion of the unequal treatment of women might be to cite some recent or striking case of unequal treatment, then show that it is typical and not unusual. A discussion of the existence of God for a popular audience might begin with some current statement or controversy.

For an audience of professional philosophers the starting point is typically the most recent philosophical work on a given topic, as it has appeared in recent books or articles in professional journals, though, of course, philosophers sometimes raise new issues or return to earlier controversies. Some articles in professional journals or philosophical monographs require considerable background, whereas others are relatively accessible even to beginners. The same is true of papers read at philosophical meetings. But even if a paper or an article is not entirely understandable to a beginner in philosophy it can be interesting to see how actual current philosophical arguments are carried on.

Many teachers prefer to use collections of articles originally published in philosophical journals as textbooks rather than single-author texts such as this one. This has many advantages, but the disadvantage is that the level of argument is often too high for beginners. With the experience of this book, however, it is to be hoped that you, the reader, will be prepared to handle actual philosophical arguments in their context and produce arguments of your own. The techniques of symbolism and proof you have learned should be useful for this purpose.

On the other hand, nonphilosophical audiences are likely to be confused by such symbols and techniques, and the logical arguments must form the backbone of a more informal exposition. Some of you may wish to explore further into the logical techniques themselves, but the logic in this book is intended primarily for *use* in analyzing and constructing arguments inside and outside of philosophy. If it is successfully used in this way, this book will have justified the work spent in writing it.

EXERCISES

A. State a thesis pro and con on each of the following topics, then give an overstatement of the thesis and a qualified statement of the thesis.
   1. The existence of God
   2. Whether we have free will
   3. Whether the soul survives death
   4. Whether life has meaning
   5. What the good life consists of
   6. What makes an act right or wrong
   7. The justifiability of abortion
   8. The justifiability of euthanasia
   9. The justifiability of war
   10. What we can know

B. Construct an argument, using Form A or Form B, for one of the theses that you developed in Exercise A.

C. Construct a counterargument to your own argument or someone else's argument on one of the theses developed in Exercise A. Make it clear which of your opponent's premises you can agree with and treat your opponent's arguments as objections to be answered.

D. Write a short essay stating what you have learned from studying this book.

I

Other Methods
of Checking Validity

In many introductory books on logic a *truth table*-method of checking for validity is used. First, the symbols such as ^, ∨, ∧, >, are *defined* in terms of their effect on the truth or falsity of statements. Thus, the definition of negation is written like this:

p	p̂
T	F
F	T

This says that by negation we *mean* an "operator" that gives a value of "false" if the original statement is true, and "true" if the original statement is false. To define "∨", "∧", ">", "<>", we must set up a systematic table of all possible combinations of truth values for the statements:

p	q
T	T
T	F
F	T
F	F

We thus define "∨" and "∧" as follows:

p q	p ∨ q	p ∧ q
T T	T	T
T F	T	F
F T	T	F
F F	F	F

This says that "∨" *means* a connective that gives a "true" value if one or both statements paired with it are true, and a "false" value only if both are false, whereas "∧" *means* a connective that gives a true value only if *both* statements joined by it are true, and a "false" value otherwise. Such definitions make the connectives *truth-functional*. Their meaning is a function of how they affect the truth value of a compound statement in which they are used.

In such a system the only workable definitions for ">" and "<>" are:

p q	p > q	p <> q
T T	T	T
T F	F	F
F T	T	F
F F	T	T

That is, a statement with ">" as a connective is false only if the first component is true and the second false, and true otherwise; and a statement with "<>" as a connective is true if the components have the same value and false otherwise.

This leads to paradoxical consequences. Any arbitrary false statement can be used as the first component in a statement of the form "p > q" and the statement will come out true whether the second component is true or false. Any two arbitrary true statements can be joined with ">" or "<>" to give a true statement. Any two arbitrary false statements can be joined with ">" or "<>" to give a true statement. These "paradoxes of material implication" and "paradoxes of material equivalence" seem highly counterintuitive to many philosophers.

For example, if

M # The moon is made of cheese

S # The sun is smaller than the moon

P # There are nine planets in our solar system

T # There are millions of stars

Then all of these statements will be *true* in a truth-functional system:

$$M > S$$
$$M > P$$
$$P > T$$
$$M <> S$$
$$P <> T$$

even though there is no real connection between the components.

To check an argument pattern for validity in a truth-functional system, we take the premises and join them with "∧," then join the premises to the conclusion with ">". Thus,

p > q		p > q
p	and	q
q		p

become

$$((p > q) ∧ p) > q \quad \text{and} \quad ((p > q) ∧ q) > p$$

We then write out all possible combinations of true and false for "p" and "q", and copy these under the letters as they occur in the statement forms:

p q	((p	>	q)	∧	p)	>	q	((p	>	q)	∧	q)	>	p
T T		T		T	T		T		T		T	T		T
T F		T		F	T		F		T		F	F		F
F T		F		T	F		T		F		T	T		F
F F		F		F	F		F		F		F	F		F

Thus, we use the truth-functional definitions of the connectives to fill in the values of compound statements, working out from the expressions inside the most parentheses: "p > q" first, then "(p > q) ∧ p", then the whole expression:

p q	((p > q) ∧ p) > q	((p > q) ∧ q) > p
T T	T T T T T T	T T T T T T
T F	T F F F T T F	T F F F F T T
F T	F T T F F T T	F T T T T F F
T T	F T F F F T F	F T F F F T F
	1 2 3	1 2 3

   Valid forms such as *Modus Ponens* will have nothing but "Ts" in the final column. Invalid forms, such as Affirming the Consequent, will have at least one "F".
   To check an equivalence to see if it is a logical rule, we write the two statements joined with "<>" (if the statements have separate lines, as in Conjunction, these are joined with "∧").
   Thus, the rule Transposition:

$$p > q$$
$$\overline{\overline{\hat{q} > \hat{p}}}$$

and the false equivalence:

$$p > q$$
$$\overline{\overline{q > p}}$$

would be written out:

p q	(p > q) <> (q̂ > p̂)	(p > q) <> (q > p)
T T	T T T T	T T T T
T F	T F F T	T F F T
F T	F T T F	F T T F
F F	F F F F	F F F F

We reverse the values of statements with a "^" above them and work from inside out as before:

p q	(p > q) <> (q̂ > p̂)	(p > q) <> (q > p)
T T	TT T T FTTFT	T TT T T TT
T F	TF F T TFFFT	T FF T F TT
F T	FT T T FTTTF	F TT F T FF
F F	FT T T TFTTF	F TF T F TF
	4　5　1 32	1　3　2

The equivalences that are rules have only "T"s in the final column; the false equivalences have at least one "F". All of the one-way and two-way rules in Chapter 2 check out as valid arguments or legitimate equivalences by truth table. However, in a truth-functional system *more* arguments and equivalences work out as valid or legitimate. Especially important are:

p	Addition	p > q	Definition
———	(Add.)	———	of Material
p ∨ q		p̂ ∨ q	Implication (D.M.I.)

p q	p > (p ∨ q)	(p> q)	<> (p̂ ∨ q)
T T	T TT T T	TTT	T FT T T
T F	T TT T F	TFF	T FT F F
F T	F TF T T	FTT	T TF T T
F F	F TF F F	FTF	T TF T F
	2　1	1	3　2

The effect of these rules is to make the paradoxes of material implication unavoidable even aside from truth-table justifications of them. For example, since the moon is *not* made of cheese, we can argue:

1 Ĝ	P
2 Ĝ ∨ S	1 Add.
3 G > S	2 D.M.I.

and

1	$\hat{G}$	P
2	$\hat{G} \vee P$	1 Add.
3	$G > P$	2 D.M.I.

Similar tactics give us the Paradoxes of Material Equivalence.

Another paradoxical consequence of Addition and Definition of Material Implication are the so-called Paradoxes of *Strict* Implication. For instance, from a contradictory premise we can "prove" *any* arbitrary conclusion:

1	$G \wedge \hat{G}$	P
2	G	1 Conj.
3	$\hat{G}$	1 Conj.
4	$G \vee S$	2 Add.
5	S	4,3 D.S.

So if we admit any contradictions into our system, absolutely anything is provable. Some see this as an advantage: It shows that admitting a contradiction leads to logical chaos!

The cancellation system of Chapter 2 does *not* contain the rules of Addition or Definition of Material Implication and thus *none* of the paradoxical consequences of truth-functional systems can be derived from the Chapter 2 system. The connectives of Chapter 2 are not intended to be truth-functional: our rule Consequence of Implication would have to become the two-way rule Definition of Material Implication.

In logic, it seems there are always disadvantages for every advantage: The system of Chapter 2 cannot show as valid certain intuitively plausible arguments; for example:

$$\frac{\hat{p}}{\bar{p \wedge q}}$$

which is closely related to Addition. As long as we keep Consequence of Implication as a one-way rule and reject the two-way rule Definition of Material Implication, we cannot get the full-scale paradoxes. So we *could* add Addition to our system. However, the Addition Rule is "ampliative": It enables us to introduce statements into the conclusion that were not in the premises. The spirit of the cancellation system is "eliminative." We take away statements but never add them. Thus, I prefer to keep Addition out of our system.

One result of this is that we cannot have certain techniques that are used in many systems of logic; for example, Conditional Proof and Reduction Proof, for if we introduce these, the Addition Rule can be proved. However, we *can* show something that is part of Reduction proofs, namely that any statement which implies a contradiction is false. The proof is as follows:

$$
\begin{array}{lll}
1 & p > (q \wedge \hat{q}) & P \\
2 & p > q & 1 \text{ I.A.} \\
3 & p > \hat{q} & 1 \text{ I.A.} \\
4 & \hat{q} > \hat{p} & 2 \text{ Transp.} \\
5 & p > \hat{p} & 3,4 \text{ H.S.} \\
6 & \hat{p} \vee \hat{p} & 5 \text{ C.I.} \\
7 & \hat{p} & 6 \text{ Rep.}
\end{array}
$$

With this and other techniques available in our system, the loss of power compared to more standard systems of logic is, in my view, more than compensated for by the elimination of paradox.

EXERCISES

1. Check out all of the Rules of Chapter 2 by truth table and show that all of them are justified by the truth-table method.
2. Take all invalid arguments mentioned in Chapter 2 and show they are invalid by truth-table methods.
3. Redo the exercises in Chapters 2 and 3, showing validity or invalidity by truth table instead of cancellation.

II

Predicate Logic and Recent Philosophy

Predicate logic is a logical system developed largely within the last century. It can give proofs and tests for validity within the realm of syllogistic logic, and the "mixed" logic discussed in Chapter 5, but it can also do a great deal more. As ordinarily developed, it depends on a truth-functional statement logic (see Appendix I) and as a result has certain paradoxical features, but these are not essential to predicate logic as such. In this Appendix we will give a brief survey of predicate logic and show what it can do and some of its philosophical applications and implications.

The crucial idea of predicate logic is of a *quantifier* that *binds* a *variable*. Consider the four standard-form statements of syllogistic logic:

Every S is P

No S is P

Some S is P

Some S is not P

We express the idea of "Every S is P" in predicate logic by a formula that says in effect "Take anything whatsoever if *that* thing has the characteristic of being S then it has the characteristic of being P." The "take anything whatsoever" is expressed by the quantifier "(x)". The two occurrences of *"that* thing," which refers back to the "anything," are expressed by two "x's" that are "within the scope" of that quantifier; we signal this "scope" by a left parenthesis after the quantifier at which the scope begins, and a right parenthesis at which the scope ends. Thus, "Every S is P" is written:

$$(x)(Sx > Px)$$

with our familiar ">" doing the work of the "if . . . then" in "For anything whatsoever *if* that thing is S *then* that thing is P."

To express the negative universal statement "No S is P" we write

$$(x)(Sx > \hat{P}x)$$

that is, "For anything whatsoever if that thing is S then that thing is not P." This should remind us of the obverse form of "No S is P," which is "Every S is non-P." The particular standard-form statements are expressed with another quantifier, "[x]", which we read as "for at least one thing." So "Some S is P" becomes

$$[x](Sx \wedge Px)$$

but, "for at least one thing that thing is S *and* that thing is P." Similarly, "Some S is not P" becomes

$$[x](Sx \wedge \hat{P}x)$$

that is, "For at least one thing that thing is S *and* that thing is not P."

Several things look odd about this notation. Here both the terms "S" and "P", which were subject and predicate in syllogistic logic, become predicatelike. In "Every human is mortal," "human" is a subject term, but in the predicate-logic form "human" becomes a predicate of "that thing."

There are true subject terms in predicate logic: Proper names are still subject terms. We would write "Socrates is human" as "Hs." This emphasizes the typographical oddities: Proper names that are capitalized and come before predicate terms in ordinary English are lower case and come *after* the predicate in predicate-logic notation. This is an historical accident; the developers of predicate logic were influenced by analogies with mathematical expressions. It does make predicate-logic expressions a little harder for the beginner to get used to.

Note that the scope of the quantifier must always be indicated by parentheses. Thus,

$$(x)Fx > Gx$$

might mean either:

$$(x)(Fx > Gx) \quad \text{or} \quad (x)(Fx) > Gx$$

In the second expression, "Gx" would be like a pronoun with no expression to refer back to: It would be puzzling or meaningless. Some systems allow expressions such as

$$(x)Px$$

to stand without parentheses, indicating scope, as there is no ambiguity, but we will use parentheses even in such cases "(x)(Px)" not "(x)Px."

Suppose now we have the simple Barbara syllogism:

> **Every human is mortal.**
>
> **Every Athenian is human.**
> _____
> **Every Athenian is mortal.**

$$\begin{aligned} \text{if} \quad &Hx \ \# \ x \text{ is Human} \\ &Mx \ \# \ x \text{ is Mortal} \\ &Ax \ \# \ x \text{ is Athenian} \end{aligned}$$

this would be

$$(x)(Hx > Mx)$$
$$(x)(Ax > Hx)$$
$$\overline{(x)(Ax \quad Mx)}$$

It looks like a simple Hypothetical Syllogism argument, but what about the quantifiers? What would we do about:

$$(x)(Hx > Mx)$$
$$[x](Ax > Hx)$$
$$\overline{}$$

What would the conclusion look like?

There are various ways of solving such difficulties, but the most practical solution seems to be a way of *dropping* quantifiers, working with the resulting expressions as if they were ordinary statement-logic expressions and then *restoring* the appropriate quantifier. The device we will use is this: To drop a quantifier we eliminate it and put the appropriate style of parentheses around each variable that quantifier bound. Then at the end of the argument we can restore that style of quantifier in front of the expression. For example, we would write out our first syllogism as:

1 (x)(Hx > Mx)

2 (x)(Ax > Hx)

3 H(x) > M(x)   1 Q.D. (Quantifier Drop)

4 A(x) > H(x)   2 Q.D.

5 A(x) > M(x)   3,4 H.S.

6 (x)(Ax > Mx)   5 Q.R. (Quantifier Restore)

To deal with our second syllogism we need the principle that *round* parentheses can be changed to *square* parentheses, but not vice versa. We will call this Universal to Particular (U.P.).

The second syllogism would then work this way:

1 (x)(Hx > Mx)   P

2 [x](Ax > Hx)   P

3 H(x) > M(x)   1 Q.D.

4 A[x] > H[x]   2 Q.D.

5 H[x] > M[x]   3 U.P.

6 A[x] > M[x]   4,5 H.S.

7 [x](Ax > Mx)   6 Q.R.

Notice we can *only* restore square brackets; the road from round brackets to square brackets is one way.

To deal with arguments about individuals we need a rule that says we can replace variables in round brackets ("universal" variables) with any proper name, and replace any proper name with a variable in square brackets, ("particular" variables) *as long as* every occurrence of the universal variable is replaced with the *same* name and every name is replaced with the *same* particular variable.

This enables us to deal with the argument:

> Every Athenian is mortal.
>
> Socrates is an Athenian.
> _____
> Socrates is mortal.

if S # Socrates

1	(x)(Ax > Mx)	P
2	As	P
3	A(x) > M(x)	1 Q.D.
4	As > Ms	3 U.N. (Universal to Name)
5	Ms	4,2 M.P.

We can also deal with the argument

> Socrates is human.
>
> Socrates is Athenian.
> _____
> Some human is Athenian.

as follows:

1	As	P
2	Hs	P
3	As ∧ Hs	1, 2 Conj.
4	A[x] ∧ H[x]	3 N.P. (Name to Particular)
5	[x](Ax ∧ Hx)	

Thus far we have had only arguments that could easily be dealt with by syllogistic logic, though the last requires a slight expansion of standard syllogistic logic. But now consider the argument:

> If any Athenian is a goddess, then some Athenian is not mortal.
>
> Every human is mortal.
>
> Athena is an Athenian goddess.
> _____
> Some Athenian is not human.

if a # Athena

  Gx # x is a goddess

we can symbolize and prove as follows:

1	$[y](Ay \land Gy) > [x](Ax \land \hat{M}x)$	P
2	$(x)(Hx > Mx)$	P
3	$Aa \land Ga$	P
4	$(A[y] \land G[y]) > (A[x] \land \hat{M}[x])$	1 Q.D.
5	$A[y] \land G[y]$	3 N.P.
6	$A[x] \land \hat{M}[x]$	5,4 M.P.
7	$A[x]$	6 Conj.
8	$\hat{M}[x]$	6 Conj.
9	$H(x) > M(x)$	3 Q.D.
10	$H[x] > M[x]$	9 U.P.
11	$\hat{H}[x]$	10, 8 M.T.
12	$A[x] \land \hat{H}[x]$	7,11 Conj.
13	$[x](Ax \land \hat{H}x)$	12 Q.R.

This fairly simple argument would be impossible to do in Syllogistic Logic alone, although with a great deal of ingenuity it might be done in a mixed logic like that of Chapter 5.

Some restrictions are needed on the new rules: For example, if we use the Quantifier Drop Rule twice on particular quantifiers we must use a new letter the second time. There are all kinds of troubles we can get into by doing quantifier drops; it is generally safer to drop quantifiers from the outside of an expression first, then drop those that were inside the scope of the dropped quantifier, and restore them in opposite order. In fact, a really rigorous set of rules for dropping and adding quantifiers has to be fairly complex, and thus potentially confusing, to handle ways in which we can stumble into bad arguments in complex proofs. In this brief survey we will pass over these difficulties.

Predicate logic was invented almost simultaneously in Germany by Gottlob Frege and in America by Charles Sanders Peirce. The notation generally used today is more like Peirce's than Frege's, but in other respects the current system is more like Frege's. This parallels in an interesting way the situation with regard to calculus, which was simultaneously invented by Leibniz and Newton. (Our notation in this chapter and also our rules are nonstandard.)

An interesting philosophical application of predicate logic was made by the English philosopher Bertrand Russell in a famous article. Russell raised the question of the truth value of statements about nonexistent things; for example, "The present King of France" (there is, of course, no such person unless you are a die-hard Royalist and believe some descendant of the Bourbons is *really* still King of France). Suppose I say, for example, "The present King of France is bald." Russell argued that in this type of phrase starting with "the," which Russell called *definite descriptions*, we make two claims: (1) There is at least one King of France, and (2) There is at most one King of France. In our predicate-logic notation, "The present King of France is bald" comes out as:

$$[x]((Kx \land Bx) \land (y)(Ky > Sxy))$$

where Kx # x is King of France

Bx # x is bald

Sxy # x is the same as y

We could read this as "For at least one thing that thing is King of France and is bald, and for anything whatsoever if that thing is King of France then it is the same as the first thing we mentioned."

Several things should be mentioned here. First, we used three different letters here, and where we do this we sometimes need the rule Letter Change (L.C.), which allows us to change any letter inside round parentheses to any other letter. Second, we needed a new letter because we had a predicate letter with *two* variables: A predicate expressing the *relation* "is the same as." The ability to handle such "relational" predicates is the great strength of predicate logic.

To return to Russell. He showed that if we symbolize "the present King of France is bald" in the way described above, it contains the false claim "there is at least one King of France." Because the claim is false, the statement as a whole is false. To show this we might argue in two steps. First, show that "The present King of France is bald" implies "At least one thing is King of France."

1 $[x]((Kx \land Bx) \land (y)(Ky > Sxy))$ P

2 $K[x] \land B[x] \land (y)(Ky > S[x]y)$ 1 Q.D.

3 $K[x] \land B[x]$ 2 Conj.

4 $(y)(Ky \land S[x]y)$ 2 Conj.

5 $K[x]$ 3 Conj.

6 B[x]   3 Conj.

7 [x](Kx)   6 Q.R.

We can take this as establishing that:

$$[x]((Kx \land Bx) \land (y)(Ky > Sxy)) > [x](Kx)$$

then use the negation of "[x](Kx)" and *Modus Tollens* to show that the longer statement is false.

We could write the negation of [x](Kx) in either of two ways:

$$\overline{[x](Kx)} \qquad \text{or} \qquad [\hat{x}](Kx)$$

The second form has some advantages for showing some interesting relations between quantifiers. For any predicate, P:

$$\frac{(x)(Px)}{[\hat{x}](P\hat{x})} \qquad \frac{(\hat{x})(Px)}{[x](P\hat{x})} \qquad \frac{(x)(P\hat{x})}{[\hat{x}](Px)} \qquad \frac{(\hat{x})(P\hat{x})}{[x](Px)}$$

These rules of Negation of Quantifiers (N.Q.) are interesting in themselves and parallel similar rules for modal operators (see Chapter 8). There are also rules for Distribution of Quantifiers (D.Q.): If F and G are any two predicates:

$$\frac{(x)(Fx \land Gx)}{(x)(Fx) \land (x)(Gx)} \qquad \frac{(x)(Fx) \lor (x)(Gx)}{(x)(Fx \ Gx)}$$

$$\frac{[x](Fx \land Gx)}{[x](Fx) \land [x](Gx)} \qquad \frac{[x](Fx \lor Gx)}{[x](Fx) \lor [x](Gx)}$$

We could use the last rule to derive [x](Kx) from the longer statement as follows:

1 [x]((Kx ∧ Bx) ∧ (y)(Ky > Sxy))

2 [x](Kx ∧ Bx) ∧ [x](y)(Ky > Sxy)   1 D.Q.

3 [x](Kx ∧ Bx)   2 Conj.

4 [x](y)(Ky > Sxy)   2 Conj.

5 [x](Kx) ∧ [x](Bx)   3 D.Q.

6 [x](Bx)   5 Conj.

7 [x](Kx)   5 Conj.

We can do this because the fact that the expressions are complex combinations of predicates and quantifiers makes no difference to the application of rules such as N.Q. and D.Q.

An interesting effect of such rules in a system of logic that contains the Addition Rules and Definition of Material Implication (see Appendix I) is that *every* universal statement about a nonexistent thing becomes "vacuously" true if, for example,

Gx # x is a gold-plated locomotive

Bx # x needs brakes

we can take "[x̂](Gx)" as a premise and argue *either*:

1 [x̂](Gx)   P

2 (x)(Ĝx)   1 N.Q.

3 (x)(Ĝx) ∨ (x)(Bx)   2 Add.

4 (x)(Ĝx ∨ Bx)   3 D.Q.

5 (x)(Gx > Bx)   4 D.M.I.

or we can argue:

1 [x̂](Gx)   P

2 (x)(Ĝx)   1 N.Q.

3 (x)(Ĝx) ∨ (x)(B̂x)   2 Add.

4 (x)(Gx̂ ∨ B̂x)   3 D.Q.

5 (x)(Gx > B̂x)   4 D.M.I.

Thus, we have proved that every gold-plated locomotive needs brakes *and* that every gold-plated locomotive *doesn't* need brakes!

This "vacuous" truth of universal statements about nonexistent things caused a certain amount of trouble in philosophy of science. Predicate logic was enthusiastically accepted by many members of the early twentieth-century philosophical movement known as *Logical Positivism*. The basic principle of Logical Positivism was that statements (other than mathematical statements) were not meaningful unless they could be proved or disproved by the methods of science. On this basis, adherents of Logical Positivism tried to sweep away a great many traditionally accepted areas of human thought and discourse: ethics, aesthetics, religion. In their battle against traditional views, followers often cited the superiority of the "New Logic," which included truth-functional statement logic and predicate logic, over traditional Aristotelian logic.

However, the Logical Positivists soon faced a dilemma. Many of the most basic laws of science seemed to be universal statements about things that did not exist in reality, because they were idealizations of, or projections from, actual situations. Newton's laws of motion, for example, speak of what will happen to a body acted on by no forces. But every real body is acted on by some forces. Thus, by the same reasoning as in our "gold-plated locomotive" example, *every* universal statement about such a body is vacuously true: Newton's laws and myriads of "laws" in conflict with them are all vacuously true as a matter of simple logic, and thus neither provable nor disprovable by the empirical methods of science. Hence, some of the most basic parts of science were "meaningless" by the Logical Positivists' own criterion!

Part of the problem was with the criterion itself, the so-called Verification Principle, which said that nonmathematical statements were meaningless if not provable or disprovable by the methods of science. Critics pointed out that the Verification Principle itself was neither provable nor disprovable by the methods of science. Thus, if applied to itself it was meaningless, and if it was an exception to its own rule why should there not be other exceptions?

But part of the problem was the truth-functional interpretation of statement logic, which, along with otherwise harmless principles of predicate logic, produced the difficulty described above. It might seem simple to change to a nontruth-functional logic, like the system of Chapter 2 in which such paradoxes cannot occur. But the Logical Positivists were deeply committed to an analysis of the meaning of statements in terms of the conditions under which such statements are true or false—their "truth conditions." This "extensional" view of meaning seemed to fit in so well with truth-functional logic that Logical Positivists had a considerable reluctance to abandon truth-functional logic. This had some interesting results: An American philosopher in the Positivist tradition, C.I. Lewis, reinvented modal logic in an effort to eliminate the paradoxes of material implication (by replacing it with strict implication) without changing the truth-functional basis of statement logic. Later efforts to eliminate the paradoxes were less plausible: Logicians in the Positivist tradition actually proposed dropping the well-established and highly intuitive rule Disjunctive Syllogism from logic and retaining the untraditional and counterintuitive Addition Rule!

Of course, in a truth-functional logic one cannot drop Disjunctive Syllogism, which checks out as valid by truth table, but the proposal to base a nontruth-functional logic on the rejection of a basic rule of logic that has seemed obvious to generations of logicians, while retaining Addition, a comparative newcomer to logic, is evidence of a habit of mind fostered by a background in truth-functional logic; a habit of accepting nonintuitive inferences on the grounds that they fit with general theoretical patterns.

An interesting result of the development of logical systems by the Logical Positivists, which would probably have surprised them, is the use of these systems to clarify and support traditional arguments for the existence of God. Analytically sophisticated theistic philosophers have used modal logic to defend the Ontological Arguments (see Chapter 8) and predicate logic to analyze the Cosmological Arguments for the existence of God. One version of a Cosmological Argument is as follows. Let

$$Cxy \quad \# \text{ x causes y}$$

$$Sxy \quad \# \text{ x is the same as y}$$

$$Ex \quad \# \text{ is a cause}$$

$$Dx \quad \# \text{ x is caused}$$

Our premises are:

1 $(x)(\hat{C}xx)$ (Nothing causes itself)

2 $(\hat{x})(Ex > [y] (Cyx \wedge \hat{S}yx)))$ (Not every cause is caused by something else)

3 $(x)(Dx > (Cxx \wedge [y](Cyx \wedge \hat{S}yx))$ (If anything is caused, it is self-caused or caused by something else)

We argue as follows:

4 $\hat{C}(x)(x)$	1 Q.D.
5 $D[x] > (C(x)(x) \vee [y](Cy(x) \wedge \hat{S}y(x))$	3 Q.D.
6 $\hat{D}(x) \vee (C(x)(x) \vee [y] (Cy(x) \wedge \hat{S}y(x)))$	5 C.I.
7 $\hat{D}(x) \vee [y](Cy(x) \wedge \hat{S}y(x))$	4,6 D.S.
8 $[x] \overline{Ex > [y](Cyx \wedge \hat{S}yx)}$	2 N.Q.
9 $\overline{E[x] > [y] (Cy[x] \wedge \hat{S}y[x])}$	8 Q.D.
10 $\overline{\hat{E}[x]} \vee [y](Cy[x] \wedge \hat{S}y[x])$	9 C.I.
11 $E[x] \wedge [\hat{y}](Cy[x] \wedge \hat{S}y[x])$	10 D.N.

12 E[x] ∧[ŷ](Cy[x] ∧Ŝy[x])	11 D.N.
13 E[x]	12 Conj.
14 [ŷ](Cy[x]∧ Ŝy[x])	12 Conj.
15 D̂[x] ∨ [y](Cy[x] ∧Ŝy[x])	7 U.P.
16 D̂[x]	14,15 D.S.
17 E[x] ∧D̂[x]	13,16 Conj.
18 [x](Ex∧ D̂x)	17 Q.R.

The conclusion of this complex proof is "[x](Ex ∧ D̂x)", that is, "There exists an uncaused cause." As we saw in Chapter 3, this is a key step in the causal argument for the existence of God. Of the premises, number 3 seems uncontroversial and number 1 would probably not be disputed by most philosophers. However, premise 2 is quite strong: It amounts to a denial of infinite causal regress. And as we saw in Chapter 3, this is still in dispute.

A great number of philosophical arguments can be considerably clarified by the use of predicate logic, but it seems clear that like logic in general, predicate logic is philosophically neutral: It can be used by theists and nontheists, skeptics and nonskeptics, determinists and nondeterminists. The view held by many Logical Positivists that the New Logic was somehow on their side turned out to be justified by historical developments.

EXERCISES

1. Symbolize and prove the exercises in Chapter 4 and Chapter 5 by using predicate logic.
2. Show the analogies between predicate logic and modal logic (Chapter 8). Which quantifiers correspond to which modal operators? Compare M.O.D. and D.Q., M.O.E. and N.Q. Are the analogies complete? What, if anything, in predicate logic corresponds to other modal logic rules such as N.E., E.P., etc.?
3. Can any of the arguments done by predicate logic in this appendix be done by the methods of Chapters 2 and 3? If so, how? If not, what stands in the way?

—— III ——

Squares of Opposition

A topic often discussed in introductory logic books is the question of *Existential Import* and the *Squares of Opposition*. Because this topic has limited application to philosophical argument, we discuss it in this appendix.

The *Traditional Aristotelian Square of Opposition* was part of traditional syllogistic logic. It consisted of a set of alleged relations among A, E, I, and O statements. A and O, and E and I were said to be *contradictory*: They could not both be true *or* both false. If A was true, O was false and vice versa; if E was true, I was false and vice versa.

A and O were said to be *contrary*: They could not both be true but they could both be false. I and O were said to be *subcontraries*: They couldn't both be false, but they could both be true. A was said to imply I, and E to imply O; this relation was called *subalternation*. These relations can be pictured on this diagram:

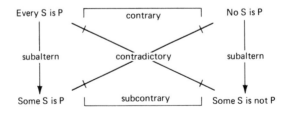

The modern critique of this Square of Opposition rests on the fact that some A and E statements seem to be *hypothetical* in nature; to say "If there are any S's, they will be P" or "If there are any S's they will not be P." Where there are no S's the I and O statements "Some S is P" and "Some S is not P" *both* seem false, since both seem to say there *are* S's. Thus, their contradictories, E and A, both seem to be true, and A does not imply I nor E imply O. This destroys all of the traditional Square of Opposition relations except for contradictories.

A rigorous demonstration of this difficulty cannot be given without rules that are not present in our system, and which are open to question: Addition and Definition of Material Implication (see Appendix I). However, something needs to be said about the difficulties raised.

There are several ways of "saving" the traditional Square of Opposition: (1) We can simply say that the usual Square of Opposition relation holds if and only if the *subject* terms of all the statements refer to actually existing things. This is enough to "save" all of the usual Square of Opposition relations, though not some rather odd inferences arrived at by combining conversion, obversion, and contraposition with the Square of Opposition relations. (2) We could take the medieval (and perhaps Aristotelian) view that A and I statements imply the existence of their subjects ("have Existential Import") but that E and O do not.

If we symbolize "S's exist" by saying "S()S" (Some S is S) we can show the result of the medieval strategy: A will now become a conjunction of S))P and S()S, and if O is to remain its contradictory, O must be the disjunction of "S((P" and the negation of "S()S":

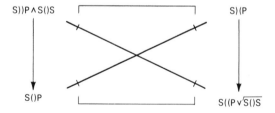

Subalternation will hold for A and I by the following cancellation argument:

$$S))P \qquad \text{S) cancels S(}$$

$$S()S \qquad \text{leaving S(and)P}$$
$$\overline{}$$
$$S()P$$

Subalternation will hold for E and O because if "No S is P" is true, either there are some S's and these are not P and thus the first component is true, or else there are no S's and the second component is true.

If subalternation and contradiction hold, all of the other Squares of Opposition relations hold; for example, if I is false, its contradictory, E, is true, and O is true by subalternation. A similar argument holds if O is false: Its contradictory A will be true and I will be true by subalternation. Thus, I and O cannot both be false and are subcontraries. E and A cannot both be true, for if E was true, O would be true by subalternation and O's contradictory, A, would be false. Similarly for A: If it was true, I would be true by subalternation and E, which is I's contradictory, would be false. However, E and A can both be false; just in case I and O are both true. So all of the traditional Square of Opposition relations hold.

The medieval view is in fact a rather neat solution to the objection, to the traditional Square of Opposition: Its drawback is that we have to make A and O into compound statements.

There is a quite straightforward Square of Opposition for Modal Logic (Chapter 8). The Modal Square of Opposition is:

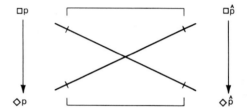

and it is easy to show that all the traditional relations hold (*Hint*: We can show "□ p" implies "◇ p" by using NE and EP).

We can also derive a Square of Opposition for Statement Logic:

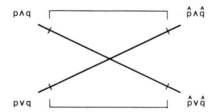

Contradictories hold because $\overline{p \wedge q}$ equals $\hat{p} \vee \hat{q}$ and $\overline{\hat{p} \wedge \hat{q}}$ equals $p \vee q$, using DeMorgan's Rule and Double Negation p q implies p ∨ q by And to Or and $\hat{p} \wedge \hat{q}$ implies $\hat{p} \vee \hat{q}$ by the same rule.

In predicate logic (Appendix II) the Square of Opposition would be

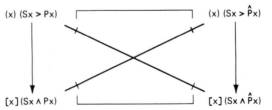

In a system with Addition and Definition of Material Implication the contradictory relations can be proved but no others. In a system without these rules we cannot show that A and O, and E and O are strictly contradictory (the problem is that "(x) (Sx > Px)" is stronger than "[x](Sx ∧ P̂x) because "p > q" is stronger than "p ∧ q̂"). Thus, in standard predicate logic there is a special problem about the Square of Opposition. Because standard predicate logic has dominated recent logic it is not surprising that the Square of Opposition has usually been in trouble in recent logic (but see Exercise 3 that follows).

EXERCISES

1. Show step by step that every traditional Square of Opposition relation holds for (a) The Statement Logic Square (b) The Modal Square.
2. Can there be (a) a Statement Logic Square with simple statements? (b) a Modal Square with compound statements? If not, show why not. If so, give the square.
3. Is there a Predicate Logic Square for "(x)(Fx)", "(x)(F̂x)", "[x](Fx)" and "[x](F̂x)"? If so, give the square. If not, why not?
4. Can you repair the Predicate Logic Square discussed in this appendix by the same methods used for the Syllogistic Logic Square? If so, how? If not, why not? (*Hint*: Either use the Rules Addition and Definition of Material Implication or else show that a weaker relation than strict contradiction is enough to restore the other relations without these rules.)

——— IV ———

Answers
to Selected Exercises

Chapter 1

A2. Doesn't seem to be obscure, negative, circular, or trivial. May be too *wide*, for an unrighteous person could ask things from the gods and give to them. Also may be too *narrow*, for it doesn't include other elements of righteousness; for example, respect for the gods.

B4. Doesn't seem to be obscure, negative, circular, or trivial. May be too wide, for a coward might *hope* to avoid harm by resistance, but not do it. Also may be too *narrow*, for not every harm we fear can be avoided by resistance.

C8. Perhaps obscure: What is meant by "in the presence of"? Doesn't seem to be negative, circular, or trivial. May be too *narrow*, for derision may not always involve hate (for example, affectionate derision of a friend's or relative's foibles). Could also be too *wide*, for extreme examples that fit the definition might go beyond derision to vituperation.

Chapter 2

A2.   L # Gods love courage

                            R # Courage is righteous

                            L > R

                            R
                            ———

                            L

Doesn't cancel: invalid (fallacy of affirming the consequent)

B4.   I # Impossible to know purity with body

                S # True knowledge possible somewhere

                D # True knowledge possible only after death

                P # Partial knowledge can be had in life

    1 I >(Ŝ ∨ D)   P cancels P>

    2 P >S   >S cancels Ŝ

    3 P   /D ∨ Î   I > becomes Î, leaving D ∨ Î

    4 S   2,3 M.P.

    5 Î ∨ (Ŝ ∨ D)   1 C.I.

    6 Î ∨ D   4,5 D.S.

    7 D ∨ Î   6 Com.

C8.   F # Dead feel nothing

                C # Death is change and migrative

                S # Eternity-like sleep

                B # Death a blessing

                G # We shall be with great

    1 F ∨ C   F cancels F>

    2 F > (S ∧ B)   leaving C ∨ (S ∧ B)

    3 C > (G ∧ B) /B   C cancels C> leaving (S ∧ B) ∨ (G ∧ B)

    4 C ∨ (S ∨ B)   1,2 C.C. We use distribution

                                and conjunction to get B out.

$$5 \quad (S \wedge B) \vee (G \wedge B) \qquad 3,4 \, \text{C.C.}$$

$$6 \quad B \wedge (S \vee G) \qquad 5 \, \text{Dist.}$$

$$7 \quad (S \vee G) \qquad 6 \, \text{Conj.}$$

$$8 \quad B \qquad 6 \, \text{Conj.}$$

Note that here, as in some other complex arguments, cancellation does not give a complete answer as to validity, for we need to prearrange what cancellation gives us to get B alone.

D1 and D2 for A2.

1. *Change* a premise

$$*R > L$$

$$\underline{R}$$

$$L$$

2. *Add* a premise

$$*R > L$$

$$L > R$$

$$\underline{R}$$

$$L$$

Chapter 3

A2.   G # God exists

U # Universe explainable without God

U/Ĝ

Invalid, doesn't cancel

B4.   D # Existence of X demonstrable

C # Nonexistence of X implies a contradiction

E # X can be thought of as existing

N # X can be thought of as not existing

(*N.B.*, this is *not* the same as Ê)

1 D > C   > N cancels N>

2 E > N   > C cancels Ĉ

3 N > Ĉ/E > D̂   D > becomes D̂

4 E > Ĉ   2,3 H.S.

5 Ĉ > D̂   1 Transp.

6 E > D̂   4,5 H.S.

Note the way in which "X" was used in the dictionary to give cross-reference between the premises. As in Exercise C8 in Chapter 2, cancellation tells us the conclusion should be provable, but some manipulation is necessary in the proof to get the exact conclusion.

C8.   P # Parts of a divided substance would lose nature of substance

I # Substance could be divided

E # Substance could be destroyed

$(P \land I) > E$

> E cancels Ê

Ê / Î

Invalid: Doesn't cancel to conclusion

D1 for A2, C8: Can't be done because no simple rearrangement of premises can yield to conclusion.
D2 for A2:

*1 G > Û

2 U / Ĝ   U cancels Û

3 Ĝ 1,2 M.T.

D2 for C8:

1 $(P \land I) > E$ P cancels P>

2 Ê   Ê cancels E

*3 P / Î   I> becomes Î

4 $\overline{P \land I}$ 1,2 M.T.

5 $\hat{P} \vee \hat{I}$ 4 De.M.

6 I   3,5 D.S.

Chapter 4

A2.   C # Composite substance

P # Perishable

S # Soul

C)) P

S)(C / S)(P   Invalid, does not cancel

B4. $\hat{K}$)) $\hat{X}$ $\hat{K}$) cancels K)

D)(H   )$\hat{X}$ cancels)X

B)) A   (H cancels $\hat{H}$)

K)(E   B) cancels $\hat{B}$)

$\hat{H}$)(A   A) cancels (A

$\hat{B}$)) X   leaving D) and (E: Conclusion D)(E or E)(D

C8.   K # Knowable things

I # Infinite

G # Known by God

M # Mind of God

K)) I

K)) G / M))I

There seems no obvious way of doing this by purely syllogistic means. D1 for A2:

D1. P)) C

S)(C / S)(P   )C cancels (C, Valid Celarent

Chapter 5

A2.

K # Knower and doer of all

G # Identical with God

<u>C</u> # Christ

K)) G

<u>C</u>)) K   K) cancels)K

<u>C</u>)) G   Valid Barbara

B4.   I # Impossible not to sin

U # Unjust to punish

1   I > U   I cancels I

2   I / U

3   U   1,2 M.P.   Note: We can ignore the "in other words."

C8.

N # X is a soul in the narrower sense

C # X has clear perception

M # X has memory

S # X is a simple substance

1   N > (C ∧ M)   C cancels $\hat{C}$

2   S > ($\hat{C}$ ∧ $\hat{M}$) / S > $\hat{N}$ M cancels $\hat{M}$

3   S > $\hat{C}$ 2 I.A.

4   S > $\hat{M}$ 2 I.A.

5   N > C   1 I.A.

6   N > M   1 I.A.

7   $\hat{C}$ > $\hat{N}$ 5 Transp

8   S > $\hat{N}$ 3,7 H.S.

Various strategies are possible on this proof: Another would use AO to get from $\hat{C}$ ∧ $\hat{M}$ to $\hat{C}$ ∨ $\hat{M}$ (We can't simply contrapose 1 or 2 since C ∧ M is not the contradictory of $\hat{C}$ ∧ $\hat{M}$).

Chapter 6
A, H2:

Let $\overline{H}$ = .1

Let the evidence be New Testament accounts of various miracles worked by Christ.

Let $\overline{H > E}$ be .9

Let $\hat{\overline{H}} > E$ be .1

$$E > H = \frac{\overline{H} \times \overline{H > E}}{E} = \frac{.1 \times .9}{.18} = \frac{.09}{.18} = \frac{1}{2}$$

$$E > \hat{H} = \frac{\hat{\overline{H}} \times \hat{\overline{H} > E}}{\overline{E}} = \frac{.9 \times 1}{.18} = \frac{.09}{.18} = \frac{1}{2}$$

Note: We got $\hat{\overline{H}}$ by the negation rule $\hat{\overline{H}}$ = 1 − $\overline{H}$. We calculated the upper part of each equation and added them to get E; .09 + .09 = .18. This assignment of probabilities gives $\overline{E > H}$ = 1/2 and $E > \hat{H}$ = 1/2 because we have assigned "symmetrical" probabilities to $\overline{H}$ and $\hat{H} > E$, that is, the hypothesis is very improbable, but so is the evidence if the hypothesis is false. If $\hat{H} > E$ is *lower* than H, the balance tips in favor of $\overline{H > E}$.

B for H14:

(i) A defender of the President might argue "Despite intensive investigation the President's enemies were unable to prove that he was involved in a conspiracy. Therefore, the probability that he was is quite low, say .1"

(ii) The most plausible alternative hypothesis might be "There was an efficient coverup, which concealed the fact of the President's involvement."

(iii) A possible argument that the alternate hypothesis has higher probability is "The investigation showed that the President had many loyal followers. It would be in his interest and theirs to cover up a conspiracy. Therefore, the "coverup" hypothesis is more likely."

(iv) H14 is *inconsistent* with *no* other hypothesis. It implies H13 and seems to imply and be implied by H15 (that is, they are equivalent).

C for H18:

(i) Let the body of evidence be that collected by the U.S. Air Force "Project Blue Book" investigation. Since the Air Force investigators collected evidence from many people who thought they had seen alien space vehicles, the hypothesis would make that evidence probable.

(ii) The most plausible alternative explanation is that accounts of alleged sightings were a mixture of honest errors and "tall tales." Because errors occur and people do tell tall tales this may seem as probable or more probable than H14.

(iii) The hypotheses are not incompatible. All alleged sightings may be mistakes or lies, but cleverly concealed alien space vehicles could still have visited us.

(iv) The hypotheses are not exhaustive: Perhaps many UFO sightings were sightings of secret Russian, Chinese, or even American experimental spy vehicles.

D8. This is very similar to an argument of Hume's discussed in this chapter. By looking at this discussion you should be able to answer much of D(i–iv) for this exercise. The question of whether Hume's view of probability is consistent cannot be answered without answering the question for other exercises.

Chapter 7
A for H2:

(a) Let $\overline{H}$ be .1

(b) Let $\overline{H > E}$ be .1

(c) Let $\hat{H} > E$ be .8

(d) Evidence: Uniformity of natural law, lack of any strong indication of different "styles" of design in the universe; on the other hand, the fact that both good and evil exist.

(e) $\hat{H} = 1 - \overline{H} = .9$

(f) $\overline{E} = (.1 \times .1) + (.9 \times .8) = .01 + .72 = .73$

(g) $\overline{E > H} = \dfrac{.1 \times .1}{.73} = \dfrac{.01}{.73} = .0136986$

B for H2:

$$\overline{H > E} \text{ is not high}$$

$$\overline{\hat{H} > E} \text{ is not low}$$

$$E \text{ is observed}$$

$$\overline{H} \text{ is not higher than } \hat{H} > E$$

Nozick's Schema does not apply.

C for H2:

Since Hume has not given any reason to think H2 probable but has simply tossed it out as a possibility, there is no reason to think H is not extremely low. (A monotheist who thinks one God designed the world and an atheist who thinks no god did can agree on this).

D for H2:

$\overline{H > E}$ seems low, for no special reason has been given to suppose that there is evidence which is especially likely if a committee of gods designed the world. Even if some form of good god/bad god view is a plausible explanation of good and evil, this implies opposition: a "committee" of gods seems to imply cooperation. For the same reasons, $\hat{H} > E$ seems high; if $\hat{H}$ is interpreted as "Either one God or no gods designed the universe" it seems to contain the most plausible alternatives.

Chapter 8
A.
*A2:

$$\Diamond p, \hat{\Diamond} p. \text{ They are contradictory.}$$

*B8:

$$\Diamond \hat{p}, \Box \hat{p}$$
$$\hat{\hat{\Diamond}} p$$

$\hat{\Box} p$ does follow from $\Diamond \hat{p}$ by M.O.E. but $\hat{\hat{\Diamond}}p$ does not follow from $\Diamond \hat{p}$ by any modal rule. This is one of Aristotle's rare mistakes.

B4.

$$\Diamond \Box G > \Box \Diamond F$$
or
$$\Diamond \Box G >> \Diamond F$$

The expression in English "If p then necessarily q" is ambiguous between "$p > \Box q$" and "$p >> q$".

C2.

B # A perfect being exists

1 $\Box$ B $\vee$ $\Box$ $\hat{B}$

2 $\Diamond$ $\hat{B}$/$\hat{B}$

3 $\hat{\Box}$B   2 M.O.E.

4 $\Box\hat{B}$ 1,3 D.S.

5 $\hat{B}$ 4 N.E.

D1 for example:

$$1 \Diamond \Box G >> \Diamond F$$
$$2 \Diamond \Box G / \Diamond F$$
$$3 \Diamond F \; 1,2 \; M.P.$$

Note premise 1 was B4. Which item in B was premise 2?

Chapter 9

A2 (partial argument):
1. Thesis: Our judgments about the sameness of souls are groundless.
2. Definitions:

Direct evidence: evidence involving sense perception or introspection.

Indirect evidence: evidence that is not direct.

3. Explicit premises: We have no direct method of observing sameness of soul.
4. Assumed premises
   A2. If we have no direct evidence for sameness of soul we have no direct evidence.
   A3. If we have no direct or indirect evidence for checking our judgments of sameness of soul, then they are groundless.
5. Conclusion: Our judgments of sameness of soul are groundless.
6. Symbolization

G # Judgments of sameness of soul groundless

D # We have direct evidence

I # We have indirect evidence

E1 $\hat{D}$

A2 $\hat{D} > \hat{I}$

A3 $(\hat{D} \wedge \hat{I}) > G/G$

7.

$\hat{D}$ cancels $\hat{D} >$ and $\hat{D} >$

$\hat{I}$ cancels $\hat{I} >$

Cancels to conclusion

8. Proof:

4 Î	1,2 M.P.
5 D̂∧ Î	1,4 Conj.
6 G	5,3 M.P.

9. Support for premises (incomplete)

EPI: Souls can't be observed.

AP2: Indirect methods must be checked by direct methods.

AP3: Judgments that cannot be supported by direct

or indirect methods are obviously groundless.

10. Objections and Replies (incomplete)

Objection, Expressed Premise 1: Perhaps we can introspect sameness of our own soul at different times. Reply: Introspection can only tell us that we seem to have the soul we remember having earlier. Anyway, the real question is about others' souls, not ours.

Objection, Expressed Premise 2: Why must "indirect evidence be checked by direct evidence"? For example, in particle physics we have indirect evidence for unobservable unintrospectable entities.

Reply: In science we have recognized procedures for checking such indirect evidence. There are no recognized procedures for indirectly checking sameness of soul.

Objection to Definition 2: This definition is negative where it could be positive and thus breaks Rule 2. It gives us no idea of what is meant by indirect evidence.

Reply: While the definition may be defective, the point is that any kind of indirect evidence must be checkable by direct evidence.

Reply to the reply: This begs the whole question . . . and the argument continues.

Chapter 10
A2.

Overstatement: Every single human action is free.

Qualified statement: At least some human actions are free.

Index